DATE DUE

MAY

 This book has been awarded
The Adèle Mellen Prize
for its distinguished contribution to scholarship.

IBERIAN POPULAR RELIGION
600 B.C. TO 700 A.D.
CELTS, ROMANS AND VISIGOTHS

Joyce E. Salisbury

Texts and Studies in Religion
Volume 20

The Edwin Mellen Press
New York and Toronto

Library of Congress Cataloging in Publication Data

Salisbury, Joyce E.
    Iberian popular religion, 600 B.C. to 700 A.D.

    (Texts and studies in religion ; 20)
        Bibliography: p.
        Includes index.
        1. Spain--Religion. 2. Portugal--Religion.
3. Celts--Spain--Religion. 4. Celts--Portugal--
Religion. 5. Romans--Spain--Religion. 6. Romans--
Portugal--Religion. 7. Visigoths--Spain--Religion.
I. Title. II. Series.
BL980.S7S25 1985   291'.09366   84-27257
ISBN 0-88946-809-5

Texts and Studies in Religion
Series ISBN 0-88946-976-8

Illustrations by Joseph Papin

        The Edwin Mellen Press
        P.O. Box 450
        Lewiston, New York 14092

Printed in the United States of America

For

Jim and Laura Graves

Maps and Illustrations

Table of Contents

ACKNOWLEDGEMENTS

This book grew out of a year's research in Spain, which was generously funded by a Rutgers University fellowship. My study was facilitated by the able librarians of the Biblioteca Nacional of Madrid, the Instituto Jeronimo de Zurita, the Instituto Enrique Florez and the Consejo Superior de Investigaciones Cientificas. Particularly helpful was the librarian of the Escorial, who generously devoted his time discussing the manuscripts and who permitted me to have several valuable manuscripts microfilmed. I would also like to thank the editors of the Journal of Medieval History for their permission to restate in Chapter IV the arguments that appeared within my article "Fruitful in Singleness," published by them in 1982. My study was also greatly enhanced by Gallegans in remote villages who were always willing to talk about life in Galicia's hills and who shared their recollections of traditions and folk tales.

I would like to thank Professors Donald Weinstein and Traian Stoianovich for their guidance throughout my years of study, for their challenging conversations and for their detailed comments on my work as it progressed. I would also like to thank my colleagues at the University of Wisconsin-Green Bay for their support and encouragement during the completion of this project.

Valerie E. Buszka prepared the maps, converting my crude drawings into clear finished products, and I would like to thank Margaret Achter for patiently and accurately completing the word processing of the final typescript. I owe special thanks to Joseph Papin, whose illustrations captured the spirit of the images far better than the small, imperfect photographs from which he worked.

It would have been impossible to devote so many years to this study without a good deal of support from friends and family. Space will not permit me to acknowledge the help of everyone, but I would like to particularly thank my friend and colleague, David Galaty, without whose intellectual and personal support this project could not have been completed. Also deserving of special mention are Ambassador Alfonso Santa Cruz and his wife, Letitia, whose help in reducing the problems that arose when I moved to Spain with two children was invaluable.

Finally, the dedication as well as my deep thanks go to my children, Jim and Laura Graves, who shared with me Galicia's countryside, remote churches and the whole experience of preparing this book.

Joyce E. Salisbury
University of Wisconsin-Green Bay

BACKGROUND

A study of rural religion during the early Middle
Ages presents particular problems. All the surviving
historical sources are written by religious or secular
leaders and reflect the religious views of the ruling
elite. The historical silence of early medieval
peasants has led most historians of medieval Spain to
assume a social homogeneity which did not exist. A.K.
Ziegler has stated the view that also defines the
position of the other major works:

> "Social life in Visigothic
> Spain was simple in the
> extreme, as might naturally be
> expected among a people whose
> principal occupation was
> agriculture. The conditions
> which prevailed offered no
> complicated problems in group
> or class adjustment...."[1]

In fact, Visigothic society was considerably more
complex than the surviving manuscripts indicate at
first glance. By using an interdisciplinary approach
to the study of early medieval society, it is possible
to get a clearer picture of the diversity of Visigothic
agricultural society. I shall use anthropological
methods and archeological evidence in conjunction with
traditional historical sources to explore Iberian
village culture and the variety of religious
perspectives that formed much of Visigothic culture.

Such an approach clearly reveals that from the
time of the Roman conquest of Spain's northern Celtic
tribes Iberian society was made up of two groups,
ruling and peasant, the first living on the

agricultural   production   of   the   second.   This
fundamental   structure remained unchanged when   in   the
fifth   century Germanic tribes replaced the   Romans   as
the   peninsula's   ruling group. While each group   was
distinguished   by   its own life-style, world   view   and
values,   the two could not co-exist by merely   ignoring
each   other.   The   ruling   group depended on   the
production of the peasants, providing in   return   some
measure   of   political and   administrative   stability.[2]
This symbiotic relationship required   interaction   and
adaptation   at many levels - economic, political,   and,
of   immediate   concern for this study, religious.   In
particular,   it is misleading to assume   that   peasants
had   the   same   religious   needs   and   views   as   the
frequently studied leaders of Visigothic society.   On
the   contrary,   practices   traditionally   treated   as
"persisting superstitions," or explained as peripheral,
archaic   or deviant religiosity, may actually point   to
deep   religious   needs   integral   to   rural   culture.
Recognizing the dual character of Visigothic society, I
shall   focus my analysis on rural religiosity and   the
Catholic Church's accommodation to it.[3]

Several questions are important to this   analysis.
First,   what   was the   relationship   between   religious
practices and the cultural framework of   the   mountain
villages   in which the practices persisted?   Second,
assuming official sensitivity to popular religion, what
kind   of   mediators   transmitted   information   between
peasant   and   elite cultures? Finally,   what   was   the
impact of rural religion on the ritual of   the   Iberian
Church?

Most   studies   of medieval popular   religion   have
dealt   with the high Middle Ages, and therefore,   quite
rightly identify   the influential religious   laity   as

townspeople.   The   Church   is   seen   struggling   to
accommodate   itself   to new needs growing out   of   town
life.   A   fine   example of   such   a   study   is   Raoul
Manselli's La Religion Populaire au Moyen Age,   (Paris,
1975), which focuses on popular religion after the year
1000.   The paucity of sources for the early Middle Ages
led   Manselli to assume that there was   little   contact
between   the   clergy   and   the   "people"   before   the
Gregorian   reform.[4]   There can be no doubt   about   the
well-documented   late medieval interaction between   the
Church   and   its congregations, but this   was   not   the
first time the Church adapted to lay impulses.   On   the
contrary,   throughout   the   first   centuries   of
Christianity,   it adjusted to needs of a   rural   laity,
and,   in   a   sense, the late medieval   struggle   was   a
re-accommodation.

Two studies that do approach early Spanish popular
religion   are   E.   Delaruelle,   "La   Vie   religieuse
populaire en Septimanie pendant l'epoque   Wisigothique"
(Anales   Toledanos,   III,   1971), and   Stephen McKenna,
Paganism   and   Pagan Survivals   in   Spain   (Washington,
1938).   While both works shed light on   the   subject,
both have unresolved problems of method that may impair
their   conclusions.   Delaruelle's article is   extremely
interesting for his imaginative use of sources such   as
archeological remains, symbols and saints' cults.   But
Delaruelle wrote about the attempts of elite   churchmen
to reach the people. He did not explore the   religious
impulses   arising   in the countryside; as a   matter   of
fact,   he   dismissed "superstitious practices"   in   one
paragraph.[5]   McKenna,   on   the   other   hand,   studied
precisely those practices that Delaruelle had dismissed
summarily.   While he catalogued various pagan practices
mentioned throughout the Visigothic period, he did   not

try to place them in a cultural context. He saw them
not as current expressions of religiosity but as the
irrelevant survivals of a previous era.

The differing approaches of these two works
suggest that a clarification of the term "popular
religion" is needed. Luis Maldonado, in his general
study attempted to define what he meant by popular
religion. He concluded that he was studying the
"church of the masses."[6] The term "masses" may be
anachronistic. My study of Visigothic Spain will deal
not with masses, but with the religiosity of rural
people. This is not to say that there were no town
dwellers during the period. The religious impulses of
town life, however, are fundamentally different from
those originating in a peasant village, and medieval
urban piety becomes much more important later, as
Manselli and others have noted. I shall, therefore,
confine myself to a study of <u>rural</u> popular religion and
its syncretic interaction with the religiosity of an
official Church.

Popular religion is at least generally understood
as that of the "masses," but there is less agreement on
the nature of the religiosity that is the opposite of
popular religion. Manselli defined elite religion as
"<u>religion savante</u>." While his analysis ranges more
widely than his term would suggest, labeling such
religious expression as intellectual or learned is to
omit a large number of uneducated elite who shared the
same religious views. Similarly struggling with the
problem of definition, Maldonado saw a parallel between
official religion and the state or nation, between
popular religion and the people: "The nation connotes
a juridical or political dimension. The people, on the
other hand, alludes to culture, land, vital space,

history,   customs and language of a human group."[7]   In
spite of the possible anachronistic application of
"nation" to the early Middle Ages, the dichotomy
suggested by Maldonado comes close to describing
realities in Visigothic Spain.   In Iberia there was a
kingdom   ruled by king and lay and spiritual nobility,
who formed the juridical/political body with a culture,
world-view and religiosity that differed in fundamental
ways from the religiosity, world-view and culture of
the rural laity.   Instead of "religion savante,"
therefore, there is the religion of the political and
economic ruling class, thus an "official religion."[8]
In the course of analyzing rural religion, I shall
explore some of the elements of Visigothic official
religiosity.

Even as a form of religious expression, popular
religion may be better grasped within the   context of
economic and social life, indeed as an integral part of
that life.[9] Moreover, the study of popular religion
requires   recognition of regional and cultural
differences.   McKenna, on the other hand, has   treated
Spain as a unit, failing to perceive that paganism in
the   more Romanized South was different from the
paganism of the North. Nor did he emphasize the   fact
that customs that disappeared rapidly in one region
persisted tenaciously in another. Delaruelle has also
succumbed to the temptation of generalizing from
regional evidence.   For example, in his article on
Septimania, he used canons from the Gallegan Council of
Braga ignoring the problem of whether Braga exerted any
jurisdiction over Septimania and, indeed, ignoring all
the evidence that it did not.[10] Once rural religiosity
is seen as an integral part of peasant culture, it
becomes necessary to deal with the problem of local
variation.

In order to attempt a precise analysis of lay
religious development, I have limited my study
geographically to the northwestern region of Spain, the
center of which is the modern province of Galicia.
However, the region under discussion is not precisely
that of the modern province, which is a political
rather than a cultural entity. The approximate
geographic boundaries extended from the Duero River in
northern Portugal northward along the Portuguese
border, then northeastward to include Leon and the
Cantabrian Mountains. This territory was approximately
the extent of the Roman province of Galicia. It also
coincides with the boundaries of the Suevian kingdom of
the fifth and early sixth centuries.[11] While these
early political divisions influenced the
distinctiveness of the Northwest, they were not the
sole determinants. This was also the area of early
Celtic colonization,[12] and a strong Celtic influence
can still be seen in place names[13] as well as in the
local Celtic-influenced dialect.[14] There are,
therefore, a number of factors that define this region
as distinctive in the larger cultural and political
entity of the peninsula.

While the boundaries of my study roughly coincide
with the above-mentioned political and linguistic
definitions, I have been interested primarily in the
study of a homogeneous culture. From this point of
view, the simplest and most accurate way to describe
the extended Gallegan province may be to say that it is
the northwestern region of ancient Celtic settlement
with stone houses and related cultural patterns. This
study, therefore, explores the religiosity of mountain
dwellers in stone villages. Throughout my work, for
the sake of convenience, I shall refer to this region

GALLEGAN STONE HOUSE WITH HORREO

as Galicia, using the old Roman term, which included northern Portugal, the Asturias and the Cantabrians.

It is not as easy to define the time span of this study. I shall focus on the Iberian Germanic period from the early fifth century through the seventh century, the years of the Visigothic Church's slow but continuing accommodation to rural religious needs. To identify the basic elements of popular religion, however, it is necessary to study religious trends over a long period in order to distinguish isolated practices from fundamental aspects of religious expression. Therefore, when appropriate, I shall feel free to trace persistent cultural or religious patterns as far back as the early Celtic settlements, ca. 600 B.C.

I shall begin my work by establishing the religious structures and cultural settings of the peasant and official cultures located in Spain's mountainous Northwest. Then I shall isolate and discuss the institutions and mediators that permitted interaction of religious impulses between these two groups. Finally, I shall analyze the ways by which rural religious practices were incorporated into the official Visigothic Church in a synthesis so sufficiently successful that Arab invaders were met by Christian Gallegans – Christian because the Church satisfied their basic needs, not because a Visigothic king declared them Christian.

Notes

1.   A.E. Ziegler, Church and State in Visigothic
Spain (Washington, 1930), p. 167. Even the recent work
by Roger Collins, Early Medieval Spain: Unity in
Diversity 400-1000 (New York, 1983) does not address
the problem of the differing interests between the
rulers of the Iberian peninsula and their rural
subjects.

2.   This model for studying peasant societies
broadly follows Kroeber's analysis: "Peasants
constitute part-societies with part cultures. They are
definitely rural - yet live in relation to market
towns; they form a class segment of a larger population
which usually contains also urban centers...but their
local units retain much of their old identity,
integration, and attachment to soil and cults." (A.L.
Kroeber, Anthropology [New York, 1948] p. 284). See
also, Jack M. Potter, et al., The Primitive World and
Its Transformations (New York, 1953); Robert T.
Anderson, Traditional Europe: A Study in Anthropology
and History (Belmont, 1971).

3.   Raoul Manselli, La Religion Populaire au Moyen
Age (Paris, 1975), p. 218, sees this accommodation as
characteristic of the Middle Ages. Although he is
writing about the period after 1000, his observations
apply to the earlier centuries as well: "Cette
relation dialectique et ce rapport continuel ont donné
naissance au christianisme medieval dans son
intégrité ; il fut un effort conjoint et soutenu pour
édifier une société intégralement et totalement
chrétienne." For an excellent analysis of the
interaction between popular culture and elite
religiosity, see Carlo Ginzburg, The Cheese and the
Worms (New York, 1982).

4. Manselli noted the shortage of sources, "Disons tout de suite que les témoignages sont plutôt rares pour toute la partie du moyen âge que précède l'an mille." He later concluded: "...le contact étroit entre le clergé et le peuple n'avait pas existé ou avait été bien insuffisant," pp. 125 and 180.

5. E. Delaruelle, "La Vie religieuse populaire en Septimanie pendant l'epoque Wisigothique" Anales Toledanos III (1971), p. 22.

6. Luis Maldonado, Religiosidad Popular. Nostalgia de lo Magico (Madrid, 1975), pp. 361-63.

7. Ibid., p. 361. "Nación connota una dimensión jurídica y política. Pueblo, en cambio, alude a la cultura, la tierra, el espacio vital, la historia, las costumbres y la lengua de un grupo humano."

8. This definition comes very close to Werner Stark's observations on "established churches" or "established religion" (Werner Stark, Sociology of Religion, Vol. I [New York, 1966]). Stark's conception of established religions as both the product and the source of conservative sentiments (Vol. I:3) is also applicable to the Visigothic official Church. I chose not to use his terms, however, because Stark further writes that the "...essence of established religion expresses itself in a sacred ruler, a sacred nation, and a sacred mission" (Vol. 1:6). These things were not true of Visigothic Spain. By Stark's definition, therefore, it did not have an "established church."

9. Julio Caro Baroja, Los Pueblos del Norte de la Peninsula Ibérica (San Sebastian, 1973), p. 15. In this study of northern Spanish people, the author suggested this relationship without pursuing its analysis: "...si se encuentra un pueblo de religion

determinada, o de determinado régimen de vida
económica, es, cuando menos, posible que a tal religion
y régimen vayan unidos una serie de otros elementos
culturales, acordes con ellos."
    10. Delaurelle, p. 21.
    11.   F. Bouza Brey, "El Estado Suevo en Galicia y
su Organizacion interna," Grial XXVII (1970), p. 29:
"El ambito territorial del Estado Suevo fue el de la
actual Galicia con parte de Asturias y León, así como
Portugal hasta Mérida."
    12.   Caro Baroja describes in detail the Celtic
settlement patterns in this region.
    13.   Stuart Piggott, Ancient Europe (Chicago,
1965), p. 72, shows the localization of Celtic place
names in this region.
    14.   Manuel Murguia, Historia de Galicia (Lugo,
1865), p. 283, analyzed the Gallegan dialect in terms
of its relationship to ancient Celtic tongues: "Hemos
visto ya que el romance Gallego se formó de los
primeros y obedeciendo a las leyes de los antiguos
idiomas célticos."   Jose Manuel Gomez Tabanera,
Ethnogenesis of the Spanish Peoples (Madrid, 1966), p.
46, provides a detailed study of the limits of this
dialect that closely coincides with the area that I
have selected for my study: "The...Galician-Portuguese
language, penetrates more or less purely into Asturias,
reaching as far as the middle and lower valley of the
Navia; to the province of León, by the transition zone
of El Bierzo and to that of Zamora, in the towns
situated to the west of Portillo del Padornelo..."

THE TRADITIONAL VILLAGE

In about 600 B.C., several Celtic tribes crossed the Pyrenees and settled in the mountains of northern and northwestern Iberia. They built complex castras (fortified towns of round stone huts and narrow, winding streets) and developed customs suited to the inhospitable hills of Galicia. Medieval Gallegan popular religion grew from a continuation of this ancient Celtic cultural foundation as well as from the social, economic and geographic elements that made up peasants' seventh century present. Both elements are crucial to an understanding of Gallegan rural religion. In this chapter, I shall describe rural patterns of life during the Visigothic era, and explore the religious needs and assumptions that had been an organic part of this rural way of life since the Celtic settlement. In his monumental work on the Mediterranean world, Fernand Braudel convincingly demonstrated that "...the fundamental reality of any civilization must be its geographical cradle."[1] Thus it may be appropriate to begin this examination of village culture with the geographic reality that shaped the broad outline of Gallegan life.

The Greek geographer, Strabo, in 18 A.D. wrote one of the earliest descriptions of this region. While his observations omitted the beauty of the countryside, they perfectly captured the harshness of the region: "...Northern Iberia, in addition to its ruggedness, not only is extremely cold, but lies next to the ocean...consequently it is an exceedingly wretched place to live in."[2] Whether beautiful or "wretched,"

the outstanding features of Galicia are its hills and
mountains ranging from rolling green hills near the
Atlantic coast to the perpetually snow-capped rugged
mountains in the Cantabrian range forming the eastern
boundary of this region.[3] The folding topography
isolated each valley, increasing the tendency of each
village to focus upon itself rather than to consider
itself part of a larger political unit. This
geographic isolation was true even of coastal fishing
villages, because the Gallegan hills do not taper off
as they reach the shore, but continue to dominate the
land until they plunge into the Atlantic. Each coastal
village was built vertically on the hills isolating it
from inland settlements.

Except for the snow and granite of the Cantabrian
peaks, the Gallegan hills are green with forests of
oak, myrtle and pine, or meadows of low weeds and
thorny bushes. The brilliant greens for which Galicia
is famous are achieved by ten months of almost daily
rain every year. So much rain required houses built of
stone with slate roofs which, while incurably cold in
the winter, at least remained dry. The earth is dark
and rich, but the excessive rain permits only one crop
per year, unlike the two or three yielded by lands
further south.

Run-off from heavy rains in the mountains feeds
large, rapidly flowing rivers whose valleys provide
access to Galicia's rugged interior. Classic authors,
Strabo, Ptolemy, Pliny and others, mentioned the great
rivers rising in the Gallegan hills and flowing to the
Atlantic,[4] and the peninsula's northwest coast is
divided by the mouths of these rivers: the Duero
(Douro in Portuguese for this river as it flows across
Portugal into the sea), the Lima, the wide Minho

separating Spain from Portugal, and the Ulla are only
the major ones. The importance of these arteries of
communication should not be underestimated. The major
Roman and Visigothic cities of the northwest interior
were located on these important avenues to the coast –
Lugo and Orense on the Minho, and Leon on the River
Berneaga, which is a wide tributary leading into the
Duero.

The Atlantic coast in this region has always been
rich in cod, sardines and shellfish,[5] but the small
fishing craft of the Celtiberians made of frames
covered with goat skin or hollowed tree trunks[6] would
have had a difficult time exploiting the rich seafood
since the shore is rocky and the sea often stormy.
Fortunately, however, the rivers that were so important
to the trade of the interior widen at their mouths to
create deep calm inlets or Rias. These Rias form
perfect natural harbors, and their often steep sides
have been locations of village settlement from
pre-historic times. The importance of Rias was
expressed in an old Christian folk tale that said God
tired a bit after five days of creation, and rested His
hand on the land for a moment. The touch of His
fingers carved the Rias.

The village way of life was based on coping with
wet, isolating, infertile hills, rushing rivers, and
devastating winter storms. Not surprisingly, from the
earliest settlement of the region, these major natural
features received religious recognition. The
Celtiberians carved inscriptions on the heights of many
mountains, either dedicating them to one of their many
Gods, or more likely, naming the spirit residing on
each peak. Rivers also were believed to have spirits,
and these were also named by sacred inscriptions.[7] In

his detailed description of Gallegan culture, M. Murguia referred to this early religion as pantheism, for him a worship of the world of nature needing neither temples nor sacred images.[8] Awe and reverence for nature is a fundamental fact of village culture, and while the forms of expression may have changed over the centuries, the basic reverence did not.

It was not enough, however, for a medieval villager to respect his natural environment. His primary concern was to persuade this difficult land to provide a living. He had to produce not only for his own consumption, but also enough to satisfy the demands of the nobility. When the Visigoths defeated the ruling Romans in Spain, the arable land was divided between Goths and Romans, allowing 2/3 to the Goths and 1/3 to the Romans.[9] Some highland or marginal lands may have remained under peasant ownership, but most villagers entered into tenant farming contracts. Custom did not dictate exactly how much rent should be paid, but it is probable that the average was a tenth of the annual produce.[10] The rent was payable annually, probably more often in kind than money.[11] This arrangement gave the tenant considerable autonomy, since his interaction with the landlord, at least theoretically, was infrequent. This rather loose contact encouraged tenants to attempt to increase their production by cultivating more land than was permitted under the terms of their leases. Families grew larger, and grown sons provided the manpower necessary to increase the area under cultivation.[12] There was always the danger, however, that the landlord would discover this extension and either increase the rent or retake possession of the appropriated land.[13] As might be expected, Visigothic laws deal abundantly with disputes between landlord and tenant regarding amounts and types of landholdings.[14] Legislation dealing with economic and juridical interaction between landowner and land-worker reflected the concern of a nobility eager to ensure its continued income. Villagers, on the other hand, remained primarily concerned with how to make a living from the land itself, and the means for successful exploitation of the land form one of the basic elements of village culture.

The land surrounding the village consisted of some common non-arable lands as well as private holdings of arable, woodland and meadow, and it was not unusual for some of the fields to be fenced or hedged.[16] The laws describe the kind of fields that were permitted to be fenced as not only fields with crops, but "...an orchard with or without fruit, or a meadow...or a field where there were no fruit trees...."[17] They also set severe penalties for destruction of legitimate enclosures. The main reason for enclosing some lands seems to have been to prevent the destruction of crops by grazing animals. Of the seventeen chapters in the Visigothic laws that generally dealt with injuries to crops, eight were concerned with animals wandering into the fields.[18] All this legislation on fencing does not mean that all the land was enclosed. On the contrary, the fact that animals were wandering about suggests the existence of substantial tracts of commons, and the sources confirm this. For example, the laws also specifically mention areas that were not permitted to be enclosed, not even by ditches, those more subtle forms of enclosure. "Where anyone surrounds open fields with ditches, travelers may disregard them, nor shall anyone presume to drive them out of said fields."[19] Furthermore, "Animals driven along the highway cannot be excluded from open pastures."[20] Actually, enclosing fields served more to preserve common grazing privileges than to limit them, since the responsibility for crop preservation lay with the owner of the crops, not with the owner of the grazing animal. This can be seen most vividly in the case of a villager whose cultivated land lay near a river: "Whoever cultivates land in a place traversed by a stream, where there is a ford through which cattle can pass, must enclose his crops with a fence. Should he fail to do this,...he shall not be entitled to damages from any person...."[21]

When a peasant left the village for the fields, which at times were some distance from the village,[22] it was likely that his wife or daughters accompanied him. In fact, if he were busy elsewhere, women may well have gone to plow, sow or harvest alone. Strabo noted that the pre-Roman Celtiberian women of this region did all the agricultural work,[23] and while the Romans insisted that the men take over the primary agricultural tasks, the tradition of women helping in the fields never completely died.[24] The family worked the field with a light Celtic plow[25] supplemented by a "laya," a two-pronged digging tool older than even the Celtic plow.[26]

After spring plowing, the main crops sowed were basically the same as had been planted for centuries before the arrival of the Romans. Flax was extremely important for making clothing as well as fish nets. Some barley was planted, most of which was used to make beer.[27] The Celtiberians also planted wheat which was also used to make a potent liquor. Orosius described its production: "...a juice artfully concocted from wheat, which juice they called caelia because it caused

LAYA - GALLEGAN DIGGING TOOL

CELTIC CART

heat.   For the power of the moistened fruit bud is
aroused by heat, and then it is dried and, when reduced
to a powder, is mixed with a pleasant juice by which
through fermentation a sour taste and the glow of
drunkenness are added."[28] The Romans attempted to
increase the production of wheat as a food crop
probably at the expense of some of the barley fields,
but the yields remained low. The crop was loaded on
wooden, two-wheeled carts and pulled by horses or oxen
to the village.[29] The harvest was then spread on a
threshing floor and animals, usually horses, separated
the grain from the stalk by treading on it. The use of
a borrowed animal on the threshing floor was forbidden
by law and in case of the infringement of the law, the
user was required to replace the animal if it died from
overwork.[30]

After threshing, the grain was stored. Even then,
the low yields were not secure, for Galicia was
constantly plagued by rodents.[31] To protect the grain,
it was stored in horreos), rectangular granaries built
above ground and supported by four posts[32] (see
illustration on page 20). These structures have
persisted until today, and are as characteristic of the
region as stone houses. The villagers, however, never
placed all their faith in such technical measures. In
addition to storing the grain above ground, they
dedicated a number of feast days to mice in order to
persuade the rodents to eat elsewhere.[33]

Since neither horreos nor festivals completely
solved the rodent problem, in times of scarcity
villagers had to turn to their oak forests for food, as
earlier generations of Celts had done, collecting
acorns, toasting them, and grinding them into flour
with which to make bread.[34] Members of the official

Figure 1

culture recognized the importance of oak trees both as food and for excellent wood, and in keeping with their legalistic outlook, made laws to protect them.[35] The rural population, on the other hand, once again had its own way of giving recognition to oak trees. Candles were lit for the tree's spirit, no doubt both in gratitude for services already received and as a plea for continued blessings.[36]

Acorns were ground at home on rotary hand mills,[37] and it is likely that the villagers sometimes used these small mills to grind their grain.[38] Visigothic Spain did have watermills,[39] which were controlled by lords. Much of the village's grain was ground at a local watermill, and severe legislation against tampering with a mill testifies to its economic importance to the lord.[40]

The Romans had introduced grapes for wine production, but most of this region was unsuitable for viticulture except in the Duero Valley of present-day Portugal. Olives also were unsuitable in this region, so cooking was done primarily with lard, as it had been during the Celtic period.[41] In sum, Roman innovations were few[42] and did not fundamentally affect the agricultural scarcity that the sources attribute to this region from Celtic times through the seventh century. Fructuosus of Braga in the seventh century was not far from wrong when he claimed that the Gallegan province "...requires more work on the soil than any other land."[43]

Not surprisingly, fertility rituals were central to Gallegan rural religion. Clifford Geertz has noted that "The source of...[religion's] moral vitality is conceived to lie in the fidelity with which it expresses the fundamental nature of reality,"[44] and

peasants faced with the problem of poor yields seem to
have seen a possible solution in the striking contrasts
that characterize this region - lush-looking green
hillsides yielded poor crops; beautiful wildflowers
grew with large thorns, dark stone proved the best
building material for a bright land. The conclusion
that excellence comes only with sacrifice is perhaps
best expressed in the traditional Gallegan explanation
for the superiority of the shellfish trapped off their
shores: the flavor is due to the constant struggle of
the mollusks against the rough, cold Gallegan waters,
unlike the bland taste of indolent fish in the warm,
still waters of the south. The religious expression of
Galicia's reality of contrasts was that perhaps
abundance could be "purchased" with abstinence. In
Galicia, most fertility rituals involved sacrificing
procreation in one place to guarantee it elsewhere.[45]
For example, traditionally it had been forbidden to
plow one of Galicia's sacred mountains,[46] a
renunciation that represented an effort to increase the
fertility of the region's other hills.

    Ritualistic efforts never solved Gallegan food
shortages. In order to make a living, a village family
could not rely solely on agriculture. Village men had
to herd, hunt and fish to supplement meager yields, and
women's help in the fields freed men to do so. All but
the poorest households had a few sheep and goats, and
milk products or meat supplemented grain. Along with
their personal livestock, many of the sons from the
villages made a living caring for the larger flocks of
landlords.[47] In the more mountainous regions,
especially in the Cantabrians, the limited pasturage
forced shepherds into transhumance on a small scale.

    While the meadowlands were used to raise sheep and

goats, Galicia's abundant oak forests were also exploited. Hogs were driven into the woods to eat acorns. Large landholders used slaves to drive the hogs, but peasant families at times sent their sons to follow the hogs into the forests.[48] Visigothic laws recognized the importance of the forests for hog raising and provided for contractual agreements between the hog owner and the owner of the woodland.[49] It was customary for the owner of the hogs to pay the landlord a tenth of the hogs annually for grazing privileges. The woodlands were rich enough to sustain the hogs through the winter, for the laws specifically stated that if the swineherd did not want to winter the hogs in the forest, he should pay a twentieth of their number.[50] Thus pork and mutton supplemented the peasant diet, and lard was used for cooking.

Often sheep and hogs were used to pay part of the taxes due to lord or church. Therefore, in order to avoid slaughtering them for meat, villagers went into the hills to hunt for game. Since the Visigothic laws regulate so many minute details of life, the absence of hunting regulations suggests that hunting was not limited to the nobility.[51] The northern mountains had abundant deer, boar and wild goats. Hunters following goats to the peaks at times encountered hermits who sought solitude in the heights. The seventh-century Saint Fructuosus was disturbed by "...a crowd of huntsmen with their dogs...." On a second occasion, Fructuosus narrowly missed being shot by an archer, for the saint was "clothed in a garment of goat's skins...."[52]

I have already mentioned the importance of fishing to Gallegan coastal villages, both for subsistence and commerce, but the abundance of inland streams and

rivers made fishing available to many villages far from
the coast. A peasant whose land bordered a river close
to the sea could build a fence halfway across the
stream to trap salmon or "other sea-fish." Deeper in
the hills, he could trap trout in the mountain rivers.
However, a peasant could not fence an entire stream,
because others who did not live along the banks also
had to have space to cast their fishnets.[53]

Honey was another product that was abundant in the
Gallegan countryside. The Celtiberians drank mead made
of honey, a drink much praised by classical
observers.[54] Hundreds of years later a medieval
chronicler noted that Galicia was famous for its
honey.[55] This continued fame suggests that between the
Celtic times and the later Middle Ages, Gallegan honey
was produced not only for local consumption but for
export. The value of honey, not surprisingly, inspired
further informative legislation. Apparently both wild
and "domesticated" bees were exploited. If a villager
were fortunate enough to find bees on his property,
"...he must make three marks, or characters, in
testimony of possession...,"[56] and he could then have
exclusive use of the product. More hazardous, however,
was the erection of an apiary near a village, since the
owner was then responsible for any injury caused by his
bees.[57] In both cases, anyone stealing honey was
subject to fines and whipping.[58]

Thus, by combining agriculture and husbandry with
hunting, fishing and gathering, a seventh-century
villager could earn a living both for himself and for
the landlord and high church officials who lived on the
taxes and dues. In the course of describing rural
life, I have tried to show how religious rituals had
traditionally grown out of the process of survival in

these hills. It is important to note that these rituals were not chance embellishments of primitive paganism but manifestations of fundamental needs growing out of the Gallegan peasants' way of life. Fertility and nature-worshipping rituals that are the expressions of rural religions grew out of two basic needs. The first was to explain the workings of nature so that natural disasters were the result of divine will, not mere chance.[59] The second was to attempt to control nature by the use of traditional ritual. Spirits perhaps could be persuaded or bribed in a way that impersonal random chance could not, and rural fertility magic and ritualized reverence for nature were direct attempts to control the events that frequently represented the difference between sufficiency and starvation. Members of the official Church may have been more interested in unifying and administering their Church and developing theology, but if Christianity was to be meaningful for the rural laity, it would have to provide both an explanation for natural occurrences and a means to control them.

Another important dimension of peasant life was social interaction. This too required ritualistic ordering. Typically, villages in the northwest of Spain were built along a hillside, perhaps near a river. The houses were of stone with thick walls and slate roofs to keep out the rain. There were no chimneys; the smoke from the cooking fires was left to escape as it could. While peasant communities were close-knit, the houses were not clustered together, but were dispersed along the sides of the hills.[60] Although the stone houses did not touch each other, the residents treated their somewhat rambling village as a cohesive social unit.

Village unity was evident in the Celtic period
when each village had its own god or goddess as a
spiritual symbol of village cohesiveness.[61] During the
Roman occupation the village disappeared as a political
or completely self-governing unit. No doubt local
matters continued to be resolved within each village,
but for official purposes, the rural settlements or
vici were placed under the jurisdiction of the nearest
city, civitas, later replaced by the Hispano-Gothic
jurisdictional unit, municipio.[62] With the
decentralization resulting from the Germanic invasions,
the rural assembly, conventus vicinorum or conventus
rusticorum, reassumed a recognized official role,
particularly in the northern provinces.[63]

According to Isidore of Seville, rural assemblies
customarily took place at rural crossroads, at a point
where "many paths in the fields meet."[64] They probably
coincided with periodic market days, and the assemblies
were used to discuss matters of interest to the whole
village, questions of property and village security.
If there were a vicious animal belonging to one of
their neighbors, the villagers would complain publicly
of its potential danger.[65] The owner of the animal
then had the responsibility to kill or dispose of it
and use the rural assembly to notify his neighbors that
the danger was passed.[66] It was also the
responsibility of trappers to announce the location of
their traps so that a neighbor might not be hurt, for,
as the law stated, "men...should not, without their
knowledge, be exposed to such dangers."[67] The spirit
behind the conventus rusticorum was a community sense
of responsibility for the well-being of each villager,
a responsibility that also extended to the property of
others. For example, if anyone found a stray animal,

he had to declare it to a "public assembly of the neighbors" so that the rightful owner might be found.[68]

It is impossible to determine how often rural assemblies took place. The everyday quality of problems presented to the assembly suggests that they were fairly frequent, probably weekly or bimonthly. In addition to regular meetings, everyone in the village was responsible for preserving the integrity of property boundaries in the area. Whenever a property question arose, a group of neighbors was summoned. Boundary problems ranged from an informal witnessing of the replacement of a landmark that had been accidentally disturbed during planting[69] to a judge's formal summons of "the oldest residents of the neighborhood to be sworn, that they will without fraud, show where the boundaries of the land in question are situated."[70]

The legitimacy of village assemblies was recognized by Visigothic rulers and their laws gave official sanction to many of the village decisions. Official recognition of the village as a legal entity was a satisfactory "ritualization" for the nobility, but it was not enough for members of the village. Traditionally, peasants have had their own methods for reaffirming community ties that formed the basis for the interactions recorded in the Visigothic law code.

From the earliest settlements, village feasts ritualized community ties. Communal feasting represented a two-directional symbol. First, the celebration expressed a victory over nature: a commemoration of the success of fertility rites combined with human labor, culminating in the harvest feast.[71] Second, the ritual meal was an institution of the peasants' social world. As such it was both a

concrete   demonstration of village cohesiveness   and   a
means   for continuing it.   E.A. Thompson   has   observed
the   importance   of feasting in clan   societies,   where
"...the communal eating and drinking were a symbol   and
confirmation of mutual social obligations."[72]   This
remained   true in the village community throughout   the
Middle Ages even after society had become more   complex
than   clan   or   tribal   organization.   Peasants   of
Visigothic   society   preserved ritual   feasting   as   an
integral part of the social ritualization.

        Along   with generous food and drink,   ritual
feasting   in Gallegan peasant culture had   always
included dancing and singing.   In   pre-Roman   times,
Strabo   observed that dances were an important part   of
Celtiberian   eating and drinking celebrations.[73]   We
lack information on the specific kinds of rural   dances
during   Roman and Visigothic times, but dancing   surely
was   an   integral physical expression of   important
rituals   and   magic   incantations.[74]   One of   the
aspirations of popular religion was the need to express
ritual   publically,[75] and the dance in effect was a
perfect   vehicle for such concrete expression.   Thus,
within   each Gallegan village there was   periodic
feasting accompanied by singing and dancing - a "feast
of fools" condemned by the official Church[76] but
vitally   necessary to the village community.   In   the
midst of communal feasting and communal dance,   the
villagers temporarily achieved a feeling of closeness,
even   unity, with their neighbors, making the village
community   somehow   more than a group of individuals
living near each other. A sense of village unity
vitally   assured all members' contributions to "the
interests   of the   community."[77]   Any reluctance to
participate in community rituals was a threat, to be
penalized by ostracization.[78]

Just as feasting and dance might join villages in space with their neighbors, the performance of similar rituals at funerals or cemeteries united villagers across time with ancestors and neighbors generations past. To commemorate a neighbor's death by funeral dances and songs comforted the living by reaffirming that the dead were still spiritually part of the village community.[79] These contacts with the dead were reaffirmed periodically by taking meals at the cemetery, thus symbolically including the dead in the feasts of the living.[80] Through such rituals traditional village communities created a form of collective immortality - an immortality of the community as a whole.

Peasant conceptions were strikingly different from the official Visigothic Church's approach to death, in which the primary goal was personal salvation. Indeed, traditional rural death rituals which symbolically included the dead in the rituals of the living, were seen as a threat to the salvation of the individual.[81] Respect for the dead was not considered the responsibility of the whole community, but rather a subject of legislation to protect the reputation and wishes of the individual. "If the guilt of any person has not been established in his lifetime, it is undoubtedly monstrous to accuse him of crime after his death...Nor shall the testimony of a living witness, in contradiction of one who is dead, ever be taken...."[82] Similarly, all the legislation regarding wills and inheritance was to guarantee that the wishes of the dead would be respected.[83]

This is not to say that on some level the Visigothic nobility did not recognize the significance of feasting and other ritualized social activities, for

they, too, had used the same kinds of mechanisms during
their tribal period to ensure a cohesive community.
However, their position as a ruling and literate elite
gave them a different view of the world. Ruling groups
increasingly relied on legislation to unify and govern
social relationships, since they were dealing with a
large kingdom instead of a close-knit community. Such
impersonal social legislation was unsatisfactory to
peasants who still relied on the cohesiveness of the
village community.

The Gallegan peasants' world was primarily
dominated by two fundamental interactions: 1) with the
natural environment of mountains, streams and infertile
soil, and 2) with the social world of the village
itself. Both these natural and social worlds had
traditionally been ritualized so that they could be
ordered, understood, and controlled. The official
Church could not eradicate by mere legislation these
old ritualizations, since they were an integral part of
village culture and had been since the earliest Celtic
settlement. The Church had to accommodate these needs
before peasants could really be called Christians.

The cross-fertilization of religious ideas between
peasant and elite was a process that took place
gradually throughout the early Christian centuries.
During this time, village life in Spain's northwest
hills changed very little. Galicia's rulers, on the
other hand, experienced rapid changes in leadership,
policies and religion. Before examining the process of
religious interaction, it will be necessary to explore
the nature and development of Galicia's official
culture.

Notes

1.   Fernand Braudel, The Mediterranean and the Mediterranean World in the Age of Philip II, trans. Sian Reynolds (New York, 1975), II:773.

2.   Strabo, The Geography of Strabo, trans. H.L. Jones (New York, 1917), 2:III, 1.

3.   The elevations range from 1000 to 3000 feet near the coast to 6000 feet in the interior.

4.   For a detailed summary of mention of classic authors, see Enrique Flórez, España Sagrada (Madrid, 1759), 55:31-51.

5.   Marcial, the classical author, mentions the export of salted fish and shellfish. Vincente Risco, Manual de Historia de Galicia (Madrid, 1952), p. 36.

6.   Strabo. 2:III, 3.

7.   Stephen McKenna, Paganism and Pagan Survivals in Spain up to the Fall of the Visigothic Kingdom, The Catholic University of America Studies in Medieval History, New Series, vol. 1 (Washington, 1938), pp. 6-7, lists inscriptions from the mountains and rivers of this region.

8.   Manuel Murguia, Historia de Galicia (Lugo, 1865), I:536.

9.   Visigothic Code, trans. S.P. Scott (Boston, 1910), Book X, title I, ch. VIII, p. 337. In using these laws for this chapter, I have tried to use only those which probably applied to the Northwest region. For example, I included those referring to oak and pine forests, since they are abundant in the North and virtually non-existent further South. I excluded those dealing with water shortage problems, since they would obviously not apply in the North.

10.   Ibid., Book X, title I, ch. XIX, p. 341.

"...a lease for 1/10 part of its annual yield, or for any other payment or consideration."

11. Ibid., Book X, title I, ch. XI, p. 338.

12. Ibid., Book X, title I, ch. XIII, p. 338. "If...he [tenant] should cultivate more land than he is entitled to under his contract, or should bring in others for that purpose, or his sons and grandsons, inmates of his house, should cultivate lands not included in his lease..."

13. Ibid., Book X, title I, ch. XIII, p. 338.

14. The whole of Book X deals with these problems, pp. 334-351.

15. Julio Caro Baroja, Los Pueblos del Norte de la Peninsula Ibérica (San Sebastian, 1973), p. 165.

16. Visigothic Code, Book VIII, title III, ch. VII, p. 277. "Whoever cuts down the posts of a fence, or the tree trunk of a hedge belonging to another..."

17. Ibid., Book VIII, title III, ch. VI, p. 277.

18. Ibid., Book VIII, title III, deals with these problems. On p. 274 is a summary of the contents of this book.

19. Ibid., Book VIII, title III, ch. IX, p. 278.

20. Ibid., Book VIII, title IV, ch. 27, p. 295.

21. Ibid., Book VIII, title IV, ch. 28, p. 295.

22. Ibid., Book VIII, title I, ch. XII, p. 269 discusses the problem of villagers being robbed when going to or from their fields, suggesting that they were some distance from the village.

23. Strabo, 2:III, 4, 17.

24. Caro Baroja, p. 151, noted that Gallegan women today take considerable part in agricultural work.

25. Most recent studies indicate that it was the Celts, not the Romans who introduced the plow to the peninsula. See Caro Baroja, p. 148, for a discussion

of archeological findings in Spain on the subject. A good summary of the Celtic "ard" type plow can be found in Stuart Piggott, Ancient Europe (Chicago, 1965), p. 150.

26. Caro Baroja, p. 148.

27. Strabo, 2:III, 3, 7.

28. Orosius, The Seven Books of History against the Pagans ed. Roy J. Deferrari (Washington, 1964), p. 187.

29. This cart was a spoke-wheeled cart introduced into the Northwest by the Celts. It replaced the indigenous solid-wheeled cart which remained predominant in southern Spain. (Caro Baroja, p. 184).

30. Visigothic Code, Book VIII, title IV, ch. X, p. 287.

31. Strabo, 2:III, 4, 17. "...the especially great number of the mice..."

32. The Roman author, Varro, in Rerum rusticarum libritres first described these structures: "Supra terram granaria in agro guidam sublima faciunt..." (Caro Baroja, p. 165).

33. Martin of Braga in the sixth century reprimanded peasants for continuing such feast days. ["De correctione Rusticorum" Claude W. Barlow, ed., The Fathers of the Church, Iberian Fathers (Washington, 1969), p. 77.] "...they [the mice] will never spare what they find simply for your dedicating a holiday to them."

34. Strabo, 2:III, 3, 7.

35. Visigothic Code, Book VIII, title III, ch. I, p. 275.

36. This practice was condemned by Martin of Braga: "Nam ab petras et ad arbores et ad fontes...cereolos incendere." ("De Correctione

Rusticorum," p. 79.) It was condemned again by the
twelfth council of Toledo in 681: "...accensores
facularum et excolentes sacra fontium vel arborum..."
[XII Tolet, XI, J.P. Migne, Patrologiae Latinae Cursus
Completus (Paris, 1844-1864), 84:478 (hereafter cited
as PL.)]

37.   Marc Bloch, "The Advent and Triumph of the
Watermill," in Land and Work in Medieval Europe (New
York, 1969), p. 147, mentions these rotary millstones
spreading later in the middle ages "...into the
humblest dwellings..." But archeological evidence
suggests that they were developed by the Iberian Celts.
This is the hand mill that would have been used by
Visigothic peasants in Galicia. For an archeological
study of this mill, see Piggott, p. 250.

38.   For a discussion of the persistent usage of
hand mills even after the advent of water mills, see
Bloch, pp. 148-150.

39.   Visigothic Code, Book VIII, title IV, ch. XXX,
p. 296, mentions mill ponds, which is clear evidence
for the existence of watermills. This law is under the
heading of "Ancient Law," which places the use of
watermills in Spain at least by the late sixth century.
This is considerably earlier than the late
eighth-century legal references noted in Germany by
Bloch, p. 137.

40.   Visigothic Code, Book VII, title II, ch. 12,
p. 242.

41.   Strabo observed that the Celtiberians used
animal fat instead of oil for cooking, 2:III, 3, 7.
The continued practice is suggested by legislation
designed to discover heretical vegetarians by seeing if
they would eat vegetables cooked in animal fat (I
Bracara XIV) PL 84:567.

42. Manuel Murguia, Historia de Galicia (Lugo, 1865) claims that virtually all Gallegan practices are Celtic in origin, and that they absorbed very little from the Romans. Strabo attributed the lack of Roman amenities to Gallegan stubbornness: "...the ocean-coast on the north has none [olive trees and grapevines] on account of the cold, and, for the most part, the rest of the ocean coast has none on account of the slovenly character of the people and the fact that they live on a low moral plane..." (Strabo, 2:III, 4, 16.)

43. Fructuosus of Braga, "General Rule," in Barlow, p. 186.

44. Clifford Geertz, The Interpretation of Cultures (New York, 1973), p. 126.

45. An analysis of a related trait of peasant societies is proposed by George M. Foster: "...peasants view their social, economic, and natural universes - their total environment - as one in which all of the desired things in life...exist in finite quantity and are always in short supply, as far as the peasant is concerned." ["Peasant Society and the Image of Limited Good," Peasant Society, A Reader, ed. Jack M. Potter, et al., (Boston, 1967), p. 304.

46. Justino, "Historiarum ex Pompey o Trogo - Epitome lib. XLIV," in Murgia, I:538, "In hujus gentibus finibus sacer mons est, quem ferro violari nefas habetur..."

47. Frances Clare Nock, trans., The Vita Sancti Fructuosi, The Catholic University of America Studies in Medieval History, New Series, Volume VII (Washington, 1946), p. 88, has a description of the saint's father who was a "military duke," which provides an example of a landlord who kept a

substantial flock of sheep. The duke went to the
"...mountain valleys of the territory of Bierzo,
seeking an accounting of his flocks...[He]...was busy
listing the flocks and investigating the reports of the
shepherds."

48. Visigothic Code, Book VIII, title V, ch. I, p.
298, says, "Whoever finds any hogs in his woodland
must...give notice to the master, or parents of the
owner..." Thus the adult responsible was presumably
usually occupied elsewhere, reinforcing the
supplementary nature of this occupation.

49. Ibid., Book VIII, title V, chs. 1-4, pp.
298-300.

50. Ibid., Book VIII, title V, ch. 1, p. 299.

51. Caro Baroja. p. 58, attributes this lack of
class stratification in hunting to the fact that game
provided an important part of the common man's diet.

52. Nock, Vita Sancti Fructuosi, pp. 94 and 100.

53. Visigothic Code, Book VIII, title IV, ch. 29,
p. 295.

54. Diodorus wrote, "The drink of the Celtiberians
is made of honey which their country furnishes in
abundance," in J.J. van Nostrand, ed., An Economic
Survey of Ancient Rome, Vol. III - Roman Spain
(Baltimore, 1937), p. 140.

55. "Chronico Aemilianense," Biblioteca Nacional
ms. no. 51, fol. 36.

56. Visigothic Code, Book VIII, title VI, ch. 1,
p. 303.

57. Ibid., Book VIII, title VI, ch. 2, p. 303.

58. Ibid., chs. I and III, pp. 303-304.

59. Geertz, p. 140: "The drive to make sense out of experience, to give it form and order, is evidently as real and pressing as the more familiar biological needs."

60. This allowance of personal space around each dwelling is strikingly different from the extremely close village structure in southern Spain. These different settlement patterns may reveal degrees of Romanization, as these differences were noted by Tacitus in the first century: "They [Germans] lay out their villages not as with us in connected or closely joined houses, but each one surrounds his dwelling with an open space..." ["Germania" Medieval History, D. White, ed. (Illinois, 1965), p. 48.]

61. The Celtic ending "brigus" usually denoted a village god, and an interesting adaptation to Roman occupation can be seen in the town Augustabriga, combining the emperor's name with a Celtic town god.

62. J. Vicens Vives, Historia Social y Económica de España y América Vol. I (Barcelona, 1972), p. 62; Marie R. Madden, Political Theory and Law in Medieval Spain (New York, 1930), p. 137.

63. Florentino-Agustín Diez Gonzáles, San Fructuoso y Su Tiempo (Leon, 1966), p. 56; Madden, p. 136, notes that in southern Spain cities municipio remained the center of organization.

64. Isidore of Seville, "Etymology" Lib. XV, c. ii, 15, in Madden, p. 139: "Compita sunt, ubi usus est conventus fieri rusticorum dicti compitas quia multa loca in agris eodem competunt."

65. Visigothic Code, Book VIII, title IV, ch. XVI, p. 289.

66. Ibid., Book VIII, title IV, ch. XVIII, p. 290.

67.   Ibid., Book VIII, title IV, ch. XXIII, pp. 292-3.

68.   Ibid., Book VIII, title V, ch. VI, p. 301.

69.   Ibid., Book X, title III, ch. II, p. 348.

70.   Ibid., Book X, title III, ch. V, p. 350.

71.   Mikhail Bakhtin's unparallelled analysis of banquet imagery in Rabelais and his World (Cambridge, 1965), p.281, expressed this aspect of feasting: "...labor and food represented the two sides of a unique phenomenon, the struggle of man against the world, ending in his victory."

72.   E.A. Thompson, "The Passio S. Sabae and Early Visigothic Society" Historia, IV (1955), p. 133. The experience of St. Sabas, a christian in a pagan village, provides a fine example of the importance of the communal/community meal. "Sabas...offended against the gods of the community by refusing to share their meal; and an offense against the gods was an offense against the community itself."

73.   Strabo, 2:III, 3, 7, "The dinner is passed around, and amid their cups they dance to flute and trumpet, dancing in chorus..." Caro Baroja, pp. 83, 237, discusses this early importance of the dance to these northern peoples and relates it to current dance rituals among Basques and other mountain Spaniards.

74.   Very useful for this hypothesis is Caro Baroja's analysis of the kinds of dances among modern northern rural Spaniards. He observed agricultural dances, social dances, and sympathetic magic dances representing various animals (ibid., p. 237). Also interesting is E. Louis Backman, Religious Dances in the Christian Church and in Popular Medicine (London, 1952), p. 2, in which he observes that "Slavonic and

Germanic races possessed a highly developed dance ritual in connection with their religious customs..."

75. Raoul Manselli, La Religion populaire au Moyen Age (Paris, 1975), p. 128: "...une des aspirations typiques de la réligion populaire est son besoin d'une exteriorisation concrête de gestes, d'actes, de rites..."

76. III Tolet, XXIII, PL 84:356. "Ut in sanctorum natalitus ballematiae prohibeantur." Manselli, p. 39, observed that medieval dance rituals were "...du monde des traditions populaires...et non pas du paganisme."

77. Visigothic Code, Book VIII, title IV, ch. XXIX, p. 295, "No one shall, for his own private benefit, and against the interests of the community..." (Emphasis added).

78. Thompson, "The Passio," p. 333. When Sabas refused to eat with the community, he was sent out of the town.

79. Again, this is not just a form of pagan worship, but a basic expression of medieval village life that persisted in spite of repeated Christian prohibitions, such as III Tolet, XXII, PL 84:356: "nam funebre carmen quod vulgo defunctis cantari solet..."

80. A sixth century prohibition describes this practice: Martin's canon no. LXIX appended to II Bracara, PL 84:584. "Non liceat Christianis prandia in monumenta portare."

81. III Tolet, XXII, PL 84:356. After prohibiting secular funeral celebrations (above note no. 79) the canon continues saying, "Sufficiat autem quod in spe resurrectionis Christianorum corporibus famulatus divinorum impenditur conticorum..."

82. Visigothic Code, Book V, title VI, ch. VI, p. 179; Book II, title IV, ch. VII, p. 60.

83.   Ibid., Book II, title V, ch. IV, p. 65, for example, directly states: "It shall not be lawful for a son, or other heir, to contest the just and legitimate provisions of the will of an ancestor, because it is presumption in him who attempts to nullify the acts of his ancestors."

THE OFFICIAL CHURCH

The principal concern of the Iberian ruling elite was power - establishing it and maintaining it. The clearest way for rulers to define their power was in their ability to command obedience from the ruled.[1] In order to command such obedience the Iberian ruling groups erected a complex administrative structure to govern the kingdom. The Visigothic sources reflect a preoccupation with power, obedience and administration which served both to define and preserve the kingdom's hierarchical structure. Indeed, one could argue that the primary concern of the ruling culture was to impose an administrative order on the natural and social orders that evolved in the village.

Before the rulers of the Iberian peninsula could actively maintain their power, they first had to establish it. The early history of the Iberian peninsula is one of a struggle for the establishment of power. Around 200 B.C., the Romans conquered Galicia. They established an administration centered on small cities in the province. Braga, Lugo, Astorga, and Leon became centers of provincial Roman administration and remained administrative centers during the Germanic kingdoms that succeeded Rome's occupation. The Sueves invaded Spain in 409 and settled in Galicia as foederati of the empire in 411. The Suevian kingdom persisted until 585 when it was conquered by the Visigothic king Leovigild and made a province of the Visigothic kingdom.[2]

In many ways the Celtiberian rural people of Galicia continued in their ways of life and belief

during these various changes in the ruling groups.
They remained primarily preoccupied with earning a
living from the poor land with the added problem of
producing a sufficient surplus to maintain the ruling
nobility. But just as the imposition of a ruling elite
added different political and economic dimensions to
the region's tribal culture, this imposition added an
additional element to the region's religious structure
- power, obedience and the administrative order
necessary to maintain it. As soon as kings converted
to Christianity, the Church became an official Church
bound not only to the official power structure, but
committed to the extraction of obedience to validate
its position as the dominant ruling religion. Church
canons parallelled secular laws pronouncing penalties
upon those who disobeyed the canons of the Church.[3]
        Obedience to religious authority, however, is
difficult to define. The subtleties and variations of
individual religious belief are difficult to use as a
measure of obedience. The most readily identifiable
yardstick of religious obedience was practice. Thus
the official Church focused on uniformity of practice
as proof of obedience and to make a reality of a Church
that claimed to rule the religiosity of the kingdom. A
coalition of lay and spiritual nobility promulgated
legislation articulating the goal of achieving a
unified Church: "We decree that no man of whatever
race or lineage, either native or foreigner...shall
openly or silently, impugn the unity of the Catholic
faith..."[4] Such sweeping abstract legislation,
however, could not bring uniformity of religious
practice to the kingdom. Church leaders would slowly
have to observe the varieties of religious practice and
slowly legislate and enforce homogeneous practices

before the kingdom could be unified religiously under the official Church.

In order to maintain its structure and to provide a means to bring practices into conformity with official expectations, the Church created an administrative structure to extend its control from the centers of power in Toledo and Braga to the villages on the geographic fringes of the kingdom. The Visigothic rulers largely kept the Roman system of administration. The kingdom remained divided into provinces governed by duces (also called comes provinciae) and further subdivided into civitates governed by minor officials. Each province was assigned judges and numerarii who were responsible for collecting taxes that contributed to the support of the nobility, the army and the administrative structure of the kingdom.[5] In the sphere of religion, official concern with administration was reflected in the abundant legislation ordering the network of bishops and priests that would guide the faithful in a unified Church and would regulate the income (tithes, land and gifts) to support the Church.

The Christianization of the kingdom, however, was a process more complex than slow systematic imposition of uniformity by the ruling powers. In a sense, the peasants of the villages too possessed a certain degree of power. It was not a power to rule but a power to persist. Rural resistance to religious change ultimately forced the official Church to expand the bounds of orthodoxy to incorporate many rural religious practices. Only then could the official Church claim the power to rule a religiously unified kingdom. Thus the administrative order imposed by the Visigothic rulers was an order of subtle struggle and slow accommodation.

From the fifth through the seventh century the Church faced several problems in its efforts to Christianize the kingdom. The Gallegan Church established during Rome's occupation had to convert the pagan Sueves when they established their kingdom in Galicia in 411. Then the Church struggled with eradicating Priscillianism, a popular local fifth century heresy. When Galicia was conquered by the Visigoths in the sixth century, Iberia's ruling Church became national instead of regional and the Visigothic rulers struggled to impose religious uniformity on the Gallegan province. Finally, throughout these changes in the ruling elite, the official Church whether Suevian or Visigothic, worked to exert its power over the countryside to bring the peasants into conformity with the orthodoxy of the elite. To understand the church's slow accommodation to rural religious sensibility, it is necessary to trace the political and legislative efforts of Iberian rulers to extend and maintain their power through the imposition of religious uniformity.

Under the Roman occupation, a Catholic hierarchy became fairly well established in Galicia. During the early Christian centuries each Roman urban center had a bishop and related administrative structures.[6] The Sueves were pagan when they established their kingdom in 411. The sources do not tell of persecution of Christians by pagan kings, and it is likely that a relatively peaceful co-existence was maintained between the two religious groups of the Gallegan elite. Not only did the Catholic hierarchy maintain itself during this period, but it is probable that Catholic leaders continued some degree of missionary activity, as is suggested by the fact that a convert, Rechiar, became king of the Sueves in 448.

In that year, Galicia officially was declared
Catholic, but the development of a strong Church in
close cooperation with the royal power was delayed by
an unstable political situation which closely followed
the kingdom's conversion. In 456, upon the death of
King Rechiar, the throne was contested, and civil war
disrupted the province for eight years. Internal
instability was exacerbated by the Visigothic invasion
of Iberia in the same year. Arian Visigoths rapidly
conquered most of the peninsula, and the unstable
Suevian kingship - with good reason - felt threatened.
In 463, Remismund managed to end the civil war and
became undisputed king of the Sueves. The Visigothic
kingdom still posed a threat, however, and, probably
for political reasons, Remismund proclaimed his kingdom
Arian and married a Visigothic princess. Galicia
remained officially Arian for about ninety years, but
the conversion of a king did not mean uniformity of
religion throughout the kingdom. Peasants were
probably not appreciably affected by this Arian
conversion, any more than they had been by Roman
paganism.[7]

Without a doubt, Catholic structure and
organization were weakened during the war years and the
Arian penetration. It would be incorrect, however, to
assume that Catholic worship disappeared and the Church
dissolved. The major sees still had bishops, and
monasteries continued to be refuges of worship in the
politically unstable country. While the Spanish
chronicles are largely silent about this Arian period
of Galicia's history, it is possible to find evidence
for survival and even missionary expansion of
Catholicism. For example, an inscription from the year
485 found near Braga commemorated the erection of a

Catholic   church   by   the   nun   Marsipalla.[8]   The
establishment   of   a new Catholic church   so   near   the
royal   capital   of   Braga   would   certainly   indicate
toleration   or,   at least,   indifference on the   part   of
the Arian kings.

One   of the most   important   sources of   information
for   this   obscure   period of Galicia's   history   is   a
letter from Pope Vigilius written to Profuturus, Bishop
of   Braga,   in 538.   Responding to questions   posed   by
Profuturus,   the Pope dealt with   issues that   suggested
that   the Catholic Church had not only   survived Arian
rule,   but   had   begun once again to expand.   In   one
paragraph,   the   Pope   discussed   the   rededication   of
churches   which   had been   destroyed   through   warfare.
This   passage   not   only   confirms   the   obvious,   that
churches   had   been destroyed   during   these   turbulent
years,   but   also   suggests   that   by   538   efforts   of
Catholic churchmen had succeeded to such a degree   that
abandoned churches needed to be rededicated for resumed
worship.   Vigilius' letter also provides other evidence
demonstrating Catholic missionary work in Galicia,   for
he discussed correct ritual for baptism, as well as how
to   receive back into the Catholic community those   who
had   been   rebaptized   into Arianism.[9]   Questions   of
baptism are a clear indication of an expanding Church.

Isidore of Seville may have felt that he summed up
this Arian period when he wrote tersely, "Then [between
463 and 559] many Suevian kings persisted in the   Arian
heresy..."[10] but   it   is   evident   that Catholicism did not
die out in Galicia with the conversion of the kings   to
Arianism.

Although   Gallegan   churchmen   slowly   worked   to
recapture Arian apostates and convert remaining pagans,
the   Frankish chronicler, Gregory of Tours,   attributed

the reconversion of Suevian kings to a miracle. According to Gregory, in 550 King Chararich's son fell deathly ill. Having heard of the wonderful miracles that had been performed in Gaul by the relics of St. Martin of Tours, the King decided to appeal to the saint. Chararich's knowledge of the Gallic saint probably may be attributed to the proselytizing efforts of Suevian Catholics. In any case, the King sent rich gifts to the shrine of Martin and promised to convert to Catholicism if his son were cured. The young prince was cured, the King converted and declared his country once again Catholic. The miraculous nature of the events of 550 was reaffirmed in the chronicler's eyes by the coincidental arrival in Braga of Martin, a monk from Pannonia who had been "divinely guided"[11] to Galicia and reached there on the same day as the relics of St. Martin. Martin of Pannonia soon became Bishop of Braga and helped the King consolidate the conversion inspired by the relics of Martin of Tours.[12]

In 550, the Arian Visigoths posed no threat to Suevian kings converting to Catholicism. By 550 Byzantium had reconquered the Vandal kingdom of North Africa and had begun to invade southern Spain. In the same year, the city of Cordoba rebelled against the Visigothic King, Agila. Cordoban citizens defeated the King, who then lost his son, his treasure and a large part of his army.[13] This began a period of expensive revolts costly to suppress and of a resulting financial crisis in the Visigothic kingdom.[14] Visigothic kings were always insecure on their thrones, but the mid-sixth century was unusually violent. Between 531-555, four successive kings were murdered. These internal problems were compounded by the fact that during this period the Franks were constantly raiding and threatening the Visigothic province north of the Pyrenees. Since this situation continued until Leovigild took the Visigothic throne in 568, the Arian Visigoths were in no position to threaten Galicia in 550. Under the influence of the miracles of Martin of Tours and the guidance of Martin of Braga, Suevian Kings Chararich and Theodimir were free to declare their country Catholic.

Without a doubt, the sixth-century, Gallegan Catholic Church was shaped by the Pannonian monk, Martin. He was well-educated, pious, popular, and extremely sensitive to religious needs not only of the Church hierarchy, but of peasants who constituted the small parishes of this hill country. Martin's career and writings have been thoroughly studied,[15] so here I shall merely discuss the nature of the Gallegan Church as it was formed in the sixth century under Martin's guidance.

In 561, King Theodimir called a council to allow newly recognized Catholic bishops to establish official Catholicism. The King did not address the council as later Visigothic kings were to do in the Councils of Toledo, nor did he seem to influence its agenda by specifying issues to be discussed. The introductory statement was delivered by Lucretius, the metropolitan of Braga, who stated the threefold purpose of the convention: 1) to define clearly the Catholic faith, 2) to consider the "worship of God," or the divine office, and 3) to organize the clerical office.[16]

These first two topics essentially dealt with the establishment of uniformity, the proof of official power. The "definition of Catholic faith" was to establish a unity of belief, and toward this end, the bishops composed seventeen canons against

Priscillianism, a persistent heresy which had plagued
Galicia for over a hundred years.[17] As uniformity of
belief is hard to identify, the council turned to the
more concrete issue of uniformity of practice, and this
council's liturgical canons are remarkably detailed.
Nine canons defined how church services should be held
and how sacraments should be administered.[18] This
legislation gave Galicia its somewhat distinctive form
of ritual practice to which Gallegans continued to
adhere long after their conquest by the Visigoths and
in spite of persistent Visigothic efforts to bring
Gallegan practices into conformity with their own
liturgical tradition. Unquestionably, part of the
reason for this province's tenacious adherence to its
own liturgy was that it was based on instructions sent
by Pope Vigilius to the Bishop of Braga in 538.[19] The
Pope's letter gave Gallegan practices the force not
only of a church council, but also the authority of
Rome.

Under Lucretius' broad category of organizing the
"clerical office," are the canons regulating church
administration and imposing penalties for disobedience,
both central concerns of the official Church. Since
the core of ecclesiastical administration was its
hierarchy, the bishops carefully ordered its structure.
The twentieth canon specified precisely how laymen
should move through ecclesiastical ranks. They would
spend at least one year as lector, then subdeacon, then
work their way up through each grade until they earned
the priesthood.[20] This provision was directed against
appointments of priests or bishops for political
reasons. It typifies the care of Gallegan bishops to
keep their Church out of royal control as much as
possible. The council also structured a ranking of the

kingdom's bishops in order to lessen rivalry among the
senior members of the ecclesiastical hierarchy. The
metropolitan of Braga was given primacy, and the other
bishops were ranked in order of their date of
ordination.[21]

Closely tied to issues of church administration
was the problem of the use of church funds. With the
new legal status of Christianity, this matter was no
longer left to the discretion of a bishop. One third
of diocesan income was for the bishop's personal use,
one third was for maintenance of the parish lower
clergy, while the final third was allotted to maintain
the church building, including such items as
lighting.[22]

The final concern of this now official Church was
to provide a mechanism to ensure obedience to the
structures and doctrine established in council. The
traditional ecclesiastical sanction against
disobedience was excommunication, and when the Church
acquired officially recognized status, the threat of
excommunication assumed both legal and social
consequences, thus increasing its effectiveness. The
council of Braga confronted the disobedient with the
threat of excommunication, adding the social penalty of
forbidding anyone to associate with an excommunicant.[23]

Now at last in 561 the Catholic ecclesiastical
structure in this region achieved legitimization and
precision of organization. For the first time, all the
churchmen in this "extremity of the world"[24] had before
them a clear statement of orthodoxy and legislation for
uniformity in organization and practice. The First
Council of Braga thus laid the foundation for a strong
centralized Church, remarkably free from secular
control.

In 570, Miro succeeded to the Suevian throne. Very likely under the influence of Martin who was then Metropolitan of Braga, Miro called the Second Council of Braga in 572. Twelve bishops attended this council, and, following the precedent set at the previous council, the introductory statement was made not by the King, but by Martin of Braga. The success of the first council is suggested by the fact that none of the issues decided in 561 had to be reconsidered in 572. The clarity achieved by the first council in determining organization and ritual for the Gallegan Church needed no further modification. The second council was called for moral rather than organizational legislation - to cope with priestly corruption. The theoretical structure established in 561 was thought to be satisfactory; this council dealt realistically with human failings of the churchmen who implemented the decrees of the first council.

The Bishops in council felt that some clergymen succumbed to greed, charging a fee to ordain priests, to bless holy oil, to consecrate churches and to perform baptism.[25] At times, priests or deacons even sold church vessels for profit.[26] The council was also concerned that clergy should be above reproach in sexual behavior. Priests were not to live with women, even family members, and charges of fornication against a member of the clergy were to be substantiated by two or three witnesses.[27] Bishops also considered the peculiarly local problem of clergy wearing their hair long around their tonsures, forbidding the practice as prideful clinging to their Germanic and Celtic custom of wearing long hair.[28]

Appended to the proceedings of the second council of Braga were eighty-four canons composed by Martin of

Braga. Both the organization and content of the canons
testify to Martin's perceptive awareness of not only
the problem of church organization, but also the
religious needs of his rural parishioners. The first
sixty-eight canons were directed toward the
organization and behavior of the clergy. They
regulated in detail everything from the election of a
bishop to the excommunication of a sinful cleric.[29]
The remaining sixteen canons were designed to instruct
the laity on proper Christian behavior. This Gallegan
Church was characterized by an awareness of, and a
concern for, the rural people who made up the body of
the Church. Such sensitivity was undoubtedly due to
Martin's familiarity with the rural laity as a result
of his travels and of his experience at his monastery
of Dumium in the countryside outside Braga. In the
canons addressed to the laity, Martin had two principal
themes: warning "superstitious" country people against
adhering to old pagan practices and urging Christian
morality upon the people, including avoiding heretics
and excommunicants.[30] Martin's awareness that church
reform required dealing separately with the different
problems of church leaders and parishioners, and his
attempts to legislate for each of the two groups of
society, religious nobility and rural laity, underscore
the fact that Gallegan religion must be examined at two
levels, not simply as a unified phenomenon.

Political events, however, once again interfered
with the development of Galicia's official Church. The
unstable political situation in the Visigothic kingdom,
which had permitted the Suevian kings to act
independently for twenty-five years, now changed. In
572, Leovigild, one of the strongest of the Visigothic
kings, took sole possession of the throne. During the

early years of his reign, Leovigild ended the possibility of any further Byzantine advances in the South and finally suppressed the rebellions in Cordoba. By 576, the King's position in the South was secure enough to permit him to turn his attention to the North, and in that year he invaded the kingdom of Galicia, then ruled by Miro's son, Eborich. Leovigild's military success was impressive, [31] and Eborich was forced to swear allegiance to Leovigild. An independent Suevian kingdom survived this initial invasion, but the reprieve was only temporary. In 584, a rebellion against King Eborich provided Leovigild the opportunity he needed to consolidate his rule over most of the peninsula. In the following year, he invaded Galicia and made it a province of his Visigothic kingdom.

Since Leovigild was of the Arian faith, the official religion of Galicia was once again changed by royal decree. While there were those who apostatized in order to please their new rulers, the Catholic Church continued to exist in this province as it had through almost two hundred years of its own kings' religious vacillations. It probably continued to be strong and relatively well organized as a result of Martin's reforms of the mid-sixth century, and Catholic bishops continued to hold their sees.[32] In any case, Arianism did not have much opportunity to gain a firm foothold in the province, since four years later, the new Visigothic king, Reccared, converted to Catholicism, and from then on there were no further changes in the ruling religion of Galicia.[33]

It has been relatively easy to follow Galicia's independent development to 585 A.D., when the Visigoths conquered the region. After that, however, Galicia

shared   in   the history of the other provinces   of   the
Visigothic   kingdom.   Gallegan bishops, as one   of   the
ruling   groups of their province, participated   in   the
national councils, bringing with them problems observed
in   their   diocese   and   returning   with   conciliar
decisions.   Since our main sources from this period are
the   decisions   of   these   national   councils,   it   is
difficult to analyze precisely the nature of the Church
in the province of Galicia.   I shall thus approach this
question indirectly, comparing provincial with national
legislation   and   local problems   with   national   ones.
Between   589   and the fall of the   Visigothic   kingdom,
eighteen provincial councils were held in Spain,   along
with   fourteen   national   councils   held   in   Toledo.
Bishops   presumably   met   in   their   own   provinces   to
discuss   issues   and problems most   relevant   to   their
regions.   Much   of   the   legislation   enacted   on   the
provincial level was a repetition and strengthening   of
canons   already   decreed   at   the   national   councils.
Therefore,   by   comparing   national   with   provincial
legislation, it is possible to begin to understand   the
ecclesiastical   situation   in each   of   the   Visigothic
provinces.   By comparing decrees   from   the   Gallegan
councils   of   Braga   and   the   episcopal   letters   and
chronicles   from   this   region with   the   national
legislation,   I   shall trace Gallegan   church   problems
through the seventh century.

        Reccared's conversion to Christianity   represented
a   final declaration of uniformity of belief among   the
ruling classes of the Iberian peninsula.   But this   did
not   end   the more fundamental   dichotomy   between   the
official   Church   and   rural   religiosity   so   clearly
perceived by Martin of Braga.   To continue to trace the
development of the official Church that struggled   with

this problem in the peninsula's northwestern mountains, we have to turn to the activity of the Visigothic church. Legislation no longer came primarily from Braga, under the direction of a churchman like Martin, who was aware of some of the religious impulses arising in the neighboring hills, many of which dated back to the Celtic settlement. On the contrary, decrees would come from Toledo, where churchmen were often more concerned with the administration of the Church and state and brutal Visigothic politics than with religious needs of peasants.

In 589, King Reccared called bishops from all of Spain, including Galicia[34] to discuss religious problems which, upon Reccared's conversion, had become national problems. The main problem considered by the council was that studied by the first council of Braga - the structuring of an official Church once again created by royal decree. As at Braga, the first business of the council was to define orthodoxy. As soon as the King converted, it was expected that his Gothic subjects would also adhere to his faith, finally giving Spain the unity of a national religion. King Reccared in his introductory address to the council promised to adhere to the councils of Nicaea and Chalcedon, thus bringing Spain into the larger Christian world. Once again, bishops used excommunication to enforce their decrees and framed twenty-three canons anathematizing those who held Arian beliefs. These excommunications were signed by both clergy (including four Suevian bishops) and viri illustres,[35] thus demonstrating the cleric and secular unity that was achieved by Reccared's conversion.

The council did, however, have to deal with several practical problems that accompanied the effort

to impose religious unity over a society larger and
more heterogeneous than the old Suevian state. The
most immediate problem involved baptism rituals. Since
baptism was one of the most important rites of passage
into the Christian society, the new national Church had
to decide what to do with Arians who had been "baptized
in heresy."[36] Was the Catholic society created by
Reccared's royal decree different enough to require
another baptism as a symbol for admission, or did the
first baptism still guarantee a place in Visigothic
Catholicism? The Third Council stood strongly by
orthodox prohibitions against rebaptism,[37] but a
prohibition simply declared what should not be done,
not what should, so the question was still not fully
resolved. In Galicia, it is very likely that churchmen
looked to their own tradition, solving the problem in a
manner suggested by Pope Vigilius in 538 - receiving
Arians into the Church by penance, instruction and
laying on of hands.[38]

There was also the problem of church buildings.
The bishops decided to preserve the Arian buildings and
rededicate them to Catholicism. The rededication
ceremony was also to extend to each diocese,[39] which,
in effect, ritually converted the land of the entire
kingdom, and at the same time, made it easy for common
people to continue to attend their local church. These
measures were the practical implementation of the
theoretical religious unity proclaimed by the Third
Council's introductory statement of faith.[40] Once the
Visigothic state Church was established, the business
of succeeding councils was largely political and
administrative.

The result of such religious unity was a blurring
of the social lines that distinguished Roman from Goth.

This is confirmed by sources outside the councils.
Archeological evidence, for example, demonstrates that
the end of the sixth century, after Reccared's
conversion, marked the final abandonment of the old
Gothic form of dress and the disappearance of the
traditional Gothic brooches and buckles.[41] It is
important to note that this increasing homogeneity at
the top levels of society represented neither the
subservience of the newly converted Goths to the older
Roman hierarchy nor a religious take-over by the
politically victorious Goths. There developed instead
a close integration in religious and political spheres
of the people who had traditionally ruled different
sectors of the now religiously unified territory. The
composition of bishops attending the Councils of Toledo
clarifies this high level cultural integration. At the
Third Council, all the Catholic bishops had borne Roman
names, which is to be expected, since until that time,
all the Goths had been Arian. By the Fourth Council,
forty-four years later, the situation had changed
considerably. Of the sixty-nine bishops who signed,
one-quarter were Germans. Reccared's conversion may
have resulted in a degree of "Romanization" of the
Goths, but it also caused many of the high offices of
the Roman Church to be filled by Germans. Most of the
metropolitan sees, however, remained in the hands of
Romans.[42] Galicia always had a higher proportion of
German bishops than the other provinces,[43] no doubt
because these positions were held by Sueves who had a
longer tradition of Catholicism than did the Visigoths.
An integration of ruling groups emerged naturally as
religious unity brought the whole society closer
together, and this trend can also be traced in the more
formal (therefore slower) records of Visigothic law
codes.

Visigothic   jurisprudence completed the   formation
of one ruling society out of two, Catholic and   Arian,
that   had   previously   co-existed   in   the   Iberian
peninsula.   All of Reccared's three   surviving   laws,
dating from about 600, were intended to apply to   both
Goths   and   Romans,[44] which began   a   trend   in   legal
unification culminating in 654 when King   Reccesvinthus
abolished   Roman law altogether.   This relatively   late
date   makes the process of legal unification seem   more
slow than it actually was.   After the Third Council of
Toledo,   Reccared   issued   a   decree   transforming   the
Council's decisions into law binding on all Christians,
which essentially meant the entire society.   Since this
practice was followed by all the Visigothic kings,   by
654,   the official date of legal   conformity,   the
decisions of eight councils of Toledo carried the force
of law throughout Iberia.   These canons were not merely
theoretically   binding; the Third Council   demonstrated
the   practical application of this new legal   synthesis
between Church and State which   transcended cultural
lines.   In   five canons,[45] the Council   called   for
cooperation between bishops and judges to combat abuses
in   both strictly secular matters such   as   taxation,[46]
and   in   religious   issues   such   as   combating   pagan
religious   practices.[47]   Thus Reccesvinthus' legal
reform only made official what had been   fact   for   a
generation.
     Indisputably,   the establishment of   a   unified
official Church in the Visigothic kingdom   helped to
consolidate the Iberian ruling class both culturally
and   legally.   This Church shared with the   earlier
Gallegan one general concerns of unity, obedience and
administration. There was one striking characteristic
of the Visigothic Church that had been lacking   in

VOTIVE CROWN OF KING RECCESVINTHUS

Galicia, the close union between Church and State.
While the Visigothic King took an active role in
religious matters, churchmen were equally involved in
secular issues. For a clear understanding of how the
official Church religion interacted with rural piety,
the nature of this Church/State synthesis must be
examined.

It is important to note that even though the
councils of bishops[48] met to discuss both secular and
ecclesiastical matters, Spain was not a theocracy.[49]
Virtually from the time of Reccared's conversion, the
Church in Spain granted practical, if not theoretical
control to its kings and always undertook legislation
and reform under the long shadow of the Visigothic
throne. National councils met only upon the King's
command, despite repeated conciliar decisions to meet
annually.[50] Frequently, kings left long intervals
between councils.[51] Once they summoned a council,
kings would usully present a request in their
introductory statement which would automatically be
incorporated into the canons. Kings influenced not
only conciliar legislation, but also controlled
ecclesiastical personnel, since from Reccared's time,
it was customary for the King to appoint bishops, who
then were confirmed by the metropolitan. The Twelfth
Council officially sanctioned the King's right of
appointment.[52]

The Visigothic State was not a theocracy, neither
was it Caesaropapist.[53] The Church was able to avoid
domination because Visigothic kings were never secure
from revolt. Theirs was not an hereditary monarchy:
each king owed his position, powerful though he may
have been, to the ecclesiastical and lay nobles in
council, and kings with a tenuous hold on their thrones

tried to use the council to provide religious justification for their rules. Royal attempts to involve Bishops in secular matters of kingship and rebellion are perhaps most clearly seen by briefly examining one of the many examples of royal instability. The fifth, sixth, and seventh Councils of Toledo, held between 636 and 646, were called during typically turbulent times.

In 636, fearing rebellion, King Chintilus called his bishops to the Fifth Council of Toledo. The King asked for and received ecclesiastical support to try to retain his crown. Of the seven decrees promulgated by the Fifth Council, six dealt with the support of the King, his family, and his followers, and with condemning usurpers.[54] A number of these canons were repeated in the Sixth Council called in 638.[55] Chintilus managed to hold his throne, but conciliar anathemas were not enough to protect his son, Tulga, who was deposed in 642 by Chindasvintus. The bishops at the Seventh Council of Toledo proved once again their obedience to the kings by forgetting their promise to pronounce anathema on usurpers and pledging their support of King Chindasvintus.[56] The spirit behind such political involvement was exemplified by an oath of allegiance to the King that everyone in Spain, lay or cleric, had to swear.[57] This oath firmly bound churchmen to the will of the King, and ironically it was reaffirmed every time a usurper took the throne.

Both in spirit and practice, Spain's official Church existed in a symbiotic relationship with the King. Kings used councils to give religious sanction to secular decisions and a king would, in turn, give ecclesiastical reforms the force of law by his traditional post-conciliar decree. Iberian lay and ecclesiastical nobles, closely cooperating with their King met fairly regularly at Toledo to discuss religious and political questions.[58] Among these issues were the problems of governing the independent Gallegan province and converting the independent northern peasants. Both problems directly concern this study.

It remains to analyze Gallegan religious developments after the Suevian kingdom was made a Visigothic province. From the time of the Third Council of Toledo, bishops from the newly conquered province of Galicia attended councils, bringing with them traditions and problems unique to their province for discussion at the national level. While Gallegan bishops during the seventh century were as concerned with imposing administrative and theoretical unity as Visigothic bishops from other provinces, representatives from Galicia were frequently interested in achieving these ends in a manner different from the rest of the peninsula - in a way that would continue precedents set by earlier Gallegan churchmen.[59] On the surface, the minutes of the national councils do not indicate any conflict between Gallegan bishops and those of the rest of Spain. No dissenting opinions were recorded, and the signatures at the end imply unanimity and conformity. But a closer examination of the canons suggests a different conclusion.

The independence of Suevian churchmen from royal control was one of the striking differences between the regional Church and the Visigothic one. Once the province was conquered by Leovigild, it was of course impossible to preserve the degree of independence to which Gallegan churchmen had become accustomed. While sitting in council in Toledo, Gallegan bishops were forced to participate in the complicated and violent politics of the Visigothic nobility. The sources indicate, however, that once they returned to their own mountainous province, these bishops attempted to stay aloof from the kingmaking politics that so preoccupied southern churchmen.

Provincial councils of the seventh century in other regions of Spain often repeated the praise and support of the Visigothic kings articulated at the national councils.[60] By contrast, the Third Council of Braga in 675 dealt solely with ecclesiastical matters. Its only reference to the Visigothic King was to acknowledge that the council had been called at his command,[61] which is to be expected, since no councils were held without royal authority. The absence of political references at this council is particularly striking, because the reign of King Wamba, who called the council, was marked by a serious rebellion in the Gallic province. In such a time of civil war, it would have been expected that provincial bishops would strongly declare in favor of the legitimate king, as happened during the provincial council of Carthagenensis held in Toledo in the same year.[62] Gallegan bishops were either cautiously waiting for the outcome of the rebellion before supporting one of the contenders, or they were adhering to the Gallegan custom of considering only ecclesiastical questions in council. Whatever the motive, the result was the same: bishops in Galicia tried to keep the regional Church aloof as much as possible from Visigothic kingmaking.

We do have evidence that at least one Gallegan churchman, the monk Fructuosus, later to become metropolitan of Braga, felt compelled by conscience to become involved in national affairs. Significantly,

Fructuosus wrote not to support, but to criticize the
royal policy of King Reccesvinthus in 651. The monk
pleaded for royal mercy on behalf of traitors held in
prison from rebellions in the time of King Chintilus
(ca. 636). Fructuosus went even further: while
calling for pious forgiveness, he attacked the oath of
allegiance which, since the Fourth Council of Toledo
(633), had formed one of the cornerstones of Visigothic
Church/State cooperation. He wrote: "It is useless to
put forth an oath as an excuse for an impious act [i.e.
showing no mercy to traitors]...If an impious oath
makes it impossible to show mercy, then it is extremely
cruel that the patronage of indulgence is denied to
your royal and priestly clemency. If you follow such
counsel, [that of southern bishops unwilling to reduce
the force of the oath by showing mercy]...what will God
think..."[63] Violation of this oath was to result not
only in civil punishment, but excommunication. Yet, in
Galicia, not only were traitors to King Chintilus not
excommunicated, but the provincial Church was pleading
for their release.

With such independence on the part of its bishops,
it is not surprising that Galicia adhered to different
practices of liturgy and ritual, which troubled the
national councils until the fall of the Visigothic
kingdom. Peninsular liturgical uniformity became an
extremely important issue from the moment Reccared tied
Church unity to his goal of a unified political unit.
If each province was to be permitted to celebrate the
church service in its own way, the social unity that
was proclaimed by each king through his church councils
would be seen to be a fiction. Therefore, from 589,
the Toledan national councils repeatedly called for
liturgical uniformity throughout Spain. Religious

uniformity would perhaps help make a reality of political unity. The conciliar canons did not specify which regions violated the demands of liturgical reform, but by comparing specific points of legislation with regional historic precedents as recorded in minutes of provincial councils, it is possible with reasonable accuracy to suggest those provinces that caused difficulty. Since Galicia had the longest standing liturgical tradition (based on the sixth-century letter from Pope Vigilius and reforms of Martin of Braga), it becomes clear that the northwestern province was a leading culprit.

One example of the diversity that was so threatening symbolically to Visigothic unity, was the form of baptism. The Fourth Council of Toledo forbade triple immersion baptism[64] because of its similarity to Arian practices. Galicia, however, was unwilling to give up this form, since Vigilius had authorized this baptismal method,[65] and Martin of Braga had written a tract, "De trina mersione" justifying triple immersion.[66] To abandon this form would have been to reject a practice defended by venerated Gallegan fathers simply to please the conquering Visigoths. Needless to say, triple immersion baptism was not easily abandoned in the North.

There are other examples of Visigothic liturgical legislation which specifically reversed decrees of the councils of Braga, making it likely that these canons were directed to Galicia. One such canon of the Fourth Council of Toledo stated that hymns composed by lay people should be permitted in church services. Furthermore, those who rejected these hymns were to be excommunicated.[67] The strength of the threat at the end of this canon suggests that it was framed to

overthrow previous practice, and indeed, at the Second
Council of Braga in 572, the Gallegan Church
specifically forbade the singing of such hymns in
church.[68] Galicia also pursued its own course in
smaller matters of ritual. In the Northwest, deacons
were forbidden to wear the orarium (stole).[69] Toledan
practice, on the other hand, permitted it, requiring
only that deacons wear only one orarium, and that it
not be too ornate.[70]

Obviously, the most effective way to achieve
standardization of services was not simply to attack
each incidence of diversity as it arose, but to issue
missals and require their use throughout the peninsula.
By 633, a missal had been compiled, probably in Toledo,
and the Fourth Council decreed that upon ordination all
priests were to receive this official book.[71] Since we
know that the Gallegan Church possessed its own missal
which had been authorized by the First Council of Braga
in 561,[72] it is very likely that this Toledan canon was
directed mainly against the newest province, and
presumably Toledan churchmen were trying to replace the
Gallegan missal with their own. This single piece of
legislation, however, was not enough to undo
traditional Gallegan practices. Toledan instructions
calling for conformity in church services were repeated
often enough between 633 and 694 to suggest that
Galicia was not eager to abandon its liturgy.[73]

Thus, even after Visigothic domination, Gallegan
bishops tried to preserve their independence as much as
possible in liturgical practices and in avoiding, for
their own region at least, the close spiritual/secular
involvement that characterized the South. While these
differences frequently frustrated the Visigothic desire
for uniformity, they did not change the fundamental

fact that the Church in Galicia remained an official
Church sharing in preoccupation with obedience,
administration and uniformity. Gallegan bishops were
perfectly comfortable joining with Toledo to add
national force to matters such as finances and taxation
which had also been passed at the provincial level.[74]
Braga was also willing to turn to Toledo for
disciplinary aid in correcting clerical immorality.[75]
Braga also allied with Toledo to try to eliminate rural
paganism, for example, by legislating nationally
against persistent idolatry.[76]

Decrees of uniformity aimed at the ruling elite
were generally successful. The principal example of
this was the Third Council of Toledo's decree against
Arianism, which was the religion of the Gothic
nobility. Except for a few practical details, Arianism
disappeared from conciliar legislation upon the
conversion of the King. (The obvious exception to the
elite's readiness to bow to conciliar pressure was the
constant legislation against usurping the throne.
Apparently nothing but the Arab invasion would end the
Visigothic love for personal rebellion.) Repeated
legislation by nobles against religious practices in
the countryside was less effective. These practices
sprang from needs foreign to noblemen meeting in
Toledo, and constant complaints were singularly
ineffective in changing persistent peasant traditions.
The existence of two different religious perspectives,
noble and peasant, required a religion claiming to be
universal to adapt itself in more subtle ways than mere
legislation from the capital. Religious accommodation
was a slow process, requiring repeated interaction and
exchange of religious information between peasants in
the villages and church leaders in the centers of

power. The administrative structure erected by the
official Church created the network through which such
communication could flow. To understand the
cross-fertilization of religious ideas that
characterized the evolution of the Church in Galicia,
it is necessary first to analyze the mediating
institutions that made it possible.

Notes

1. Raoul Manselli, La Rél11gion populaire au Moyen
Age: Problèmes de méthod et d'histoire (Paris: 1975),
p. 131, noted that obedience is a hallmark of the
"religion savants." "...par obeissance aux
commandements de Dieu, aux conseils evangeliques et aux
canons de l'Eglise."
2. Joannes Biclarensis Abbas, "Chronicon,
continuans ubi Victor Desinit," PL 72:867, "Leovigildus
rex Gallaecia Vastat... Suevorum gentem, thesaurum et
patriam suam in potestatem redigit, et gothorum
provinciam facit."
3. I Bracara PL 84:568 expresses one of the many
proclamations of excommunication upon anyone who
disobeys the canons of the Church.
4. Visigothic Code, trans. S.P. Scott (Boston:
1910) Book XII, title II, ch. 2, p. 365.
5. For a summary of the administrative structure
of the Visigothic kingdom, see A.K. Ziegler, Church and
State in Visigothic Spain (Washington: 1930), pp.
19-21.
6. The names of some of these early bishops have
survived: Basilides in Leon in 252, and Paternus in
Braga in 390. Enrique Florez, España Sagrada (Madrid:
1759), 34:82-97.
7. Mario Martins, Correntes da Filosofia Religiosa
em Braga dos sec. IV a VII (Porto: 1950), noted:
"...quanto ao Arianismo...nunca chegou a perverter o
povo católico..." and without a doubt, Arianism also
failed to "pervert" the poor.
8. William A. Hinnebusch, "St. Martin of Braga -
The Apostle of the Sueves," (Master's thesis, Catholic
University of America, 1936), pp. 11-15. He describes

the arguments concerning the validity of the date of this inscription. Based on the use of the word "serenissimus," Ludwig Schmidt suggests that the date on the inscription was wrong, and should have been MXXIII instead of DXXIII. Due to the fact that this title was used in the East to refer to Emperors, and keeping in mind that several Gallegan churchmen had visited the East, it seems not unlikely that this term would have been used at this early date even though the Visigoths did not use it until two hundred years later to refer to their kings. The inscription reads: "In nomine domini perfectum est templum hunc per Marispalla deo vota sub die XIII kalendas Apriles era DXXIII regnante serenissimo Veremundu rex." I think that more than the negative evidence presented by Schmidt is required to dismiss the inscription as incorrect.

    9.   Epistola Vigilii Papae ad Profuturum Episcopum," PL 84:831-33.

    10.   Isidore of Seville, "Historia Gothorum, Wandalorum, Suevorum," in Monumenta Germaniae historica (hereafter cited as MGH) auct. ant. X:90 "Multis deinde Suevorum regibus in Arriani Haeresi permanentibus..."

    11.   Gregorii Turonensis, "Historia Francorum," MGH, ss. rer. Merov., I, xi, p. 596.

    12.   Isidore, p. 90. "Qui confestim Arrianae impietatis errore destructo Suevos catholicae fidei reddidit innitente Martino monasterii Dumiensis episcopo fide et scientia claro."

    13.   Ibid., p. 98.

    14.   E.A. Thompson, The Goths in Spain (Oxford: 1969), pp. 16-19 describes in detail the series of revolts.

    15.   The best works remain C.P. Caspari, Martin von Bracara's Schrift De Correctione Rusticorum

(Christiana, 1883) Claude W. Barlow, ed., <u>Martini</u>
<u>Bracara Opera.</u> <u>artini Episcopi Bracarensis Opera</u>
<u>Omnia</u> (New Haven, 1950).

16. I Bracara, <u>PL</u> 84:562, "...prius, si placet, de
statutis fidei catholicae perquiramus: tunc deinde
sanctorum Patrum instituta, recensisis canonibus,
innotescant: postremo quaedam etiam, quae ad obsequium
Dei, vel officium pertinent clericale, diligentius
pertractentur..."

17. Priscillianism will be discussed in detail in
Chapter VI.

18. I Bracara I-V, IX-XII, <u>PL</u> 84:565-67.

19. I Bracara IV, <u>PL</u> 84:566: "Item placuit, ut
eodem ordine missae celebrentur ab omnibus, quen
Profuturus quondam hujus metropolitanae Ecclesiae
episcopus ab ipsa apostolicae sedia auctoritate
suscepit scriptum."

20. I Bracara XX, <u>PL</u> 84:567.

21. I Bracara VI, <u>PL</u> 84:566.

22. I Bracara VII, <u>PL</u> 84:566.

23. I Bracara XV, <u>PL</u> 84:567.

24. I Bracara <u>PL</u> 84:568, "...qui in ipsa
extremitate mundi..."

25. II Bracara III, IV, V, VII, <u>PL</u> 84:571-73.

26. "Canones Martini," II Bracara XVII, <u>PL</u> 84:577.

27. "Canones Martini," II Bracara XXXII, <u>PL</u>
84:579, and II Bracara VIII, <u>PL</u> 84:572.

28. "Canones Martini," II Bracara LXVI, <u>PL</u> 84:583.

29. "Canones Martini," II Bracara I, XXXV-XXXVI,
<u>PL</u> 84:574 and 580.

30. "Canones Martini," II Bracara LXX, LXXVII,
LXXXI and LXXXIV, <u>PL</u> 84:584-86.

31. Joannes Biclarensis, <u>PL</u> 72:865. "Leovigildus
rex in Gallaecia Suevorum fines conturbat..."

32. At the Third Council of Toledo, nine Catholic bishops signed from Galicia, thus demonstrating that the Arian conquest did not end Catholic organization. Arian bishops had just been placed in the major northwestern cities, Tuy, Lugo, and Oporto, alongside their Catholic counterparts, which explains why at the Third Council there were two bishops signing from those cities. The signatures may be found in PL 84:357-60.

33. Joannes Biclarensis, PL 72:868. "Recardus...converti ad catholicam fidem facit, gentemque omnium Gothorum et Suevorum ad unitatem et pacem revocat Christianae Ecclesiae."

34. Ibid., c. 869. "...sancta episcoporum totius Hispania, Gallia, et Gallaeciae..."

35. III Tolet., PL 84:350.

36. IV Tolet., XIX, PL 84:372. The importance of baptism as both a symbol and means toward a unified society was also accepted from the Arian point of view. The Arian king Leovigild tried to unify Spain under Arianism, and toward that end, he changed Arian baptism regulations to make it easier for Catholics to covert to Arianism. They would no longer have to be rebaptized (a ritual unacceptable to Catholics). These events were observed by the chronicler John Biclara: "Leovigildus rex...dicens de Romana religiona ad nostram catholicam fidem venientes non debere baptizari, sed tantummodo per manus impositionem..." (Joannes Biclarensis, PL 72:866)

37. III Tolet XV, PL 84:347.

38. "Epistola Vigillis Papae," PL 84, pars, III, c. 831. "Quorum tamen reconciliatio non per illam impositionem manus, quae invocatione sancti Spiritus fit, operatur, sed per illam, quae poenitentiae fructus acquirit, et sanctae communionis restitutione

39. III Tolet, IX, PL 84:353.

40. III Tolet, PL 84: 341-42.

41. Thompson, p. 108.

42. Ibid., pp. 291-92.

43. Thompson analyzed the names of the bishops who signed all the councils, and broke down the figures by province. One example of the higher proportion of Galicia's German bishops can be seen by comparison with the province of Baetica, where there were seventeen Germanic bishops and forty-four Roman ones. In Galicia, there were thirty Germanic bishops for forty-three Roman ones. (Ibid., p. 290.)

44. Visigothic Code, Book III, title v, ch. 2, p. 107; Book XII, title 1, ch. 2, p. 360 and Book XII, title 2, ch. 12, p. 369.

45. III Tolet, V, XVI, XVII, XVIII and XXIII, PL 84:352-56.

46. III Tolet, XVIII, PL 84:355.

47. III Tolet, XVIII, PL 84:355.

48. While from 653, lay palace officials attended and signed the record, the councils were still dominated by the churchmen in both numbers and spirit.

49. S.P. Scott saw the Visigothic state as a theocratic one in which all the power of "the once independent and liberty-loving Goths" was given up to the clergy. This is a clear misunderstanding of the king's role in the church councils. (Visigothic Code, p. xi.)

50. IV Tolet, II, PL 84:365.

51. For example, nineteen years lapsed between the tenth and eleventh councils, and forty-four years between the third and fourth councils.

52. XII Tolet, VI, PL 84:475.

53. E.A. Thompson took a position opposite from

Scott's in his analysis of Visigothic church/state structure: "Seventh century Spain was not an example of ecclesiastical rule and clerical terror. It was the kings not the bishops who governed Spain and with it the Spanish Church." This view is also a little extreme. (Thompson, p. 282.)

54. V Tolet, II, III, V, VI, VII, PL 84:389-91.

55. VI Tolet, XVII, XVIII, PL 84:401.

56. VII Tolet, I, VI, PL 84:403 and 408.

57. IV Tolet, LXXV, PL 84:383.

58. A.K. Ziegler gives perhaps the best analysis of the interaction of church and state, without real domination by either. While virtually all works of the period acknowledge the arrangement to have been fairly efficient, Ziegler gives it extremely high praise: "Under the aegis of this union of the spiritual and temporal powers the kingdom attained a height of civilization and culture singularly advanced for the period." (Ziegler, p. 133.)

59. The accomplishments of Gallegan churchmen were recognized throughout the peninsula. For example, Bishop Braulio from the province of Tarraconensis in the seventh century praised Galicia's past: "The province...has been the birthplace of most eminent and most learned men...the priest Orosius, the Bishop Turibius, Idatius, and Carterius, another bishop of laudable old age and holy erudition." ("Letter no. 44," The Fathers of the Church - Iberian Fathers vol. 2, trans. C.W. Barlow [Washington, 1969], pp. 111-12.)

60. See, for examples, the two councils of Caesaraugustanum (Saragossa) in 592 and 691 and the council of Emeritense (Merida) in 666. (PL 84:315, 317, 615.)

61. III Bracara, PL 84:591.

62. XI Tolet, XVI, PL 84:465.

63. "Letter of Fructuosus to Recceswinth" in Barlow, Iberian Fathers, pp. 210-11.

64. IV Tolet, VI, PL 84:367.

65. "Epistola Vigillii Papae," PL 84:831

66. "De trina mersione," in Barlow, Iberian Fathers, pp. 99-102.

67. IV Tolet, XIII, PL 84:370.

68. "Canones Martini," II Bracara LXVII, PL 84:583.

69. I Bracara IX, PL 84:566.

70. IV Tolet, XL, PL 84:377.

71. IV Tolet, XXVI, PL 84:374.

72. I Bracara IV, PL 84:566. "Item placuit, ut eodem ordine missae celebrentur ab omnibus, quem Profuturus quondam hujus metropolitanae Ecclesiae episcopus ab ipsa apostolicae sedis auctoritate suscepit scriptum."

73. The Fifth Council of Toledo introduced a new litany for a September fast, and King Chintilus must have expected some reluctance to accept this innovation, because he closed the Council with an additional statement requiring that all provinces adhere to the litany: "...litaniae per omnes regni nostri provincias omne debeant celebrari devotionis cura." (V Tolet, I, PL 84:389, 394.) The Sixth Council again called for obedience in this matter. (VI Tolet, II, PL 84:395.) The Seventh Council, too, stressed the importance of uniform practices: "Cum enim omnes unum in Christo, nihil contrarium diversitas format, ubi efficaciam prosperitatis unitas fidei repraesentat..." (VII Tolet, II, PL 84:406.) This was repeated again at the Tenth Council and at the last council of the Visigothic reign in 694: "De diebus

litaniarum per totos duodecim menses celebrandis...per
universas Hispaniae et Galliarum provincias pro statu
Ecclesiae Dei, pro incolumitate principis nostri atque
salvatione populi..." (X Tolet, I, PL 84:441, XVII
Tolet, VI, PL 84:558.)

74. VI Tolet, V, PL 84:397 and II Bracara II, PL
84:571.

75. Bishop Potamius of Braga was brought before
the Tenth Council of Toledo in 656 and found guilty of
fornication. The statement is appended to the council
decisions. (X Tolet, PL 84:448-49.)

76. II Bracara I, PL 84:571; III Tolet, XVI, PL
84:354; XII Tolet, XI, PL 84:478 and XVI Tolet II, PL
84:537.

MEDIATORS — PARISH PRIESTS

By the sixth century, parish churches had been built in the largest or most centrally located villages in the Gallegan hills.[1] Since these small churches had become the center of peasants' social as well as religious life, it is appropriate to begin a study of rural Christianity with them. The surviving examples of Visigothic churches were not the larger structures of bishops in cities; those have long since been destroyed and replaced. The churches that exemplify Visigothic architecture and religious expression are in the remote parts of the country, and are the ones that served peasants who came on Sundays and Holy Days from their nearby villages.[2]

The two basic floor plans of Visigothic churches are the rectangular and the cruciform styles.[3] Two such typical churches are San Juan de los Banos near Palencia, and Santa Comba on the River Lima near Orense. (See illustrations, pp.78 & 79.) Like the village houses, both churches were built of local stones, rough-hewn and not too carefully aligned. However, both differ structurally from the easily comprehensible rectangles of village houses, adding angles, arches, shadows and columns, which make the churches more mysterious than the stone homes with which the worshippers were more familiar. G.G. King in her description of the architecture of Santa Comba beautifully captured the feeling of the structure: "...Tau-shaped or like a cross inscribed with vaulting at various levels, with dim heights and sudden sweeping corners of vault."[4]

VISIGOTHIC CHURCHES

San Juan de
los Baños

S. Comba de
Bande

VISIGOTHIC CHURCH
FLOOR PLANS

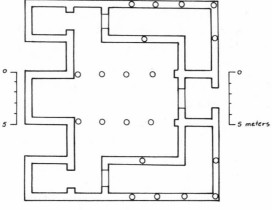

San Juan de los Baños

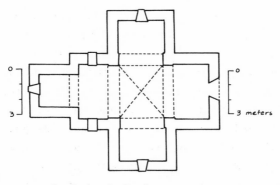

S. Comba de Bande

SOURCE: G.G.King

Both San Juan and Santa Comba are clear examples
of the hybrid nature of Gallegan religiosity. The
locations of both churches were probably sacred from
Celtic times. King Reccesvinthus erected San Juan de
los Baños to commemorate a healing mineral spring in
the area,[5] and G.G. King suggests that the site of
Santa Comba had previously been dedicated to a
pre-Christian goddess.[6] The columns in each church
reflect the region's Roman heritage; San Juan's columns
were designed in a Roman style, and Santa Comba's were
brought from the nearby Roman baths at Bande.[7] The
capitals of the columns are Visigothic. The church
architects probably came to these remote sites from
larger Visigothic cities, bringing ideas that
ultimately derived from the large urban centers in the
East.[8] The actual construction, however, was done by
local stonemasons who used the rough techniques that
were traditional in the villages. Thus each building
demonstrated aspects of both Roman and Visigothic
occupation, and reflected the interaction between elite
and peasant cultures that characterized the Visigothic
kingdom.

Diocesan bishops assigned a priest to each parish
church. The priest was responsible for the spiritual
well-being of his parishioners, to instruct them in the
Christian faith, to guide them through a Christian life
and to help them attain salvation. In performing his
pastoral duties in the village, a priest became a
principal mediator between elite and peasant cultures
and established a link that facilitated the exchange of
religious expressions between the two. Beyond
fulfilling the abstract concept of spiritual care, the
official Church expected its priests to perform
specific administrative, disciplinary and mediating

functions, and peasants looked to their priest to
perform acts that ritualized social interactions of
village life.[9] An analysis of these official and
village duties sheds light both on the religious needs
of the two groups comprising Visigothic society and on
the mediating role of the parish priest.

A priest's central position between elite and
peasant cultures was often characterized by a tension
arising from his attempt to balance both roles. The
ambiguity that arose from a priest's central position
was evident from the moment of his selection. Should a
candidate be chosen on the basis of his acceptability
to bishops or to villagers, both of whom the priest was
to serve? Visigothic bishops appointed their priests
to be sure that they would be suitable representatives
of the official Church and bearers of orthodox
religiosity. To further guarantee sacerdotal
suitability, the Second Council of Toledo established a
method for educating candidates for the clerical
offices:

> We decree that the following
> is to be observed in the case
> of those whom their parents
> have given from their earliest
> years to the clerical office:
> As soon as they have been
> tonsured and dedicated to the
> ministry of the Church, they
> are to be educated by a master
> in the ecclesiastical
> residence under the
> supervision of a bishop.[10]

The Fourth Council of Toledo similarly ordered that young candidates for the clergy were to be taught by "an elderly man of proved character who will be their teacher and a witness to their life."[11]

In spite of the decree of the Second Council of Toledo, it is unlikely that each parish priest had been educated by living in a bishop's household. While that may have been the case for some priests, most were probably taught by the parish priest in the churches where they served. Their education was probably fairly rudimentary, enough to read the holy offices and generally to serve their parishes. Sacerdotal education was, by and large, practical, based upon a clerical apprenticeship that provided a means for priests to educate their successors in the parish. A candidate had to spend years rising through the ranks of the lower clergy, at least one year as lector, then as subdeacon and as deacon before he finally became a priest, no earlier than at the age of thirty.[12]

While bishops tried to select candidates well schooled in official thought and administration, peasants wanted a priest qualified to serve also as the focus of village social life. Apparently villagers were frequently successful in choosing a candidate, for St. Isidore complained: "In these times there are many who are invested with the priesthood because only of public opinion."[13] A seventh-century Gallegan chronicler, Valerius of Bierzo, criticized a local priest who was chosen "...for the sake of a boisterous humor, and because he was adept in the soft art of eliciting music from the lyre."[14]

Although popular election was forbidden by the Second Council of Braga,[15] it never was completely eradicated. The official Church tried to retain some

control over the candidate by requiring that the clergy
who were selected by popular acclamation (pro
contentione populi) not take office until their
election had been confirmed.[16] Thus the actual
practice of the appointment of priests ranged from
total episcopal responsibility to a compromise which at
least gave bishops some veto power over a popular
candidate. This compromise indicates the combination
of roles that was embodied by a local priest.

Once a priest had been approved, the next problem
was how he was to live in the village - as a member of
a family in a style admired by his village, or alone,
adhering to a more abstract morality admired by the
official Church. This introduced a question that was a
constant source of difficulty - that of clerical
celibacy. The council of Elvira in 304 (attended by
one Gallegan, Decentius from Leon) officially initiated
the problem by decreeing that "bishops, priests,
deacons and all clerics," be celibate.[17] This
statement opened an issue that was never completely
resolved or even clarified during this period.
Fornication was easy to prohibit universally. Since
fornication was forbidden to the laity, it was an even
greater sin for the clergy. A cleric found guilty of
fornication was to be beaten and deprived of his office
by his bishop.[18]

The question of married clergy was more
complicated than the simpler one of fornication. From
the time of the First Council of Toledo in 397, the
Spanish Church required bishops to remain celibate.[19]
If a married clergyman were raised to the episcopate,
he was to live chastely with his wife. This also
applied to married Arian bishops upon their conversion
to Catholicism.[20] A pattern of chaste marriage seems

to have been fairly common. The fifth-century chronicler, Hydatius, for example, praised a newly ordained Gallegan bishop who, in accordance with this principle, lived chastely with his "wife made sister."[21]

By the Fourth Council of Toledo in 633, the Visigothic Church came closer to the strict spirit expressed by the Council of Elvira. Priests, who were the representatives of celibate bishops, should not only avoid the sin of fornication but be completely celibate.[22] This position fulfilled doctrinal morality, but it was difficult to sustain at the village level where a priest guided community social life.[23] It was certainly more convenient for priests to live in a household where, if there was not a wife, there was at least a woman who would share the work as well as the social interactions involved in village life. The precedent of earlier bishops living chastely with their wives seemed to provide a model for local priests; a Gallegan priest would thus often surround himself with a "family" by adopting a woman, taking her into his house calling her sister, or mother or daughter.[24]

The frequent prohibitions of this practice[25] suggest that celibacy was not simply an issue of conscience; even the appearance of fornication had to be avoided. No woman, not even a female slave, could be in the household of a priest.[26] This prohibition seems to have been less a problem for bishops living in the cities. However, there were sometimes scandals on the episcopal level, such as the case of Bishop Potamius of Braga who, at the Tenth Council of Toledo, confessed to carnal sin.[27] For a village priest it was more difficult to live alone, since living in a family group was a fundamental part of the village culture, which the priest shared.

The priest's principal service for the village was to ritualize the community's social ties. As the priest cleansed the souls of his parishioners by baptism, he was, in fact, also ritualizing the individual's membership in the Christian community. As he was performing the sacrament of marriage, a priest created social ties that bound villagers together. When he gave the last rites to help a dying parishioner gain immortality, a priest also presided over the communal mourning of the death of a neighbor.[28]

Since he was a central figure in these highly important moments of the village's social life, it is not surprising that priests were expected to participate actively in the feasts and celebrations that traditionally had been the principal way to reinforce and confirm community ties. Although the disapproving official sources may exaggerate somewhat the degree of sacerdotal participation in popular festivals, there can be no doubt that priests frequently took part. Valerius gives one example of a priest, Justus, who seems to have let himself be carried away by the festivities:

"...forgetful of his orders wrongfully received, in a vulgar fashion [he] whirled about in the obscene giddiness of theatrical immodesty, while swinging his arms this way and that, in another place circling his wanton feet, going around with mincing steps timed to the routine of

the   tripudium and hopping   on
shaky   feet,   singing   wicked
ditties,   the frightful   songs
of   a sinful dance he   carried
on   with the   devil's   ruinous
obscenity."[29]

Valerius'   disapproval   mirrored   the   official
Church's attitude toward priestly involvement in   these
festivities,[30] but conciliar legislation does not   seem
to   have had much effect.   The Church began to   try   to
regulate   the   degree of clerical   involvement,   rather
than eliminate it altogether.   For example, priests who
attended   a   marriage   or other   feast   were   to   leave
decorously before any entertainment began.[31]

By such compromises with official policy,   priests
were   able   to   continue   to   supervise   the   important
moments   of   each   person's   interaction   with   the
community.   The importance of the priest's social   role
was eloquently summarized by Lison in his general study
of parish priests:

All   the   faithful   hear   the
voice of the same pastor, they
meet together and receive   the
sacraments in the same church,
celebrate   the same   festivals
and   are   buried in   the   same
cemetery.   The priest is their
main   authority...[and]   they
have   him as   an   intermediary
between   the   parish   and   the
outside world.[32]

Lison's   reference   to   the   "outside   world"
acknowledges   that   priests could not spend   all   their
time   answering to village needs.   The official   Church

also had expectations. Without a doubt, the bishops
expected their priests to perform all the rituals
described above, but the official Church viewed them
more as spiritual than as social rituals. Beyond
these, moreover, each priest was responsible for the
administration of his parish. Upon his ordination, a
priest was assigned to a parish where he was to live
and serve. Visigothic legislation was designed to tie
the priest closely to his parish, for it was forbidden
for him to hold another church or office at the same
time,[33] and he was advised repeatedly to stay in his
assigned village and not to travel excessively.[34] The
frequency of the legislation against traveling clerics
argues against its effectiveness, but the significant
fact is that in the Church's view, the responsibility
of a priest lay in the administration of his own
assigned region. Consistent with official concern for
effective administration, priests were to be given the
information needed to perform this function:

> It is...decreed that priests
> and rectors shall not only
> have the opportunity to
> inspect such documents
> [defining rights of property
> and income of the parish], but
> shall also be entitled to
> copies of the same, confirmed
> under the hand of the bishop,
> to enable them to direct the
> affairs of the church
> committed to their care
> without any uncertainty...[35]

A priest was to care not only for his church and
its sacred contents under pain of excommunication,[36]

but   he was also to guard the property attached to   the
church.   Each parish church was supposed to have enough
property   to   provide   an income.   There   were   fields
and/or   vineyards to supplement the tithes,[37]   but   the
property   measure   that bishops had   set   to   determine
whether   a church had enough income was the   number   of
slaves   it   possessed.   If a church did   not   have   ten
slaves,   it   was   to be united to   a   nearby   parish.[38]
Since   the official Church felt that wealth   determined
the existence of a local church, a major responsibility
of   a   local priest was to care   for   church   property.
Each   priest   was to guarantee that church   lands   were
properly   worked.   For example, he   was   not   to   use
ecclesiastical   slaves   to   work   any   private   land.[39]
Furthermore,   if a priest had to lease some church land,
it   was to revert to the church upon the death   of   the
leaseholder[40] to avoid any possibility of   complicating
the   title   of   church   lands.[41]   Close   control   of
ecclesiastical   property   is   most   evident   in   the
treatment of church slaves.   Manumission was   contigent
upon   freed slaves presenting themselves to the   bishop
annually   for   renewal   of their freedom.[42]   Thus,   a
priest   was to guard his parish's property in order   to
pass it on to his successor intact.[43]   To ensure   this,
a   newly appointed priest was to take inventory of   the
church   property in the presence of five   witnesses   as
soon   as he assumed office.   If anything were   missing,
the   heirs   of   his   predecessor   would   have   to   make
restitution.

Along with the church's fixed property, it was the
responsibility   of   the   priest   to   collect   and
redistribute   church   income.[45]   The   parish   received
income   both from tithes and from its own produce,   and
the wealth of the church was counted in both money   and

crops.[46]   In Galicia, church funds were divided into
thirds, one for the bishop, one for the maintenance of
the local clergy, while the final third was to light
the church and provide for the other necessities of the
services.[47] The misuse and alienation of church income
was a constant theme of conciliar legislation,[48] and it
was the responsibility of the bishops to be sure that
parish churches were not suffering from neglect due to
such misuse.[49]

   In return for granting a parish to a priest,
Visigothic rulers and churchmen required complete
loyalty.   A priest was expected to take the oath of
allegiance to the Visigothic king. If he broke this
oath, he would immediately be unfrocked and, if the
king desired, exiled.[50] Bound by oath and official
expectations, a cleric was even forbidden to exchange
messages with foreigners.[51]

   The official status of parish priests also
required them to be diligent in upholding the laws of
the kingdom.   Their position in the village was
especially useful for law enforcement.   For example,
priests were indespensable in helping the kingdom
enforce its fugitive slave laws. Since the priest knew
everyone in the parish, he immediately recognized a
stranger. If a stranger came to reside in the village,
the priest had to take him within eight days to the
local judge (who probably resided in the nearest large
town, the bishop's see) to determine whether he was a
fugitive.[52]   In this way the close legal cooperation
established in Toledo between the Church and State
authorities was continued at both the provincial[53] and
the parish level, where priests not only participated
in traditional community matters, but represented
official legal authority.

Along with considerations of administration and
loyalty, parish priests were expected to enforce the
decrees of ecclesiastical uniformity that so
preoccupied churchmen meeting in council in Toledo.
They were expected to use the official missal so that
they would not "through ignorance offend divine
sacraments."[54] Bishops were to check periodically on
their priests to be sure that they were using the
correct forms for baptism and the mass.[55] If services
throughout the kingdom were alike, a traveling
clergyman who stopped to attend church services in
another city, (as he was required to do)[56] would have
been perfectly familiar with the rituals. By observing
ecclesiastical uniformity, he perhaps would see that
his village was indeed part of a larger kingdom instead
of the solitary unit that its mountainous isolation
suggested.

Along with standards of uniformity in ritual and
dress, bishops expected priests to represent the ideals
of the official Church in their daily life, and thus be
examples of Christian morality for their villages.[57]
Clerical misconduct was seen as an offense against the
official Church, which expected priests to exhibit and
exemplify the highest standards of behavior. Bishops,
moreover, had the discretionary right to remove priests
from office temporarily not only for sins but even for
unusual behavior. Priests who behaved strangely were
considered "to be subject to torments" and were removed
from office for one year. Thereafter, they could be
reinstated at the discretion of the bishop.[58]

Once clerical behavior was under control, and
priests could teach parishioners by example, there
remained the question of instructing congregations
directly. The task of preaching remained primarily the

responsibility of bishops,[59] a responsibility which
they sometimes delegated. For example, Bishop Valerius
of Saragossa asked his deacon, Vincent, to preach in
the villages.[60] Furthermore, in order to preserve
orthodoxy by instruction, the official Church expected
parish priests . to be able to read the Holy
Scriptures.[61] In the small, dark churches, peasants
heard selections from the Bible (read probably by
lectors rather than by the priest himself). They also
heard stories of saints' lives, which were read on
appropriate feast days. To supplement these readings,
bishops provided their priests with prepared homilies,
suitable for each occasion in the liturgical year.[62]
The most effective of the homilies were those that
adhered to recommendations made by Martin of Braga for
preaching to "rustics." The sermon was to be preached
in everyday language and was to be short. Martin
wrote: "Long indeed is the story as related in the
Holy Scriptures, but in order that you may retain at
least a small portion of it in your memory, we are
imparting to you a few facts out of many."[63] Most of
the homilies in the Visigothic collection meet Martin's
specifications for brevity, for some are only two and a
half or three minutes long.[64] By reading these short
homilies to rural parishioners. Priests fulfilled
their charge to instruct and served as the conduits
which passed the bishop's words to the peasants.

     In addition to their responsibilities to village
and bishop, priests also performed functions more
directly related to their role as mediators. A
traditional responsibility of the village community was
the care of needy members. An ill or hungry villager
was the concern of the whole community and the parish
priest was expected to alleviate the condition of the

village poor. Each priest had to use some church
tithes for charity. In this way, the community
actually contributed to the support of its poor through
the priest's mediation.

Visigothic rulers also showed concern for the
kingdom's "pauperes,"[65] and they tried to limit the
oppression of the poor by authorizing judges to
moderate the "severity of the law...especially where
said parties are oppressed by poverty..."[66] Like
peasants, rulers delegated care of the poor to the
priest. The Fourth Council of Toledo charged priests
with care of the poor, telling them to rebuke noblemen
who oppressed the people, and if abuses continued, to
inform the king.[67] The legal code converted the spirit
of the Fourth Council's canon into a more concrete
policy: If priests observed official abuses (i.e.
"misconduct of judges or of other officials") without
reporting them, priests "...shall be compelled to make
reparation from their...own property for such losses as
the poor may have suffered through their silence."[68]
While officials insisted that the priests should
protect their parishioners against exploitation, there
can be no doubt that peasants, too, expected their
priest to intercede for them with more distant
officials. Concern for the underprivileged was thus a
social issue recognized by both peasant and elite, and
both entrusted this care to priests as part of their
mediating duties.

The priest's role as mediator between village and
official structure required that he communicate with
the church hierarchy on a reasonably regular basis.
Although a local priest was to remain in the parish to
which he was assigned, there were times when he had to
travel to consult with his ecclesiastical superior.

During these contacts, the local priest further
fulfilled his mediating role. These moments of contact
fall roughly into two broad types: irregular and
regularly scheduled.

The irregular contacts stemmed from the priests'
duties to act as intercessors for their parishioners.
To report an abuse, a priest had to travel to or at
least correspond with his bishop. There were other
problems that required a priest to make an unscheduled
contact with his superior: if transport duties and
taxes were being imposed on the local clergy (who were
supposed to be exempt from these impositions) priests
were to report this abuse to their bishops.[69] Priests
also had to report the presence of strangers or Jews in
their parish.[70] While these reports were initiated by
the priest, it was not unusual for a local clergyman to
be summoned by the king to answer at council. A priest
who ignored such a summons was subject to
excommunication, although exceptions were made for
priests in Galicia where traveling may have been
prevented or made difficult by excessive rain, which
caused the rivers to flood.[71]

Irregular meetings between priests and bishops
took place to deal with special problems. There were
also more regular contacts between parish priests and
their bishops, although the wet winters and swollen
rivers of Galicia probably reduced communication during
the winter months. During Lent, however, a priest
could expect a visit from his bishop. The Second
Council of Braga required bishops to visit each parish
at least twenty days before Easter to determine whether
during the winter the clergy had become lax in
observing the correct order for the mass, and whether
priests knew the correct form for the traditional

Easter baptism.[72] At about the same time, each   priest
had to send a representative (usually his   deacon   or
subdeacon) to the episcopal see to pick up blessed
chrism for use at the Easter services,[73] for a   priest
who consecrated his own chrism was subject to the
strong penalty of deposition.[74] Presumably, priests
took advantage of this meeting to send word of problems
they faced, and during his Lenten travel through the
diocese the bishop could discuss questions that may
have arisen that winter. In any case, these two Spring
visits annually re-established the communication
between bishop and parish, which usually lapsed during
the months of inclement weather.

The Fourth Council of Toledo also required that
each bishop or his representative travel annually
through the diocese to determine whether any   churches
needed repair.[75] Presumably, the bishop could check on
the condition of the churches during his Lenten visit,
but since the canon stipulated that the bishop could
send a representative on the inspection tour, which he
could not do for the Lenten trip, we may perhaps
conclude that this inspection took place at a different
time of year. A logical time would have been in late
summer or early fall, before travel became too
difficult. This would provide a final opportunity for
priests to discuss village conditions with their
superiors before the winter interruption.

These visits seem to have been occasions for much
ceremony and episcopal extravagance.   The Seventh
Council of Toledo, in a canon directed specifically to
Gallegan bishops, cautioned them to take no more than
fifty attendants on their visits, and to stay no more
than one day at any church, lest they impoverish a
parish.[76] The Second Council of Braga gives further

insight into episcopal visitation abuses: Bishops were
forbidden to accept more than two solidi from a priest
during   his   visit,   and they   were   cautioned   against
treating local clergy like slaves.[77]

   To   be effective mediators of   official   religious
policy,   parish   priests   had to   be   informed   of   new
decisions   by   church   councils   in   Toledo   and   Braga.
Councils   therefore decreed that within six   months   of
each national or provincial council each bishop was   to
call together all "abbots, priests, deacons, and   other
clergy"   to   hear of the council's decisions.[78]   This
legislation   explains   the   network   that   transmitted
religious policy from its formulation in Toledo to   the
episcopal   sees in each province, and finally   to   each
parish,   ideally   within   six months   of   the   original
legislation.   The six-month deadline gave a good   deal
of leeway for difficult travel and weather conditions.

   There   is   conflicting   legislation   as   to   the
recommended   date for councils.   The Fourth Council   of
Toledo   ordered   that   provincial   councils   be   held
annually   on   the 18th of May,   "...when the   grass   was
green and pasture available."[79]   This authorization for
Spring   councils   was   contradicted   by   the   Third   and
Twelfth   Councils,   which   required   national   and
provincial   councils to be held on November 1.[80]   The
actual   dates   of the council   meetings   parallel   this
indecisive legislation.   Seven of the national councils
convened between November and January, five in May   and
June,   and   two in September and October.   There   were
none   between February and April, nor   in   the   summer
months   of   July and August.   The   provincial   councils
show   more   consistency.   Twelve met in the   recommended
month   of   November   (in these I   have   included   three
councils of Toledo, IX, XI and XIV, which were actually

provincial councils of Carthagenensis). The other
eight were distributed throughout the year.[81] Two of
the three Gallegan councils of Braga met in the late
spring, on May 1 and June 1. Unfortunately, the
records of the Third Council of Braga do not indicate
the month in which it was convened. It was probably
also held in the spring, not only because of the
precedent set by the two previous Bragan councils, but
also because the other provincial council of the
mountainous north, at Gerona in the Northeast, met in
June, suggesting that the northern provinces adhered
more closely to the spring recommendation of the Fifth
Council of Toledo instead of the November meetings
favored by the southern provinces.

It remains to explore how these figures translate
into actual patterns of communication with the Gallegan
parish structure. The three provincial councils held
in the spring were so few that they do not constitute a
real catalyst for repeated meetings between bishops and
their priests. Presumably, in the summer following
these councils, the bishops did summon their rural
clergy to explain the results of provincial
deliberations.

The national councils met more frequently,
providing bishops with a good forum to speak to the
clergy of the diocese at one time. To relay
information on the councils that met in the winter, the
diocesan meeting was probably held in early spring, as
soon as travel through the mountains was practical.
For spring councils, local meetings were probably held
in summer or early fall. This analysis involves a
paradox which requires an explanation: If travel in
Galicia's hills was so difficult that bishops probably
did not call mid-winter diocesan meetings, how did

these same bishops go to Toledo for the national councils in November or January? The best explanation comes from settlement patterns set during the Roman occupation of the region. The Romans established the cities that would later become Galicia's episcopal sees. More important, the Romans joined these cities by roads.[82]

The map on p.98 shows the proximity of the Gallegan episcopal cities to the existing road networks. These roads probably made it easier for bishops to go to Toledo in November than it would have been for a priest in a neighboring valley to travel to the city. Thus, while Gallegan attendance at national councils fell off a little in the winter (six to eight Gallegan bishops attended the winter councils, as opposed to eleven or twelve in the spring), the roads permitted bishops in this remote province to participate in formulations of national policy and then to return to their province to relay the information to their priests for implementation at the village level.

Thus from the information we have available, it seems as if the mediating function of the parish priest was fulfilled by three or four annual visits with his bishop and by his availability to answer for any problems that arose. It was also the priest's responsibility not to go outside this established hierarchical network. He was not to be in communication with any bishop other than his own.[83] This not only reduced the possibility of priestly involvement in treason, but may have contributed to a greater efficiency of the diocesan/parish administrative structure. In any case, the principal mediating contacts with the priest and his bishop probably were made between early spring and late fall,

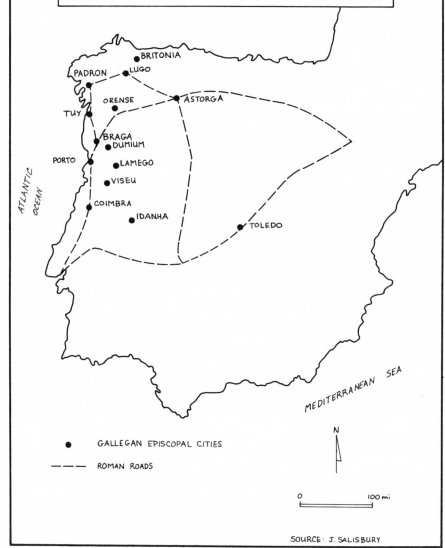

PROXIMITIES OF EPISCOPAL
CITIES TO ROMAN ROADS
(IBERIAN PENINSULA)

BRITONIA
PADRON   LUGO
ORENSE   ASTORGA
TUY
BRAGA
DUMIUM
PORTO   LAMEGO
VISEU
COIMBRA
IDANHA
TOLEDO

ATLANTIC
OCEAN

MEDITERRANEAN SEA

N

● GALLEGAN EPISCOPAL CITIES
- - - ROMAN ROADS

0   100 mi

SOURCE: J. SALISBURY

leaving the parish priest as the villagers' only
contact with the official Church during Galicia's cold,
wet winter. This comparative isolation reinforced the
importance of the local priest's functions of official
representative for his bishop. Since a priest's
mediating role placed him within the larger context of
the kingdom as a whole, it is important to examine how
the parish fit into larger regional divisions.

The lack of sources usually makes it difficult to
study parish organization during the early Middle Ages.
For Galicia, however, we are fortunate to have a list
of all the episcopal cities of the Suevian kingdom (the
Gallegan region before it was incorporated into the
Visigothic kingdom) and a list of the parishes attached
to each see. This document, the Parochiale Suevorum,
has been preserved in the text of a twelfth-century
forgery of two fictive sixth-century councils of Lugo.
The circumstances of the text's survival led it to be
neglected by historians for years.[84] Pierre David,
however, in his study of sixth-century Galicia, has
argued convincingly for the accuracy of the listing,
suggesting that it was incorporated into the
twelfth-century documents to strengthen the credibility
of the forgeries. His excellent textual and manuscript
analysis demonstrates that the Parochiale itself was
written between 572 and 582, making it an extremely
valuable source for early Spanish church
organization.[85]

The Parochiale identifies thirteen bishoprics.
Eleven correspond to the main Gallegan cities and have
anywhere from three (at Egitania) to thirty (near
Braga) churches under their jurisdiction. The other
two bishoprics, Britonia and Dumium, were monasteries
whose abbots also held the position of bishop but had

no jurisdiction over any parish churches. It is impossible to locate each parish in each diocese, but the patterns that emerge permit us to make some general statements about sixth-century parish structures, which probably also apply to the seventh century. Some diocese have many more parishes than others (see the map on p.101 for the breakdown of parishes per diocese) and it seems likely that in the sixth century, as well as in the seventh, the determining factor for the establishment of a parish was the amount of wealth it possessed, since the most numerous parishes were in the richer dioceses of the broad valley of Braga and the comparatively rich port of Oporto.

Population density and wealth probably account for the variety in the number of parishes per diocese, but not for the actual location of the parishes relative to the diocesan see. Pierre David concluded that the parishes were located neither on the basis of some general nor juridical rules, but purely on the basis of convenience.[86] Keeping in mind the important parish function of communication with official hierarchy and tracing the diocesan structures on a map, it appears that the most "convenient" standard for diocesan jurisdiction was that each parish be no further than one day's journey from its episcopal see. On the attached map, the circles around each city represent twenty Roman miles, which the Visigoths acknowledged to be an average day's journey.[87] The exceptions to the twenty-mile figure, between Padron and Lugo and between Leon and Astorga, lie along Roman roads. It thus would have been possible to travel more than twenty miles and still reach the city in one day's travel. This analysis permits us to grasp more clearly the communication between each priest and his bishop. A

DIOCESAN STRUCTURE

BASED ON PAROCHIALE SUEVORUM

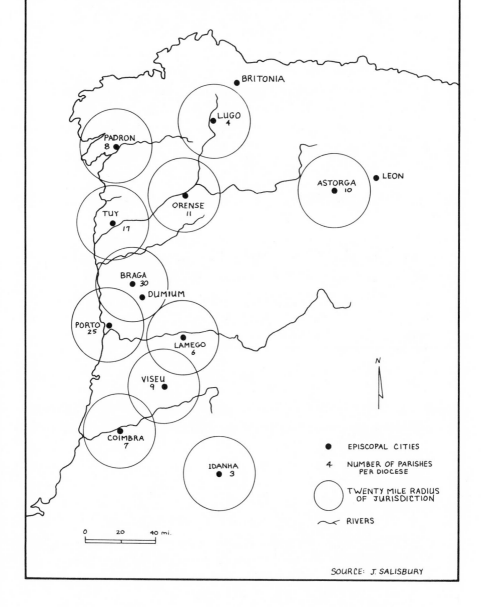

BRITONIA

LUGO
4

PADRON
8

ASTORGA ● LEON
● 10

TUY
17

ORENSE
11

BRAGA
● 30

DUMIUM

PORTO
25

LAMEGO
6

VISEU
9 ●

N

COIMBRA
7

IDANHA
● 3

●   EPISCOPAL CITIES

4   NUMBER OF PARISHES
    PER DIOCESE

◯   TWENTY MILE RADIUS
    OF JURISDICTION

〰 RIVERS

0   20   40 mi.

SOURCE: J. SALISBURY

priest could reach the city in one day, while a bishop
travelling around his diocese could be well assured of
the hospitality of one of his priests each night.

The day's journey from the parish to the episcopal
see represents the transition from village to official
culture.   Twenty miles was enough of a distance to
remove bishops from the agrarian activities that shaped
village religiosity. Expressing the religious views of
the official Church, bishops wrote of personal abstract
theology[88] and worked to bring religious uniformity to
the kingdom.   They also directed much of their energy
toward administrative and fiscal tasks, both concerns
of an official religion.

While bishops and parish priests performed many of
the same liturgical and ecclesiastical tasks, bishops
were less torn between village and elite value systems.
Bishops were expected to be even more virtuous than
their priests,[89] and their administrative duties were
more complex than those of parish priests, for bishops
were responsible for the effective functioning of the
whole diocese. Like parish priests, however, bishops
were to reside in their dioceses[90] and maintain the
integrity of church property and wealth.[91]   Preserving
church property took precedence even over matters of
conscience, as was demonstrated in 656, when the will
of the Gallegan abbot/bishop Recimiro of Dumium was
challenged at the Tenth Council of Toledo.   Abbot
Recimiro left so much of the Church's income to the
poor that the bishops in Toledo felt that such
generosity would impoverish the church of Dumium and
declared the will invalid.[92]

Beyond these administrative tasks, the primary
responsibility of bishops was to guide their parishes
effectively and complement the mediating function of

their priests. To do this, bishops were constantly warned not to abuse their position of authority. For example, Gallegan bishops were advised not to beat their priests or lower clergy, lest they lose their respect.[93] Nor were bishops to charge their priests for the Easter chrism.[94] Such legislation suggests official recognition of the importance of the relationship between bishops and their priests, and the necessity for keeping these contacts amicable and effective.

Just as parish priests were expected to be obedient to their ecclesiastic superiors, bishops were to obey the official hierarchy represented by the provincial metropolitan bishop.[95] The metropolitan of Galicia was the bishop of Braga. Due to Braga's location south of the River Minho, it was difficult for the metropolitan to maintain close control over his bishops residing in the northern part of the province. Therefore, between 562 and 572, Martin of Braga divided the province at the River Minho. The south remained under the jurisdiction of Braga, and the north fell under the direction of the bishop of Lugo. Lugo was not raised to metropolitan status, however; Braga continued to maintain primacy in the province.[96]

The metropolitan bishop of Braga was responsible for the administration and orthodoxy of the whole province. Since the quality of the provincial clergy was the metropolitan's responsibility, no one but he could appoint and ordain a bishop.[97] Bishops themselves were forbidden not only to ordain other bishops, but they were not even permitted to recommend their successors.[98]

Appointing worthy bishops did not exhaust the metropolitan's responsibilities. Just as each bishop

was to travel through his diocese to supervise priests,
metropolitans had to inspect the whole province
periodically to be sure all the divine laws were being
kept, and that the churches were properly run.[99]
Metropolitans were to be particularly vigilant against
diversity in the church services within their
provinces.[100] To maintain effective control, the
metropolitan was supposed to call a provincial synod
twice a year.[101] Although the records show that the
number of provincial synods never approached this
ideal, the intention of the legislation is clear;
metropolitan bishops were to guide their clergymen by
maintaining close contact with their bishops.

To complete the hierarchical pattern of religious
centralization, the Twelfth Council gave the
metropolitan of Toledo primacy over all the provincial
metropolitan bishops,[102] while the Visigothic kings
appointed the metropolitan of Toledo. Thus, by the
seventh century the administrative structure of the
official Church was well established. The center of
the Church's power was in Toledo guided by the king and
the metropolitan bishop. From there, religious control
was exerted through the provincial capitals to the
episcopal sees, ending finally in the local parishes.
There peasants accepted their priest not only for his
spiritual guidance, but because he fulfilled the need
for ritualized social interactions that grew out of
village life. At the same time, priests attempted to
fulfill the expectations of the bishop who had ordained
them. Since local priests touched both village and
official cultures, they could convey official religion
to villagers while expressing rural religious needs and
practices to bishops. In this way, although the Church
hierarchy consciously created the office of parish

priest to transmit official religion to the countryside, in fact, the reverse was often true. Priests transmitted peasant religion to the elite. Parish priests in small, stone churches located in remote villages were principally responsible for the exchange of religious sensibilities that characterized early Iberian Christianity.

Notes

1. Pierre David, Etudes historiques sur la Galice et le Portugal du VI au XII siècle (Lisbon, 1947), p. 16: "La paroisse rurale a été plus d'une fois organisee dans un chef-lieu de district, de pagus."

2. G.G. King, Pre-Romanesque Churches in Spain (Bryn Mawr, 1924), p. 72: "These churches are all unimportant; they are either private foundations or situated in places out of the way and poverty-stricken."

3. S.R. Jernigan, "Origins of the Early Christian Architecture of the Iberian Peninsula," (Ph.D. diss., University of Missouri-Columbia, 1974), gives detailed descriptions of these styles and traces the eastern and African architectural influences.

4. King, p. 19.

5. An inscription on a stone above the apse-arch dates the building in 661, and acknowledges the patronage of Reccesvinthus.

6. King, p. 211, suggests this hypothesis based on Gallegan folk-lore which attributes to Sta. Comba powers of witchcraft which the saint gave up on her conversion to Christianity.

7. Ibid., p. 46.

8. Jernigan, ch. II, discusses Gallegans like Martin of Braga, Etheria, Orosius and others who traveled to the Holy Land and Constantinople probably bringing back ideas of Eastern church architecture.

9. Peter Brown, "The Rise and Function of the Holy Man in Late Antiquity," Journal of Roman Studies LXI (1971), p. 80, discusses the question of mediators between villagers and the outside world. In the East, Holy men/hermits fulfilled this function, but Brown, p.

95, correctly notes that "In the West, the hierarchy serves the functions of the Eastern holy man." Actually, at the village level, it is the local priest who is the Western counterpart of the holy man as mediator.

10. C.M. Aherne, "Late Visigothic Bishops: Their Schools and the Transmission of Culture," Traditio, 1966 (22), p. 437. See also, II Tolet, I, PL 84:335.

11. Aherne, p. 437 and IV Tolet, XXIV, PL 84:374.

12. I Bracara, XX, PL 84:567; "Canones Martini," XX, PL 84:577. This canon was reaffirmed at IV Tolet, XX, PL 84:373.

13. Isidore of Seville, "De Ecclesiasticis Officiis," I, II, 7, PL 83:782.

14. C.M. Aherne, Valerio of Bierzo: An Ascetic of the Late Visigothic Period (Washington, 1949), pp. 86-7.

15. "Canones Martini," I, PL 84:574.

16. "Canones Martini," X, PL 84:675.

17. Eliberitanum XXXIII, PL 84:305, "Placuit in totum prohibere episcopis, presbyteris et diaconibus vel omnibus clericis positis in ministerio abstinere se a conjugibus suis..." A. Garcia Villada, Historia Ecclesiastica de Espana (Madrid, 1932), p. 236, claims that this is the earliest written law in favor of clerical celibacy.

18. VIII Tolet, IV, PL 84:422. This is milder than the earlier penalty set by the council of Elvira, Eliberitanum XVIII, PL 84:304, which excommunicated fornicating clergy until the end of their lives.

19. I Tolet, I, PL 84:329, states that if priests or deacons father children after their ordination, they shall not be raised to bishop, which suggests that celibacy was strictly enforced only at the episcopal level.

20. III Tolet, V, PL 84:352.

21. Idatius "Chronicon," PL 84:879, "...conjuge factor soror..."

22. IV Tolet, XXI, PL 84:373, "Nec ullo eos fornicationis contagio pollui, sed caste viventes mundos semetipsos celebrandis exhibeant sacramentis."

23. Peasants did respect celibacy, but their reverence was directed to hermits and virgins whose celibacy was an integral part of a life of abstinence. I shall discuss this question more fully in the next chapter.

24. "Canones Martini," XXXII, PL 84:579, "Nullos episcopus neque presbyter neque diaconus neque omnibo aliquis...habeat intromittendi ad se quasi adoptivam aliquam mulierem, quasi in loco filiae aut sororis aut matris..."

25. II Tolet, III, PL 84:336, repeated in III Bracarensis IV, PL 84:589.

26. II Tolet, III, PL 84:336.

27. X Tolet, appendix, PL 84:448-9.

28. The specific practices surrounding these rituals are discussed more fully below in Chapter VIII.

29. Aherne, Valerio of Bierzo, pp. 90-1.

30. "Canones Martini," LXI, PL 84:583, "Non liceat sacerdotes vel clericos sed nec religiosos laicos convivia facere de confertis."

31. "Canones Martini," LX, PL 84:583, "Non liceat sacerdotibus vel clericis aliqua spectacula in nuptiis vel in conviviis spectare, sed opertet antequam ingrediantur ipso spectacula surgere et recedere inde."

32. Carmelo Lisón Tolosana, Antropología Cultural de Galicia (Madrid, 1971), p. 86. "Todos los feligreses oyen la voz del mismo pastor, se congregan y reciben los sacramentos en la misma iglesia celebran

las mismas fiestas patronales y reciben sepultura en el mismo cementerio. El sacerdote es su primera autoridad...lo tienen como intermediario entre la parroquia y el mundo exterior..."

33. Visigothic Code, trans S.P. Scott (Boston, 1910), Book V, title I, ch. V, p. 146.

34. The legislation for stability is frequent. The following are only a few of the examples: "Canones Martini," XXXIII and XXXIV, PL 84:579, VIII Tolet, VI, PL 84:423, and XI Tolet, V, PL 84:459.

35. Visigothic Code, Book V, title I, ch. VI, p. 150.

36. "Canones Martini," XVIII, PL 84:577.

37. II Tolet, IV, PL 84:336.

38. This requirement is in both the laws, MGH Legem Sectio I, Book V, title I, ch. V, p. xxxiv, and in the councils, XVI Tolet V, PL 84:539, "...decem habureit mancipia, super se habeat sacerdotem; que vero minus decem mancipia habuerit, aliis conjugatur ecclesiis." Scott, Visigothic Laws, p. 146, translated this passage as"...any congregation which possesses ten pieces of property is entitled to a priest, but such as have less than ten shall be united with other churches." There are medieval precedents for translating "mancipia" as property: (The Lexicon Mediae Latinitatis by W.H. Maigne D'Arnis (Paris, 1866), p. 1354, recognizes "villa, mansus" and "tenementum" as well as "servi homines" as translations of mancipium). However, the more common use of the word is "slave," as A.E. Giffard demonstrated in his article "Mancipium. A propos de travaux recents," Revue de Philologie, 1937, pp. 396-400. The translation, slave, seems to apply best to the Visigothic documents, for although slaves are normally

referred to as "servi," the two other times the word
manicipia is used in the councils (I Hispalense I and
II, PL 84:591-92) clearly refer to slaves.

39.   III Tolet, XXI, PL 84:356.

40.   II Tolet, IV, PL 84:336.

41.   Visigothic Laws, Book V, title I, ch. VI, p.
147, recognize landholding for over thirty years as a
legal right of possession, not contestable.

42.   VI Tolet, IX, PL 84:398.

43.   IX Tolet, VII, PL 84:437.

44.   Visigothic Laws, Book V, title I, ch. II, p.
144.

45.   IX Tolet, IV, PL 84:436.

46.   "Canones Martini," XVI, PL 84:576, "...lucra
ecclesiae vel fructus agrorum."

47.   I Bracara, VII, PL 84:566.

48.   VI Tolet, V, PL 84:397, IX Tolet, I, PL
84:434-35, and IX Tolet, VIII, PL 84:437.

49.   Visigothic Laws, Book V, title I, ch. V, p.
146.

50.   X Tolet, II, PL 84:442.

51.   IV Tolet, XXX, PL 84:375.

52.   XIII Tolet, XI, PL 84:498.

53.   III Tolet, XVII, PL 84:354, and Visigothic
Laws, Book XII, title I, ch. II, p. 361. Both explain
the cooperation between bishops and judges in legal
cases.

54.   IV Tolet, XXVI, PL 84:374, "Quando presbyters
in parochias ordinantur, libellum officiale a sacerdote
suo accipiant...ne per ignorantiam etiam ipsis divinis
sacramentis offendant..."

55.   II Bracara, I, PL 84:571.

56.   I Tolet, V, PL 84:330.

57.   IV Tolet, XXIII, PL 84:374, "Ut presbyter vel

diaconus vitae suae habeant testionium." This was repeated again in XI Tolet, X, PL 84:462-63, "Ut omnes pontifices rectoresque ecclesiarum tempore quo ordinandi sunt sub cautione promittant quam justissime vivere debeant."

58. XI Tolet, XIII, PL 84:464

59. E. Delaruelle, "La Vie Religieuse populaire en Septimanie pendant l'époque Wisigothique," Anales Toledanos III (1971), pp. 26-8, has a particularly useful analysis of preaching in Visigothic Spain.

60. "Acta S. Vincentii," Acta Sanctorum, Januarii, Tom. III (Bruxelles, 1931), p. 394.

61. IV Tolet, XXV, PL 84:374, "...qui docendi officium in populis susceperunt: sacerdotes enim legere sancta Scriptura admonet..." This passage does not refer only to priests reading to educate themselves but also to reading directly to parishioners in church. This becomes more clear in the Second Council of Braga which calls for reading the apostles in church ["Canones Martini," XLIV, PL 84:581]. The Fourth Council of Toledo discusses the book that the parish priests were supposed to use to educate their parishioners. [IV Tolet, XXVI, PL 84:374]. A provincial council best summarized the Church's position on clerical literacy: "...non potest nisi legendo aedificare populum." [Narbonense XI, PL 84:612.]

62. Reginald Gregoire, Les homeliaires du Moyen Age, Inventaire et analyse des manuscrits (Rerum eccl. documenta...Pontif. Ath. S. Anselmi, Series Major, Fontes VI) (Rome, 1966), pp. 196-230.

63. Martin of Braga, "De Correctione Rusticorum," in Martini Episcopi Bracarensis, Opera Omnia, ed. by C.W. Barlow (New Haven, 1950), p. 184.

64. Delaruelle, p. 28.

65. Official and peasant cultures did have a differing perception of who were the poor. Jose Orlandis, La Iglesia en la España Visigótica y Medieval (Pamplona, 1976), p. 216, discusses the legal references to the poor, and from the synonyms used for pauperes, (humiles, humiliores, inferiores, vilioses personae) concluded that the laws referred to "...no una minoría de indigentes...sino la gran masa del pueblo, gobernada y a menudo oprimida por una oligarquía dominante detentadora del poder social." In the broadest sense, however, both groups were concerned with anyone poorer than themselves, and it was the care of the less fortunate that was delegated to the parish priests.

66. Visigothic Laws, Book XII, title I, ch. I, p. 359.

67. IV Tolet, XXXII, PL 84:375.

68. Visigothic Laws, Book XII, title I, ch. 2, p. 361.

69. II Tolet, XX, PL 84:355.

70. Visigothic Laws, Book XII, Title III, ch. 26, p. 407.

71. XIII Tolet, VIII, PL 84:495, required the appearance of a summoned cleric, while acknowledging the excuse of "...fluminum aut aerum procellosa immensitas..." This admonition as well as the exemption was also included in the Visigothic Laws, Book II, title I, ch. 31, p. 37.

72. II Bracara, I, PL 84:571.

73. I Tolet, XX, PL 84:332.

74. I Bracara, XIX, PL 84:567, repeated in "Canones Martini," LI and LII, PL 84:582.

75. IV Tolet, XXXVI, PL 84:376.

76. VII Tolet, IV, <u>PL</u> 84:407-8.

77. II Bracara, II, <u>PL</u> 84:571, "Ut episcopus per diocesem ambulans duos solidos tantum accipiat; neque tertiam partem oblationibus quaerat, et ut clerici non cogantur more servili."

78. XVI Tolet, VII, <u>PL</u> 84:541, "...infra sex mensium spatia omnes abbates, presbyters, diacones atque clericos, seu etiam omnem conventum civitatis ipsius..."

79. IV Tolet, III, <u>PL</u> 84:366, "Quinto decimo autem calendarum Juniarum congreganda est in unaquaque provincia synodus propter vernale tempus, quando herbis terra vestitur et pabula germinum inveniuntur."

80. III Tolet, XVIII, <u>PL</u> 84:355, and XII Tolet, XII, <u>PL</u> 84:479.

81. Two in June, and one in each of the following: January, August, October, December and May. One regional council was undated.

82. J.J. Van Nostrand, <u>An Economic Survey of Ancient Rome, Vol. III Roman Spain</u> (Baltimore, 1937), pp. 208-17, lists the milestones found on these roads which demonstrate that they remained in use and repair through 394 A.D., and it is likely that they remained the primary communication network throughout the Visigothic era.

83. I Tolet, XII, <u>PL</u> 84:330.

84. Flórez, <u>España Sagrada</u> (Madrid, 1759) IV:130-76, dismissed the whole document as a forgery.

85. David, pp. 51-2.

86. <u>Ibid.</u>, p. 17, "...si n'est pas cependant une regle generale ni surtout une regle juridique: l'autorité diocesaine s'inspirait des convenances et des opportunités."

87. <u>Visigothic Laws</u>, Book IX, title I, ch. 8, p.

310, computed the pay for returning a fugitive slave on twenty miles a day. This measure was also used for payment for taking a borrowed animal too far; one solidus was to be paid for each ten miles, thus making twenty miles for the round trip to return the animal. [Book VIII, title IV, ch. 2, p. 285.] The same round-trip figure was used for travel expenses in legal disputes: one solidus per ten miles [Book II, title II, ch. 7, p. 42].

88. Good examples of official religious interests can be found in the letters of Braulio of Saragossa, in which he discusses such questions as how Methuselah could have lived fourteen years after the flood if all life perished. [Braulio of Saragossa, "Letters" in The Fathers of the Church: Iberian Fathers, Vol. 2, trans. Claude W. Barlow (Washington, 1969), p. 197.]

89. See above, p. 83 for the earlier requirement of chastity on the part of bishops.

90. "Canones Martini," XI, PL 84:575 and XII, PL 84:576, both censure bishops who complain about or refuse their assigned sees.

91. "Canones Martini," XIV, PL 84:576. This canon was original with Martin, so it is likely to have been particularly applicable to the Gallegan situation.

92. X Tolet, appendix, PL 84:449-50. A. Garcia Gallo, "El Testamento de San Martin de Dumio," Anuario del Historia de la Derecha Española (1956), pp. 369-85, analyzed the legal precedents set by this decree of the Tenth Council, noting that the king was made an executor of both the will and the ecclesiastical property. This set a precedent which both demonstrated and reinforced the close church/state ties under the Visigothic kings.

93. III Bracara, VI, PL 84:590.

94.   II Bracara, IV, <u>PL</u> 84:571.

95.   "Canones Martini," IV, <u>PL</u> 84:575.

96.   W.A. Hinnebusch, "St. Martin of Braga--The Apostle of the Sueves," (M.A. thesis, Catholic University of America, Washington, 1936), p. 75, accepted the signature on the Second Council of Braga in which the bishop of Lugo signed as Metropolitan and assumed that there were two metropolitans within the province. David, p. 66, however, demonstrated from his comparisons of the manuscripts that the title on the signature was a later addition, and that throughout the Visigothic period Lugo was not a metropolitan see.

97.   "Canones Martini," II, <u>PL</u> 84:574 and III, <u>PL</u> 84:575.

98.   "Canones Martini," VII and VIII, <u>PL</u> 84:575.

99.   XI Tolet, II, <u>PL</u> 84:458.

100.   XI Tolet, III, <u>PL</u> 84:458.

101.   "Canones Martini," XVIII, <u>PL</u> 84:577.

102.   XII Tolet, VI, <u>PL</u> 84:475.

MEDIATORS — HOLY MEN AND WOMEN

In seventh-century Spain monasteries began to
serve as influential mediators between peasant and
elite cultures. Unlike parish priests, who were
officially designated as mediators, monasteries were
effective primarily due to the awe and respect shown by
villagers to the holy men and women who lived in them.
Long before the establishment of monastic institutions
however, holy men and women lived in Galicia's towns
and villages and in its hills. In order to understand
rural Iberia's respect for monks and nuns, it is
necessary to analyze the roles of their predecessors,
the holy virgins and hermits.[1]

We have become so accustomed to associating
virginity with Christian morality that we lose sight of
the fact that virgins inspired awe long before Christ
was born, and in regions untouched by Christianity. It
is perhaps even more difficult to try to examine the
reasons for such respect prior to the overlay of
Christian notions of purity, but we must make the
effort if we are to understand popular veneration of
virgins and virgin saints in Galicia.[2]

Earlier, I described the importance of fertility
rites to peasants, and I suggested that one form of
fertility magic dating from the Celtic period was that
of sacrificing fertility in one sphere in the hope of
achieving it elsewhere. Virginity was regarded as the
highest sacrifice, essentially a human sacrifice that
could perhaps purchase fertility (of crops as well as
procreative fertility) for the whole community. From

the   pre-Christian   centuries   in   Gallegan   folklore,
virgins   were   linked   with   water   images   and   the moon   to
form   a   triad   of   interwoven talismans   that   were   to
guarantee fertility.

        Early   Celtic   creation myths   clearly   state   the
creative   role   of   virgins   working   through   their
traditional medium: "A water virgin was fertilized   by
a wind - the sea then became the mother of all life."[3]
This Celtic myth survives in great Britain, but a later
myth from Galicia, which was incorporated into a local
Christian   heresy   in   about   the   fourth   century,   has
enough   symbolic similarity, in spite of a   superficial
Christian   overlay,   to   indicate   that   Iberian Celts
probably shared much the same mythological heritage:

                When   God   wants to   give   men
                rain, he shows a   Light-Virgin
                to the Prince of Darkness, who
                desires her so that he   sweats
                with   excitement making   rain,
                and   when   deprived of   her,
                causes   thunder   by   his
                groaning.[4]

The Light Virgin was probably an allegorized version of
the   moon   which   had   traditionally   been   a   female
fertility figure.[5]   In both texts, virgins do   not
directly   generate   fertility, but in a   passive sense
control   water, which in turn makes the   land   fertile.
This, then, is the relationship between the three   main
fertility   symbols   in Galicia: virgins represent   the
moon (in   fact, the images are so intertwined, it   is
impossible   to determine which symbolizes which).   The
moon   controls water; water brings fertility.   Beyond
establishing the relationship between virgins, the moon
and   water,   this   wonderfully   telling   myth   clearly

attributes   fertility   to frustrated sexuality.   This
basic   relationship   persisted throughout   the   seventh
century, albeit in a Christian form.

There is no way to be certain that prior to the
Roman Conquest some women lived as dedicated virgins in
Galicia,   but the richness of references to virgins   in
Celtic mythology[6] and the general respect given to
women who remained virgins makes it probable that   at
times   a village woman would remain virgin either by
choice or circumstances.   With the   coming of the
Romans,   however, what may have once been   an   informal
dedication   to virginity became formalized.   A woman
might   renounce family life to remain independent,
virgo, whether she was virgo intacta or not.[7]   Roman
women may have had any number of reasons for their
dedication to virginity, but it is not farfetched to
imagine that Gallegan pagans revered such women as
fertility symbols. The Roman ideal of virginity may
indeed   not have been so far from the Gallegan
association   between   virginity and its   opposite,
fertility.   In   examining the epitome of Roman
virginity,   the Vestal Virgins, Pomeroy, in Goddesses,
Slaves and Whores, wrote:

> Most paradoxical, perhaps, was
> their   involvement   in
> agriculture   and   fertility
> rites.   It   appears   that
> virginity is not synonymous
> with   sterility,   and   not
> incompatible with fertility.
> Purity and intactness can be
> viewed   as   stored-up
> fertility...[8]

The   relationship between virginity and   fertility

continued throughout the early Christian centuries, as
did popular respect for dedicated virgins. An
indirect, but clear expression of popular sentiment is
provided by the cults of saints in the period. While
the surviving hagiographic records were obviously
written by official churchmen, they often reflect
popular sentiment since they usually were written to
give official sanction to an established cult.
Therefore, hagiographers eulogized a saint for the
traits for which she was already being worshipped. The
earliest Spanish saints were those martyred during the
persecutions of the later empire, especially those of
Diocletian. Some of the earliest hagiographic
materials are the hymns of Prudentius written in the
late fourth century. As Marique in <u>Leaders of Iberian
Christianity</u> accurately observed, "The martyr poems of
Prudentius crystallize the legend at the stage which
had been reached at that time in narrating the life and
passion of a saint."[9] Prudentius' poem about the
virgin martyr, Eulalia, articulated and Christianized
the ancient relationship between virginity and
fertility:

> Mighty and populous the city
> she blessed
> Drenching the soil with her
> blood there outpoured,
> Hallowing it with her virginal
> tomb.[10]

Through the medium of poetry, Prudentius made more
explicit what was probably the underlying symbol that
had pervaded the earlier virgin/water images: the
magic, fertile "water" passively controlled by virgins
was blood. Menstrual blood which spontaneously flowed
monthly represented a mysterious sacrifice that bought
fertility for the community.[11]

Prudentius' verse, at one level, is about martyr's blood and a city hallowed by the martyr's burial. At a deeper level, it is about a city made prosperous (fertile) by the blood from a virgin's womb. There is a repeated mythological and literary association between birth and death, between womb and tomb. As Jean Marshall noted, "the jar, the pitcher, the hole in the ground, the cave, the underwater grotto...all symbols of woman, are also symbols of death."[12] The images expressing Eulalia's martyrdom are well within this tradition. By her virgin, sacrificial death, Eulalia joined and exceeded the many virgins of Celtic mythology who guarded the "fountains" of their own flowing sexuality[13] so that the community might remain fertile and prosperous. It is not surprising that peasants addressed the same petitions to Eulalia as they had previously offered to Ataecina, a fertility goddess.[14] It would not have required much official pressure to replace the pagan Ataecina with the Christian Eulalia, because, in function, Eulalia was Ataecina.

There were many virgin saints during the Iberian persecutions, so many, in fact, that one wonders whether only virgins held firm in their faith. More likely, in the telling virginity was attributed to all female martyrs, thus reinforcing the sacrificial virgin image so important in this region.[15] Eulalia was the hagiographical and symbolical archetype for these many virgin saints, so she will suffice here to demonstrate the pervasive hagiographic association between fertility and abstinence. It is easy to understand how peasants who were so concerned with scarce crops had a great deal of respect for both virgin saints and local virgins.

Obviously, women who married also possessed the capacity to be fertile. By bearing children, these women brought fertility to the private sphere of the family, insuring its survival. Virgins, on the other hand, by renouncing private regenerative fertility brought prosperity to the communal or public sphere of the village as a whole.

Many of the women who dedicated their lives to abstinence between the fourth and seventh centuries were city women. While at times they moved to remote areas near a village to live out their chosen way of life, those who chose chastity did so not explicitly to insure a good harvest, but for more personal reasons. A virgin gained considerable independence, the companionship of a community of women or a perception of a closeness to God. These private explanations, however, do not detract from the public result. Virgins residing in a community brought prosperity. We are severely handicapped in exploring the experience of dedicated virginity by the scarcity of writing by women during this early period. The few but eloquent surviving texts will have to speak for all the Gallegan virgins.

The best known fourth-century Spanish virgin was Etheria, who left Galicia to make a pilgrimage through the holy lands. She was gone for over three years[16] and during her trip, she wrote a long letter to her "reverend sisters" in Galicia with whom she had presumably lived in a loose-knit community. Etheria's letter is not an introspective eulogy of celibacy, but rather a joyous travelogue. Etheria seems to have been a virgo in the classical Roman sense, an independent woman belonging to no man. The tone of Etheria's letter suggests that by rejecting traditional social

relationships,   a   virgin   need   not   forego   warm
companionship.   Etheria's poetic   references   to   her
sisters   as   "lumen meum" and "dominae   animae   meae"[17]
hint   at strong ties of affection that united women   in
their   vows   of   chastity.   These   informal   ties   of
affection   and commitment were perhaps   often   stronger
than   monastic   rules which would later   bind   nuns   to
their convents.

Personal autonomy was a motive for holy women, but
the phenomenon of dedicated chastity was complex.   In a
Christian tradition, virginity is frequently a path   to
mystic   knowledge   of God.[18]   A virgin   was   considered
"whole"   (intacta), existing in a state closer   to   the
oneness   (i.e., wholeness) of God, thus more   receptive
to   a mystic union.[19] Two letters from   fourth-century
Gallegan   virgins   survive   which   typify   this   mystic
motivation for chastity.   Instead of choosing merely to
be   their own women, these two anonymous   women   became
brides of Christ,[20] and as Jerome (whose writings   were
well-circulated   in Iberia) described the Virgin   Mary,
remained   "simple, pure, unsullied, drawing no germ   of
life   from without, but like God himself,   fruitful   in
singleness."[21]   Jerome's   description   is   remarkably
applicable   to the experience of chastity as   described
by   the   two   Iberian   virgins,   particularly   his
association of fertility (fruitfulness) with   chastity,
and   his sexual imagery ("drawing no germ of life   from
without").

The   first   of   the letters   seems   to   have   been
written by an avowed virgin, probably one not living in
a   formal community.   She wrote to her dear friend   and
spiritual   mentor in affectionate language   reminiscent
of Etheria.[22]   She thanked her friend for a letter   and
attempted   to   express   her   mystical   knowledge,   the

"prophetic testimony in the mystery of the Bride of
Christ,"[23] by symbolic images. The image she chose
most frequently was that of fertility. In the short
three-page letter, she used some form of the words
"fructus" and "fecunditas" eight times, as well as less
direct references to water, pregnancy and the womb,
which were clearly further associations with fertility.
The complex images can be distilled into one central
throught: by foregoing carnal knowledge, a virgin
receives God's spirit into her uterus from which she,
in turn, gives birth to God's word to benefit others,
in a spiritual emulation of Mary's virgin birth.[24] The
virgin author of the letter believed that the benefit
to others by "spiritual" rather than "carnal" knowledge
was didactic. Everyone could benefit from knowledge
gained by a virgin. The author praised her friend's
teachings in her obscure, sexually symbolic way:
"...fruit pours forth from your womb; that you may
carry your child [i.e., knowledge] about and show it in
Egypt [the world], that is, to us survivors of a
darkened generation, you may show the fruit of your
doctrine."[25]

These basic themes appear in the second letter,
written also by a fourth-century religious woman to an
acquaintance. The writer was urging her friend
temporarily to withdraw from the world to a monastery
ceil,[26] to isolate herself, fast and pray for three
weeks between Christmas and Epiphany.[27] This fast and
isolation were in imitation of the Virgin Mary's
post-partum recuperation. It was to be a restorative
period as well as a commemorative time, when women who
could not dedicate their lives by being brides of
Christ could benefit from a period of reflective
chastity. The writer urged her friend to be like Mary,

"calm...in the tenth month with the box of your body in
flood...you will not go out in public...."[28] By this
withdrawal, prayer and fasting, she would heal her body
and perhaps receive a revelation.[29]

In spite of the intensely personal mysticism that
pervades this second letter, the writer nevertheless
implied a benefit larger than the personal one:
"...just as within the secret cell of the monastery,
something is formed in us, which shall bring us to
health and in the tenth month, new works will appear
from our fruits, at which the world will wonder."[30]
This passage summarizes the views expressed in both
these difficult but fascinating letters, and if they
are indeed representative, they are remarkably
consistent with traditional associations between
personal sexual abstinence and community prosperity.

Even though we have few documents which express
the motivations and feelings of these women, the amount
of legislation at the Council of Elvira (ca. 300)
directed to dedicated virgins suggests that there were
probably many women who had chosen this way of life.[31]
It is difficult to describe precisely how these women
lived, since there was no prescribed mode of life for
virgins dedicated to God before the establishment of
convents.

Probably the most common way of life was for a
consecrated woman to remain with her family. It was
difficult to resist family pressures to marry, and
legends of early Christian "heroines" reflect this
struggle that must have been repeated in many
households when a woman announced that she refused to
marry and chose to remain at home supported by her
father. One, Castissime, had to run away disguised as
a man to avoid her father's insistence.[32] Another,

Benedicta, was betrothed to one of the king's guard and
ran away to avoid marriage.[33] Helie, in language
strongly reminiscent of pagan fertility symbols, was
described as being "as beautiful as the moon"[34] and
remained at home after winning her right to remain
virgin in long dialogues with her mother and a judge.
Helie's mother marshalled examples from saints and
scriptures to support her position: "Either receive
marriage; or you shall be damned."[35] In spite of
Helie's protestations that truth was not discovered by
disputation, she responded with an impressive number of
biblical examples to support her somewhat extreme
anti-nuptial position: "Profess virginity; or be
damned."[36] Her parents despaired of convincing her,
and presented her to a judge to see if she might be
seized as a wife.[37] The third book of Helie's Vita is
her dialogue with the judge. She persevered with long
eloquent speeches, exempting herself from the judge's
scriptural admonition that "It is better to marry than
burn," by saying: "It is true that scripture says it
is better to marry than burn; but not for everyone,
that is, not for holy virgins."[38] To demonstrate that
such scriptural demands did not apply equally to
everyone, Helie pointed to an inequality in applying
secular laws: "Men are not bound by laws promulgated
for women."[39] Her arguments won her the right to have
as her husband "...one who presides not on earth, but
in heaven."[40]

Even if a girl bowed to social pressure and
married, she could still live as "virgo intacta." St.
Jerome heard of this Spanish practice and described it
with a good deal of skepticism: "They live in the same
house, enclose themselves in the same room and
sometimes sleep in the same bed... [Nevertheless] the

women do not deny, but affirm that their virginity was
intact."[41] Even if a marriage were consummated, a
woman could still decide to live chastely and dedicate
herself to God although she no longer was technically
"virgo intacta." As implied by the second of the two
letters of anonymous Spanish virgins, living chastely
seems to have been accorded only slightly less status
than perpetual virginity, and the Christian legends
have numerous examples of men and women taking vows
after years of marriage.[42] Most of these consecrated
women lived ordinary lives, tending their family homes,
walking through town or shopping, although members of
the community knew of their special dedication. The
women may have worn a special article of clothing
distinguishing themselves, perhaps a veil, since a
later law of the sixth century forbade "...widows from
wearing religious clothing on top of their regular lay
clothes to pretend that they have taken vows...."[43]

Living within the family, however, was by no means
the only possibility for early Spanish virgins.
Sometimes holy women chose to live with holy men. As I
noted in a previous chapter, priests, especially in the
countryside, frequently had women living with them.
Often these women took vows of celibacy and were called
agapetas or subintroductas.[44] While the Church
legislated frequently against this practice, [45] through
the fifth century it must have been common, and
undoubtedly it was popular with villagers who would
thus have their parish priest and holy virgin together,
accessible to benefit the community. There were also
hermits living in this region, and they seem to have
not been unwilling to provide a home for consecrated
women. Braulio, the seventh-century hagiographer of
St. Emilian, praised, perhaps excessively, Emilian's

ability to withstand temptations of the flesh: "He lived with holy virgins and, from his eightieth year on...he calmly accepted...all the services of the maidservants of God...yet...he never experienced a trace of dishonorable passion...."[46]

Apparently, serving holy men was considered a worthy occupation for holy women, but it is difficult to imagine an independent pilgrim like Etheria living out her vows as a lady-in-waiting. For such women, it was possible to live alone, isolated in rural areas,[47] but this seems to have been rare, or temporary. For example, Benedicta, who fled from her high-born betrothed, lived for a while in a small hut in the forest. Soon, however, "when her reputation was heralded with praise...such an ardent desire inspired other young maidens of various families that from all sides a splendid troop of women gladly came, so...the number of holy women in the congregation reached eighty."[48] It was probably to one of these loose-knit anchorite communities that Etheria belonged.

There were no rules for any of the virgins, wherever they lived, and no vows except a commitment to chastity. They traveled when it pleased them, whether as far as the Holy Land, or simply to visit nearby friends as did the anonymous author of Letter No. 1.[49] Whatever their way of life, as holy virgins they performed an extremely important mediating function. Conferring fertility to the community by their chastity, they were held in awe and respect by villagers in their vicinity. They also moved frequently, bringing town views to their rural communities, and bringing their observations on rural life to their town friends. These same activities, however, made them a threat to the nascent official

Church of the early fifth century which, together with the newly converted Visigothic monarchy, was trying to bring uniformity and orthodoxy to the kingdom. The men of the official Church did not encourage the association of all-important fertility magic with women holding themselves aloof from both official social structures and official religiosity.

One of the most informative documents about official conceptions of virginity was the sixth-century Rule[50] of St. Leander of Seville, written to his sister Florentina. Leander demonstrates the struggle to transform highly respected, independent virgins into obedient, orthodox, isolated nuns. By the late sixth century, most of Iberia's virgins were living formally in convents, but some of Leander's images recall an older view of virginity which was never completely eradicated. In his preface, which was a long praise of virginity, Leander recognized the sacrificial quality of a dedicated virgin, "...the oblations acceptable to God and consecrated on the altars of heaven,"[51] yet he avoided making the traditional association of sacrifice with the purchase of fertility. The official Church consistently attempted to ignore the magic potential of virginity, but as Leander demonstrates, it was never completely able to do so, managing to go only halfway, accepting a virgin as a sacrifice, but leaving it unclear for what she was sacrificing.

Leander also continued the old practice of associating virginity with health. To phrase it obversely and more theoretically, the penalty of carnal knowledge was death.[52] Referring to the dangers of childbirth, Leander wrote: "...the mother perishes with the child and all the pomp of marriage ends in death."[53] Finally, in his explanation of the purpose of marriage Leander voiced a strong echo from a time when virginity was praised as an end in itself, not as a means to a celestial end (that is, "to be numbered among the 144,000 who... [sing] the song that virgins alone may sing...").[54] He could not completely dismiss marriage for fear of falling into dualist heresy that had plagued Spain during the early Christian centuries. His argument in favor of marriage, drawn from Jerome, recalls a time when virginity was praised not solely as a path to salvation: "From a marriage a virgin is born."[55] But virginity had to be incorporated into and controlled by the Church hierarchy, and Leander clearly recognized this necessity.

The obvious first step in regulating and controlling dedicated virgins was to eliminate the diversity of their styles of life. A woman who dedicated her sexuality to God was no longer to live at home nor with others who remained within the world. Leander accurately identified such informal living arrangements as belonging to a pre-Christian era: "Virgins should flee a private life; not only because they might imitate others they see in the cities, but because it is a pagan custom merely tolerated by the Church for those converts who wished to continue to live alone [or at least outside a community]."[56] Leander was not alone in urging informally dedicated virgins to become nuns. Early legislation on this subject is abundant. Consistent with the legalism of the official Church, women were to take formal and legally binding vows of virginity.[57] Increasingly, church law condemned the breaking of vows rather than the fall from chastity itself.[58] While there were probably always women who chose a private life of chastity, by and large from the seventh century, dedicated virgins lived in communities bound by legal vows and under episcopal discipline.

The Church wanted to modify not only the virgins' way of life, but also the ideal of virginity itself. Once it may have been enough for a woman to preserve her virginity in order to be held in awe for her sacrifice. St. Jerome, however, was representative of the early Church fathers in believing that "...the virgin must keep herself [free] not only from every physical contamination but also from every other kind of sin. In fact, corporal purity is of little value if not accompanied by purity of life."[59] Virginity was to be a means to an end, to smooth the way to salvation, rather than an end in itself.

To what degree Visigothic nuns accepted this expanded view of virginity of the spirit as well as of the flesh is difficult to say. For example, in an old Visigothic Codex Regularum[60] of a convent, there is a section containing seven saints' lives.[61] All seven saints were women, and curiously, in an age of martyrs, none had been martyred. The unifying theme of these lives was that of each woman successfully preserving her virginity (or at least her chastity) in the face of demanding husbands (Melania), irate fathers (Castissime), persistent mothers (Helia) or society in general (Mary of Egypt). In these stories it was considered virtuous for these women to lie, steal and disobey the authority of family or spiritual leaders in order to preserve their chastity. These activities hardly fulfill Jerome's mandate that virgins should keep themselves free from all sins, not only those of the flesh. Within the convents, however, the stories were copied and preserved as testimony to the high value placed on virginity itself. Furthermore, these

stories were read for instructional purposes, thus
perpetuating behind convent walls many of the values
that had existed in this region since the time virgins
had lived in the world.

Clearly, Galicia was a region whose people always
had a high regard for virginity as a spiritual, if
somewhat mysterious state, and as a sacrifice that
brought fertility to the ungenerous land. By the
seventh century, the official Church had largely
succeeded in regulating and institutionalizing Gallegan
ritual virginity. As nuns, women were subject to the
discipline of the local bishop. They were bound by
vows carrying the force of law and by laws directly
ordering their lives.[62] Within the convents, however,
the feelings and motives that had moved fourth-century
women to dedicate their sexuality to God was never
completely transformed. Strong abbesses who ruled
their own houses and sometimes presided over a double
monastery of men and women[63] would have surely been
familiar to the independent pilgrim, Etheria, who
befriended just such an abbess in the Holy Land.[64]
Marriage to Christ continued to provide an opportunity
for independent women to remain that way. Also, from
the monastic writings faithfully copied, one can still
feel the mystic strain. Virginity was a blessed magic
state both sufficient in itself and yet a means to
divine instead of carnal union. The convents
themselves became a collective symbol of sacrificial
virginity. As such, they continued to be revered by
neighboring villagers, yet they were more controllable
than independent virgins, and therefore less of a
threat to the official Church.

Gallegan villagers also revered holy men who had
removed themselves from society and proven themselves

to be bearers of supernatural power. During the Visigothic centuries, hermits' huts were scattered in the forests of Galicia and in the Cantabrian peaks. The importance of these hermits was only partially due to their withdrawal from society.[65] If they had remained completely isolated, their impact would have been minimal. Iberian holy men, for the most part, remained hermits in the true sense of the word for only a period of their lives. In fact, they frequently traveled throughout the countryside or received visitors; they preached in the apothegmatic tradition of eastern holy men, and they performed miracles, not the least of which was the miracle of overcoming natural needs in order to live an ascetic life. In this continuing interaction with society, holy men functioned as influential religious leaders alongside the officially designated parish priests.

There was little overlapping of roles because Iberian priests and holy men functioned as two different types of religious leader: one ritualistic and the other charismatic. These functions have been variously studied and defined,[66] but perhaps the clearest description of the functional dichotomy comes from anthropoligical analyses of shamanism. Willard Z. Park, for example, in his study on Shamanism in North America, wrote: "The priest is regarded as one who has knowledge of the rituals and leads ritualistic performances; his office is therefore primarily dependent upon learning, not upon direct personal experience with supernatural forces. The shaman [or in the case of Visigothic Iberia, the holy man] on the other hand, works by virtue of his possession of supernatural power. With this power he usually performs curative rites and acts as prophet and

seer."[67] This definition roughly parallels the roles
played in Iberia by the priests and local holy men and
provides a useful theoretical context within which to
analyze the development and nature of Iberian holy men.

Members of the ruling elite accepted priests'
roles   easily,   since   priests' ethical, legal   and
ritualistic   functions   were consistent with   elite
philosophy. An individual holy man privately in touch
with the supernatural, on the other hand, was not
readily accepted by the official Church because such a
leader   could   easily represent a threat to orthodox
homogeneity. Peasants, however, needed both.   Priests
ritualized social interactions and holy men interceded
with natural forces.

It is not as easy to trace pre-Christian Celtic
antecedents to Iberian holy men as it was to trace the
ideal of virginity. Strabo mentioned neither priests
nor charismatic religious leaders in his description of
early Celtiberians, but it is improbable that these
tribes were totally lacking a priesthood. Since they
were Celts, it seems likely that their priests were
similar to Druids.   From descriptions we have of
British Druids, they seem to combine both priestly and
charismatic functions. Their knowledge of important
rituals was derived from years of study as would be
appropriate for a priest, yet they seem to have had
elements of supernatural power which suggests that they
were also holy men. Druidic supernatural powers seem
largely to have involved controlling the weather and
prophesying, both of which were also the skills of
Iberian holy men. Early Christian holy men, like
shamans, were actively involved in curing, but if
Celtiberian Druids existed, they seem not to have been
known for miracle curing. Strabo observed that illness

among Celtiberians was a social matter. A sick person
was carried outside the round, stone huts and laid
alongside the narrow pathways that wound through the
citanias. There, passing neighbors observed the
patient and if they recognized the illness, they would
recommend a cure.[68]

With the exception of curing (which indeed may
have been presided over by some sort of priest figure
in spite of Strabo's omission) all the elements of
Iberian religiosity from legalistic and ritualistic, to
charismatic prophecy were performed by the same
religious leader. This raises the question of how and
why these functions became separate and began to adhere
roughly to Park's dichotomy of priest vs. shaman. The
most likely conclusion is that in Galicia holy men were
imported with Christianity.

The confrontation of two different religious
conceptions and cultures created a division in the
traditional functions of a priest. No longer would a
priest in the Celtic manner be both priest and prophet,
for the Church restricted the personal charismatic
authority of priests. Priests were to be merely
conduits of the power of the Church, thus reducing the
danger of heterodoxy that might arise from unrestricted
prophesying and miracle-working.[69] This Church policy
preventing priests from using personal power to
intervene in controlling nature led essentially to a
division of labor between the functions of priest and
holy man. Virtually from the time a Christian
priesthood was established on the peninsula, there were
men who felt themselves chosen to separate themselves
from the community to acquire spiritual power. These
men were quickly venerated as holy men. The earliest
Christian holy men were martyrs.

Many Iberians suffered martyrdom under the Roman emperors, especially during the reign of Diocletian. Some were remembered anonymously <u>en masse</u> such as the eighteen martyrs of Saragossa. However, some individuals' lives and passions were recorded and these martyrs became objects of cults, providing spiritual examples for those who might also try to be "soldiers of Christ" centuries after the age of martyrdom. The lives of the martyrs provided a model for the path to sanctity: first, the martyr was called to martyrdom. Then followed a period of torture, during which he proved his spiritual strength. Finally, he became a vessel of supernatural power manifested by miracles. The oral tradition that preserved saints' cults established a pattern that would be followed by ascetic holy men throughout the Visigothic period. The close relationship between martyrdom and asceticism was articulated during the Visigothic era. St. Isidore in his <u>Etymologies</u> described two modes of martyrdom, one by "visible passion" and the other by "virtue hidden in the soul," or the ascetic life.[70] While local traditions provided abundant examples of martyrs exhibiting "visible passion," much of the inspiration for living an ascetic life was imported from the East where there had always been a strong tradition of holy hermits.

There were many travelers from Galicia to the Holy Land and North Africa who returned with tales of ascetics.[71] In the middle of the fourth century, two travelers from the East came to Galicia and instructed a Gallegan noble, Priscillian, in dualist heresy. Priscillianist heresy was extremely popular in Galicia, and heretical holy men wandered about the countryside demonstrating the power of a charismatic prophet in

direct touch with the supernatural: "The dead were
resurrected with the same ease that our fields put
forth flowers...The saints spoke with the animals, old
magicians were vanquished in spite of their
sorcery..."[72]

In spite of its disapproval of wandering holy men,
the official Church also contributed to the
establishment of the tradition in Galicia. In the
sixth century, two influential men traveled to Spain
and firmly, if unintentionally, established the
tradition of wandering holy men. The first, Donatus,
travelled from North Africa with a group of monks, and
established a coenobitic community in Spain. His
contribution to the eremetic tradition lay in the Books
of Saints he brought with him.[73]   These probably
included several of the virgins' lives preserved in the
Escorial manuscript a II 9 discussed above, as well as
lives of heroic Eastern holy men that were copied and
circulated. The second, Martin of Braga, brought a
complete eremitic exemplar to Galicia from Pannonia.
This was a Greek copy of the Sayings of the Desert
Fathers which Martin's monk, Paschasius, translated
into Latin.[74]   The Sayings (Apothegmata) is a
collection of short anecdotes about Eastern hermits.
These holy men did not present models of complete
reclusion: the anecdotes were about hermits who
interacted with society, gave advice, prophesied and
performed miracles. The sayings were widely copied and
read in Spain[75] along with hermits' Lives.

Due to this combination of forces, by the fifth
century a functional separation was achieved between
priest and holy man, one ritualizing social
interactions, the other interceding with natural
forces. Both were as indispensable to peasants as were

old Celtic priests who probably performed both
functions. As was true with dedicated virgins, people
revered holy men because they possessed supernatural
power. Unlike virgins, a hermit's power was not the
ability to bestow fertility, but it was the ability to
control nature. Just as the quality of their magic was
different, the power of holy men was also derived
differently from that of virgins. Virgins inherently
possessed their unexpended, thus potentially magic,
fertility. They needed only to preserve it. Men,
however, had to fight to gain their power. They were
soldiers, rather than brides of Christ. If they
remained chaste, it was not to be symbols of fertility,
but to retain their strength for battles with various
demons.

Seventh-century sources testify to men choosing to
go out into remote areas as hermits, wandering about to
preach, and sometimes founding monasteries. Valerius
of Bierzo, a seventh-century chronicler, wrote of
"monasteries constructed in remote desert places as
God's work by a few elect and perfect men."[76] These
"elect and perfect men" were some of Galicia's holy men
and their stories were all written in the seventh
century, either contemporaneously or within one hundred
years of their lives. First and most famous was
Fructuosus of Braga, born of a wealthy family (his
father was a "dux exercitus Hispaniae")[77] who was to be
in turn hermit, monastic founder, and bishop. Another
was Emilian, a poor shepherd who became widely
venerated. Finally, Valerius of Bierzo, a wealthy,
educated man, is perhaps the most interesting of the
three because he wrote of his own life as an occasional
hermit. While there were many differences between
these three men, their common experiences may

illuminate the essential qualities of all Gallegan holy
men.

Valerius called the hermits and monastic founders
"elect" which suggests that they were called by God to
their role. This election was distinguished by a
conversion experience. Fructuosus had his call as a
child, when he was in the mountains of Bierzo with his
father inspecting flocks of sheep. The child was
suddenly inspired by God to consider suitable places to
build a monastery.[78] Emilian, too, was in the
mountains caring for flocks when "...his cithara was
changed into an instrument of learning and his mind was
filled with the urge to contemplate the supernal."[79]
Valerius, after being "engrossed in worldly pleasures
during...[his] adolescence, [was]...driven by a desire
for divine grace to attain the beginnings of the
religious life."[80] These inspirations, however, were
only the beginning. Each man had to prove himself by a
series of struggles before he qualified to be a true
soldier of Christ. The conversions were simply turning
points which provided the commitment to begin the
battles.

According to these sources, after conversion a
potential holy man sought out instruction from an
established churchman. Fructuosus "surrendered himself
to the saintly man, Bishop Conantius, to be instructed
in spiritual discipline."[81] Emilian became a disciple
of another hermit, Felix, from whom he learned "...how
to guide his steps unfalteringly towards the kingdom
above."[82] Valerius entered the monastery of Compludo
after his conversion, "hoping...to attain at length the
light of truth."[83] Although all three sources mention
a brief period of instruction, it is unlikely that all
holy men went through this stage, since a holy man's

power,   unlike that of a priest could not   be   learned.
The sources' emphasis on guidance more likely reflected
the concern of the official hagiographers of Fructuosus
and Emilian to encourage the tutelage of would-be holy
men in order to maintain orthodoxy. Braulio, Emilian's
hagiographer,   stated   plainly   that   "...no   one   can
correctly guide his steps to the blessed life without
the instruction of his elders."[84] Valerius, on the
other hand, writing of his own experience, belittled
his   apprenticeship   period,   dismissing   it   as
unsatisfactory ("I was not able to reach the   port   I
desired.").[85]

Inevitably,   an   aspiring holy man had to   go   off
alone to achieve in solitude the personal contact with
God that was promised at the moment of his   conversion;
for, as Valerius wrote: "...a holy man and an
unconquerable warrior in order to exercise and prove
himself,   desires   to find tribulation and misery."[86]
This period of solitude was crucial in a holy man's
development. The aspiring soldier of Christ fought the
twin demons of natural forces: externally he faced
cold,   storms,   and wild beasts; internally he had to
cope with lust, hunger, thirst, fatigue and fear.   A
man   might   fail to overcome his body's demands and
return home to a normal life and probably anonymity; or
he would persevere and win, prove his power as a holy
man, and perhaps achieve immortality. When a man left
his community to seek solitude in the hills, he made a
pilgrimage from the secular space of the   village   to
holy space in the wilderness, where in solitude he
could be closer to God.   If he succeeded   in
withstanding the trials, he then no longer belonged to
the community of men, but to the company of the Lord.

Fructuosus, Valerius and Emilian succeeded   in

their   lonely struggles to become soldiers   of Christ.
Each man withdrew to a difficult solitude.   Fructuosus
"...entered   barefoot   into   a   forest   overgrown   with
vines,   wild and rough, where he spent his time among
caves   and rocks in trebled fasts,   multiplied vigils,
and prayers."[87] Emilian climbed Mount Dirce and lived
alone near its peak.[88] Valerius, too, climbed one of
Galicia's   many   mountains   and   "...found   a
rock...situated on a lofty height at the top of a
mountain,   bare of human habitation, baked in the
harshness of complete sterility...."[89] It was during
such periods of solitude that holy men acquired both
their power and their reputations as soldiers of
Christ.   From this moment on, the language chosen to
describe holy men and their experiences is filled with
the terms and symbols of warriors. The Sayings of the
Desert Fathers provided abundant examples: "The hard
working monk...is a warrior." "If I am in a place
where there are enemies, I become a soldier."   "One
hour's sleep is enough for a monk if he is a good
fighter."[90] The warrior theme is continued in the
Iberian Lives.

        Holy men's struggles were both internal and
external. As Braulio wrote of Emilian, "What invisible
battles he experienced there [on Mount Dirce] and what
visible ones..." In the Gallegan hills the latter were
abundant.   Emilian was "...drenched with incessant
rain, troubled by the blasts of wind...the bite of
cold..."[91] Valerius, too, was "...struck by the
violent tempests of all the winds threatening from
every side, and often smitten by storms of pelting rain
and by tremendous blizzards, and at the same time
gripped by all the rigors of intolerable cold."[92] The
internal battles against passions and bodily needs were

just as common and no less difficult. Indeed, Valerius
gave these battles priority: "For the first palm of
victory is to conquer by conquering oneself."[93]
Emilian, too, in the face of "temptations of various
ingenious kinds...directed all his emotions...all his
desires...all his inspiration."[94]

As important as the ascetic trials themselves was
the manner in which these struggles were described for
it was here that the warrior image definitely applied.
Valerius "bore up courageously," fought back "manfully,
wrestling with difficulties."[95] After Emilian won his
victory, he was dubbed "wrestler of the Eternal
King."[96] Villagers saw these lone men, without the
support of village networks, braving mountain tops long
dedicated to old spirits, storms, exposure, and
starvation. Not only did holy men fearlessly seek
those elements which kept village death tolls so high,
but they emerged victorious over the forces of nature
that peasants for centuries had worked carefully to
placate. A holy man had demonstrated his power: he was
an object of veneration and awe. He was looked upon as
an excellent mediator between the village and the God
who controlled the natural world that the holy man had
vanquished. In practice, he was also often a mediator
between the village and the official Church.

After a certain period of time, which the sources
describe vaguely in terms of years, a hermit's solitary
victories were recognized by local people, usually the
peasants of the neighboring countryside. From this
moment on, a man was no longer merely a hermit, but a
holy man who was served by his people, and who was
expected to use his intimate relationship with the
supernatural to benefit the community.[97] Fructuosus
tried to avoid this recognition by withdrawing deeper

into the woods, but small black birds which he had
befriended "betrayed his holy hiding
places....Thereupon all hastened to the man with great
joy."[98] Emilian, too, became famous: "...the report
of his holiness spread so far and wide that almost
everyone learned of it."[99] Valerius gave a fascinating
picture of villagers gathering around a local holy man
and offering him reverence, service, and food, no doubt
to keep him and his beneficial powers in the vicinity:
"...a varied crowd of persons of both sexes, flocking
together, began to gather there, to offer help to
me...to tender service, and to furnish food."[100] After
being transformed by recognition from hermit to holy
man, the acknowledged soldier of Christ seldom lived as
a solitary ascetic again. He was provided for by
villagers, or acquired disciples, or, as Emilian, was
served by dedicated virgins.

As holy men, Fructuosus, Emilian, and Valerius
possessed a particular status in the community, with
powers and expectations centered around their proven
ability to overcome nature. This is a stage in their
careers significantly different from their eremitic
trials, and it must be analyzed separately within the
context of the social structure to which they had
become important[101] but of which they were never fully
a part. Essentially, the activities of holy men were
to remain peripheral to the social structure of both
village and elite cultures. Their role was to preach,
prophesy, wander about and perform miracles.

Holy men were powerful due to personal contact
with the supernatural, and this contact often took the
form of supernatural knowledge[102] which was frequently
contrasted with knowledge gained by education, that is,
the knowledge of clerics. For example, Braulio said

Emilian had gathered "...from the fields the flowers of
the   wisdom   of   ineffable   divinity...[until
he]...surpassed   the   ancient   philosophers...for   what
they achieved by world industry, he was granted by   the
divine graces from above...."[103]   Knowledge of the
supernatural was bestowed by visions, and the   sources
are full of descriptions of hermits' prophetic visions.
Valerius,   for   example,   described   in   vivid   detail
several   monks' visions of heaven and hell.[104]   While
such   visions   of   an   afterlife   could   easily   be
categorized as predictions of the future,   there   were
also instances of more immediate portents.   To Emilian,
for example, were revealed matters as political as   the
"downfall of Cantabria" by Leovigild and as personal as
the imminence of his own death.[105]   The most   important
consequence   of   the   recognized   visionary   ability   of
hermits was that people sought them out for   advice.[106]
People came to a hermit's secluded site to plead for   a
"word."   In speaking, holy men automatically became
mediators   not   only   between   God   and   humanity,   but
between   peasant   and   lord.   Valerius,   the   highly
educated townsman, could not help imparting his   elite,
literate   views   to peasants who came to   venerate   and
listen to him.   Nor could Emilian, the   illiterate
shepherd,   avoid expressing his unsophisticated views
when receiving priests and bishops.   Since the words of
holy   men   carried the force of secret   knowledge   from
God,   their   preaching   was   not   only   assured   of   an
interested audience, but it was also certain to   arouse
fear and repression on the part of the official Church.
Prelates who were unwilling even to allow their priests
to preach extemporaneously, surely did not want   laymen
speaking with the force of divine inspiration.
    Another   characteristic   of   holy   men   that

contributed both to their mediating roles and their
threat to official homogeneity was their predilection
for wandering. Fructuosus traveled throughout most of
western Spain (see map on p. 145 for Fructuosus'
travels) and even wanted to visit the East[107] as the
virgin Etheria had done before him. Although he was
unable to make the pilgrimage, his desire to widen his
travels suggests how little stabilitas was considered a
prerequisite for being a holy man. Valerius, too,
moved about several times, and the frequent mention of
"wandering monks" in Visigothic sources[108] indicates
not only that Fructuosus and Valerius were but two of
many such traveling holy men, but also that the
official Church recognized that their potential for
spreading heterodoxy increased with the distances they
traveled.

While prophecy and wandering characterized Iberian
holy men, these soldiers of Christ could be most
clearly recognized by their periodic demonstrations of
power which they had gained from their ascetic
struggles. These demonstrations took the form of
miracles that were indisputable testimony to a holy
man's personal contact with God.[109] Iberian holy men's
miracles fall broadly into two categories, those that
were willed and those that occurred spontaneously when
the holy men were in the vicinity.

From the example of the Apothegmata, there was
abundant precedent for the most dramatic suspensions of
the natural order. Desert Fathers could turn sea water
sweet or command the sun to stand still.[110] Iberian
spiritual athletes, too, specialized in nature
miracles. Most of their miracles were cures similar to
those performed by martyrs. Moreover, it is not
surprising to find Emilian, Fructuosus and other holy

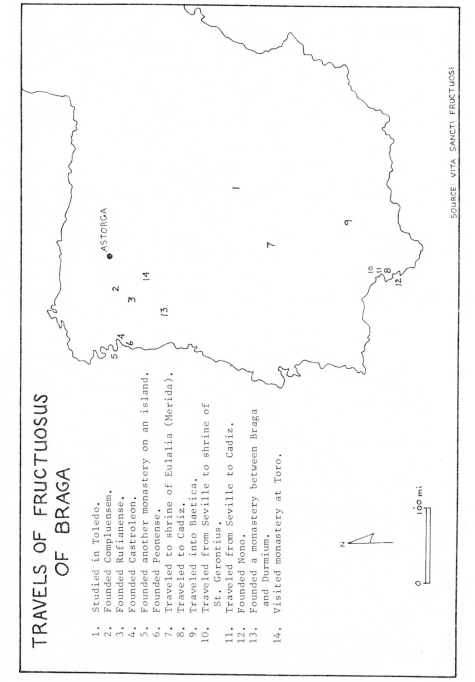

TRAVELS OF FRUCTUOSUS
OF BRAGA

1. Studied in Toledo.
2. Founded Compluensem.
3. Founded Rufianense.
4. Founded Castroleon.
5. Founded another monastery on an island.
6. Founded Peonense.
7. Traveled to shrine of Eulalia (Merida).
8. Traveled to Cadiz.
9. Traveled into Baetica.
10. Traveled from Seville to shrine of
    St. Gerontius.
11. Traveled from Seville to Cadiz.
12. Founded Nono.
13. Founded a monastery between Braga
    and Durmium.
14. Visited monastery at Toro.

SOURCE: VITA SANCTI FRUCTUOSI

men exorcising demons as well as effecting cures, since
many ailments were attributed to demonic possession.
It is significant that these curing miracles cut across
the boundary between peasant and elite cultures. Holy
men belonged to neither the village nor ruling
communities, so their miracles were not confined to one
group. Emilian, for example, cured and exorcised
demons for senators, servants, churchmen and rural
people.[111]

Illness was not the only practical problem on
which holy men were consulted. Emilian once saw a
villager who had been cutting beams to build his horreo
or above-ground granary. The peasant had inadvertently
cut one too short. Emilian prayed over the beam and it
miraculously stretched to fit.[112] Emilian had
suspended the laws of nature so that a worker would not
lose the benefit of his labor. Fructuosus, too, could
intervene in the natural course of things, as when he
commanded storms to cease, to protect crops, or
suspended water's wetness so that precious books would
not be damaged.[113]

There can be no doubt that, in the minds of their
contemporaries, holy men could use their hard-won power
to intervene in day-to-day events and occasionally
reverse the order of nature. This power, however, had
become so much a part of the holy man's person, that
miracles might happen without his direct intervention.
Unwilled miracles were important because they
demonstrated that holy men, like martyrs before them,
were not simply magicians who performed unusual feats,
but were in touch with God; their bodies were actual
receptacles of divine power. The most immediate
results of the special affinity of hermits for the
supernatural was that they had to be treated with

special care. Any wrong done to a holy man would bring
certain penalty. In Iberian sources, holy men were
never depicted as wishing punishment on their enemies,
but punishment happened as surely and inexorably as a
fire burning a careless hand. For example, when a man
who was foolish enough to steal from Valerius' small
vegetable garden was fatally bitten by a snake, the
hagiographer averred, "no one else was found who had
been wounded by a serpent in these mountains."[114]
Unwilled, automatic miracles performed good deeds as
well, usually through secondary objects. Emilian's
staff cured a lame woman, and the granary beam that
Emilian miraculously stretched was so imbued with his
power, or to be doctrinally correct, with God's power
filtered through Emilian, that "...hardly a day goes by
without its providing a cure for those who are ill."[115]

These, then, were the qualities of Iberian holy
men, warriors of Christ. They were men who for a
period went into the hills and proved their spiritual
strength by reversing the natural order and overcoming
hunger, thirst, cold, fear and demons of the hills.
Armed with knowledge of their own power, they reentered
society (or were drawn back by popular demand) and
became influential and respected, if unofficial,
participants in the continuing dialogue between peasant
and elite. They fulfilled the need of villagers to
have some means of interceding with the supernatural
forces controlling nature. Holy men were sufficiently
influential to be a threat to the homgeneity of the
Visigothic Church unless they were brought into its
structure.

There were three principal steps taken by the
Church to co-opt the influence of individual holy men:
1) they were ordained; 2) their individual power was

reduced by their being collectivized and stabilized   in
coenobitic   communities; 3) the veneration   of   Saints'
cults was encouraged, thus the influence of dead   holy
men   was enhanced at the expense of live   ones.   The
first attempt, ordaining holy men priests, was not very
successful. Emilian, for example, was "forced against
his will to obey in being appointed to the   office   of
priest..."[116]   A poor shepherd, Emilian lacked the
elite values which ordinarily came with training   for
the   priesthood and open-handedly gave church funds   to
his   poor   parishioners, totally disregarding   the
financial needs of the temporal church.   His   own
clerics   complained to   the   diocesan   bishop   that
Emilian's   church "was   suffering ruin   and...[its]
property was being complete squandered." Emilian was
"relieved of   his   ministry" and   retired to   his
hermitage.[117]

A Visigothic lord tried to make Valerius a   priest
also,   but   Valerius remained firm in   his   resolve to
avoid what he saw as an easy life "...enriched by   many
fat offerings."[118] On the other hand, Fructuosus was
successful in the ecclesiastical hierarchy, probably
due   to his noble upbringing and his organizational
experience as a founder of a monastery.   Nevertheless,
Fructuosus, too, fought the pressures of divine office.
His   reputation was too great, however, for him to
continue his former free life in the direct service   of
God.   Thus, when he wanted to go to the Holy Land,   the
king "fearing lest such a shining light should withdraw
from   Spain, gave orders to arrest him."[119]   Shortly
after that, Fructuosus was named metropolitan of Braga.
It   is   important   to note,   however,   that   his
miracle-working and other supernatural manifestations
disappeared   while   he   was   preoccupied   with

administrative duties, until he received a premonition of his impending death.

Popular veneration of virgins and holy men established a solid foundation for them to be mediators between peasants and rulers. Before they could be satisfactory conduits of orthodoxy, however, the Church had to bring them into its control, and during the late sixth and early seventh centuries, the Visigothic Church was much preoccupied with this effort.

Notes

1. Justo Pérez de Urbel, <u>Los Monjes Españoles en la edad media</u>, Vol. 1 (Madrid, 1933), p. 88, "...los ascetas y las vírgenes se nos presenta como los precursores de los monjes."

2. Raoul Manselli, <u>La Religion Populaire au Moyen Age</u> (Paris, 1975), p. 117, noted the importance of women in popular piety without really analyzing the reasons behind it. "...un des phénomènes - et non des moins significatifs - que caractérisent la religion populaire: L'importance dont y fut revêtue la femme." See also p. 124: "Elle constitue une des forces primordiales de cette religion et en permet la transmission orale."

3. Jean Markale, <u>Women of the Celts</u> (London, 1975), p. 44.

4. Orosius, "Memoria Apostolorum" <u>CSEL</u> 18, 158, 12-14.

5. Strabo, <u>The Geography of Strabo</u> (New York, 1917) III, 4, 16.

6. Markale described in detail all the references to virgins and their symbolic mythology in Celtic Britain.

7. Markale, p. 127, discusses usages of the word "virgo" meaning independent woman, as opposed to "virgo intacta," which referred to a woman's sexual, not political or economic, status.

8. Sarah B. Pomeroy, <u>Goddesses, Whores, Wives and Slaves: Women in Classical Antiquity</u> (New York, 1975), p. 211. See also, Marina Warner, <u>Alone of All Her Sex</u> (New York, 1976), p. 48: "There was one particular attitude toward virginity that the...Christian religion did inherit from the classical world: that virginity

was powerful magic and conferred strength and ritual
purity."

9. Joseph Marique, ed., Leaders of the Iberian
Peninsula (Boston, 1962), p. 129.

10. Sister M. Clement Eagan, trans., The Poems of
Prudentius (Washington, 1962), p. 129.

11. Mikhail Bakhtin, Rabelais and His World,
trans., Helene Iswolsky (Cambridge, 1965), p. 279,
noted the relationship between blood and fertility in
popular legend: "[Rabelais] relates that after Abel's
killing the earth absorbed his blood and became
fertile." For a discussion of peasants' fear and
respect of blood, including menstrual blood, see
Foster, "Peasant Society and the Image of Limited
Good," in J.M. Potter, et al., eds. Peasant Society
(Canada, 1967), p. 309.

12. Markale, p. 59.

13. See ibid., pp. 45-46, for Celtic myths about
virgins guarding fountains.

14. Stephen McKenna, Paganism and Pagan Survivals
in Spain up to the Fall of the Visigothic Kingdom, The
Catholic University of America, Studies in Medieval
History, vol. 1 (Washington, 1938), p. 26.

15. Werner Stark, The Sociology of Religion (New
York, 1966), IV:127, noted the importance of symbolic
references in the study of religions: "Not literal
truth, but symbolic truth is what matters in religion.
Differently expressed, a legend, though incredible on
the level of literalness may well convey in an
allegorical fashion a very hard and fast fact."

16. M.L. McClure, The Pilgrimage of Etheria (New
York, 1919), p. 30.

17. Ibid., pp. 5, 6, 23 and 37.

18. John Bugge, Virginitas: An Essay in the

History of a Medieval Ideal (The Hague, 1975), pp.
42-45, has an excellent analysis of noetic communion
with God which is more accessible through the virgin
state. On p. 46, Bugge summarizes: "A chief trait of
the virgin saint or virgin martyr is an intimate
knowledge of the mind of God."

    19.   Ibid.,   p.   16:   "Methodius
describes...virginity [as] an ontological kinship with
the divine existence which gives it the ability to
comprehend Perfection."

    20. G. Morin, "Deux lettres mystiques d'une ascete
espagnola," Revue Benedictine 40 (1928), p. 293,
"Christi sponsa." Bugge, p. 59, writes "The
designation of the Christian Virgin as the bride of
Christ goes at least as far as the Third Century..."

    21. Jerome, "Ep. XXII, xix, Ad Eustochium" PL
22:405-6.

    22. Morin, p. 294. The author addresses her
friend as "non soror, sed domina."

    23. Ibid., p. 293. "...propheticum testimonium
illa in mysterio Christi sponso..."

    24. Ibid., pp. 293-4. "Concepimus in utero,
domine et parturivimus spiritum salutis tuae...Tu verbo
dei feta, tu sermonem eius enixa, sic nobis scientiam
dei parturis."

    25. Ibid., p. 294. "...ventris tui fructus
effudit; ut circumferas et demonstres in Aegypto filium
tuum, hoc est, nobis in saeculi obscruitate viventibus
doctrinae tuae fructus ostendas."

    26. While she uses the word "monasterius" twice in
this letter, ibid., pp. 298 and 301, it seems clear
that she is referring to an isolated hermit's retreat
rather than a coenobitic community.

    27. Ibid., p. 300. "...nos in coniunctione decimi
et undecimi mensis orationem ieiunio copulemus...."

28. Ibid., p. 298. "sedeat...in decimo mense arca
corporis tui in deluvio...non egradiaris in publico..."

29. Ibid., p. 301. "...membris nostri corporis
medeamus, verum etiam per adnuntiationem angeli, id
est, revelationem spiritus futurorum nobis arcana
pandantur." The healing benefits are reiterated on p.
301, "...in quo nobis requies nostrae salutes
ostenditur."

30. Ibid., p. 297. "...velut intra occultam
vulvam uteri, sic intra secretam monasterii cellulam
aliquid formetur in nobis, quod proficiat ad salutem,
et in decimo mense novum opus ex fructibus nostris,
quod mundus miretur, apparet."

31.   P. Francisco de B. Vizmanos, Las Vírgenes
Cristianas de la Iglesia Primitiva (Madrid, 1949), p.
604, "No puede ponerse en duda que las jovenes
consagradas a Cristo baja el velo de la pureza se
contaban en gran numero, va que el ano 300..." On a
European scale, J.J. Schulenburg, "Sexism in the
Celestial Gynaeceum - from 500-1200," Journal of
Medieval History (June 1978), p. 120, also recognized
this trend noting that for early candidates for
canonization "...the primary profession was that of
consecrated virginity outside of an organized monastic
community."

32. "Vita Sancte Castissime Virginis." Ms. Esc. a
II 9, fol. 115 v.

33.   Sister Frances Clare Nock, The Vita Sancti
Fructuosi (Washington, 1946), p. 116.

34. "Vita Sancte Helie," Ms. Esc. a II 9, fol. 73.

35. Ibid., fol. 86 v. "Aut suscipies nuptias; aut
damnabis."

36.   Ibid., "Virginitas profitenda est; aut
damnada."

37. Ibid., fol. 90, "...ut dum puella tribunalibus presentaretur; sibi eam raperet in uxorem."

38. Ibid., "Quod vero scriptum dicis nubere melius esse quam uri; non omnibus, id est non sacris virginibus..."

39. Ibid., "Quomodo lex mulieribus promulgata, masculos non constringat?"

40. Ibid., fol. 90 v., "Est mici sponsus, qui non in terra presidet; sed in celo."

41. Pérez-Urbel, pp. 91-2.

42. Ibid., pp. 89-90, describes several fourth-century husband/wife ascetic partners, for example, Damaso and Laurencia, Paulino and Teresa, and Lucino and Teodora.

43. S.P. Scott, Visigothic Laws Book III, Title V, ch. 4, pp. 109-10.

44. Pérez-Urbel, p. 92.

45. I Tolet, VI, PL 84:330.

46. Braulio, "Life of St. Emilian," The Fathers of the Church, Iberian Fathers, vol. 2, pp. 133-4.

47. Vizmanos, p. 609, interpreted the "Monasterium" in the second letter of the anonymous virgin discussed above as "...un lugar solitario para una sola persona, segun la significación griega del vocablo."

48. Nock, pp. 116-18.

49. Morin, pp. 295-6, "...ut cum me iuxta consuetudinem visitaveris..."

50. "Sancti Leandri, Hispalenses Episcopi, Regula sive Liber de Institutione virginum et Contemptu Mundi," PL 72:873-94. This is not a monastic rule in a real sense of the word, for it does not attempt to establish in detail a monastic way of life. The Rule contains a preface and 21 short chapters, in which

Leander selectively discusses certain aspects of life in a virgin's community — aspects which either were of particular interest to Leander, or perhaps to his sister, Florentina, to whom the tract is addressed.

51. Ibid., PL 72:875.

52. See Bugge, p. 19, for an analysis of theological relationships between sex and death.

53. "Sancti Leandri," PL 72:889.

54. Schulenburg, p. 121.

55. "Sancti Leandri," PL 72:888. Jerome, PL 22:403.

56. "Sancti Leandri," PL 72:890.

57. Concilium Eliberitanum, XII, PL 84:303, (Held ca. 300 A.D.) calls it a "pactum virginitatis." Jose M. Fernandez Caton, Manifestaciones asceticas en la iglesia hispano-romano del siglo IV (Leon, 1962), p. 53, recognized this designation as a "public contract" which is a significant change of status.

58. See IV Tolet VI and X Tolet V, PL 84:397 and 443.

59. Schulenburg, p. 129.

60. Visigothic monasteries and convents were not governed solely by a particular Rule, in spite of the fact that several Iberian monastic "Rules" were written. Instead, each house had a Codex Regularum, a collection of rules, saints' lives and other writings considered useful to monks and nuns. Members of the house would try generally to live in a way consistent with the writings in their Codex. This particular Codex is Escorial Manuscript a II 9.

61. Ms. Esc. a II 9, Melania, Castissime, Helie, Egeria, Pelagia, Maria Aegyptiae, and Constantinae. I am currently preparing a book in which I will publish and analyze these Lives.

62. For example, Scott, Book III, Title V, 2, p. 107: "Anyone marrying a woman...dedicated to God shall be perpetually exiled."

63. Joan Morris, The Lady Was a Bishop (New York, 1973), p. 8: "Certainly the prayer of ordination of abbesses in the Wisigothic Sacramentary declared that before God there is no discrimination of the sexes..."

64. McClure, p. 210.

65. Peter Brown, "The Rise and Function of the Holy Man in Late Antiquity," Journal of Roman Studies 61 (1971), p. 87, discusses the importance of holy men remaining outside established social structures and deriving much of their power from this aloof position.

66. Max Weber, The Sociology of Religion (Boston, 1963), has the classic discussion of the charismatic leader, defining the two types of leaders as prophet vs. priest. Two other studies defining and discussing the question of charismatic leaders are Stark, vol. 4 and Jeffrey Burton Russell, A History of Medieval Christianity - Prophecy and Order (New York, 1971). Both books deal abundantly with the historiography of the question.

67. Willard Z. Park, Shamanism in Western North America (New York, 1975), p. 9.

68. Strabo, III, 4, 18.

69. This development was described by Max Weber, p. 77, as he discussed the replacement of "genuine by official charisma."

70. Isidore, "Etymology" VI, c. XI "De Martyribus," PL 82:290, "Duo autem sunt martyrii genera, unum in aperta passione, alterum in occulta anima virtute."

71. For a full discussion of pilgrimages between the holy land and Galicia, see Casimiro Torres

Rodriguez, "Peregrinaciones de Galicia a Tierra Santa en el S.V." Compostellanum (Abril-Junio, 1956), pp. 401-48.

72.   Mario Martins, Correntes da filosofia Religiosa em Braga dos sec. IV a VII (Porto, 1950), "Os mortes ressuscitam com a facilidade com que nos campos desabrocham milhares de flores...Os santos falam com os animais..."

73.   Sancti Isidori, "De Viris Illustribus Liber," in Henrique Flórez, España Sagrada, Vol. V. App. 6, pp. 475-76, "...copiosisque librorum codicibus..."

74.   Paschasius, Monk of Dumium, Prologue to his translation of the Vitae Patrum, PL 73:1026.   Also reprinted in Claude W. Barlow, ed., Martini Episcopi Bracarensis, Opera Omnia (New Haven, 1950), pp. 293-94.

75.   Valerius certainly had a copy of the Apothegmata, because in the end of his work "Residuum," he told a story of the blessed Arsenius which is from the Sayings (although Valerius did make a few changes in the story, both the saint's name and the basic elements of the tale are the same).   C.M. Aherne, trans., Valerius of Bierzo - An Ascetic of the Late Visigothic Period, The Catholic University of America Studies in Medieval History, New Series, vol. xi (Washington, 1949), p. 156.

76.   Valerius, "De Genera," PL 84:457:   "...a paucis electis et perfectis viris in desertis locis rara ope domini constructa sunt monasteria..."   The references to "desert" places are formulaic, referring to deserted areas.   In Galicia, where Valerius was writing, he meant forests and mountains.

77.   Nock, p. 89.

78.   Ibid., p. 88.

79.   Braulio of Saragossa, "Vita Sancti Emilian,"

The Fathers of the Church: Iberian Fathers, Vol. 2 (Washington, 1969), pp. 120-21.

80. Aherne, p. 68.

81. Nock, pp. 88-90.

82. Braulio of Saragossa, p. 121.

83. Aherne, p. 68.

84. Braulio, p. 121.

85. Aherne, p. 70.

86. Ibid., p. 82. This need for solitude is also a characteristic of shamans, who have many parallels with early Christian holy men. Park, p. 21, writes: "Acquiring shamanistic power and the exercise of power, is an individual affair... Power is... the result of private personal experiences."

87. Nock, p. 94.

88. Braulio, p. 122.

89. Aherne, p. 70.

90. Benedicta Ward, trans., The Sayings of the Desert Fathers (London, 1975), pp. 17, 163, and 9.

91. Braulio, p. 123.

92. Aherne, p. 70.

93. Ibid., p. 72.

94. Braulio, p. 122.

95. Aherne, pp. 70 and 72.

96. Braulio, p. 125.

97. Brown, p. 80.

98. Nock, p. 100.

99. Braulio, p. 123.

100. Aherne, p. 72.

101. Park, p. 10, "...the shaman is one who acquires supernatural power through direct personal experience. This power is generally manipulated in such a way as to be a matter of concern to others in society."

102.   Braulio, pp. 120-21.   "Emilian's mind was
filled with the urge to contemplate the supernal."

103.   Ibid., pp. 123-24. Humble or "natural" wisdom
was also frequently praised in the Apothegmata, for
example, Abba Arsenius said: "I have indeed been
taught Latin and Greek, but I do not know even the
alphabet of peasants." Ward, p. 8.

104.   Valerius "Dicta ad Beatum Donadeum scripta,"
"De Bonello Monacho" and "De Coelesti Revelatione," PL
84:431-38.

105.   Braulio, pp. 135-36.   Fructuosus, too,
received special knowledge from God, Nock, pp. 112 and
126.

106.   Brown, p. 93.   "The 'God-bearing' hermit
usurped the position of the oracle..."

107.   Nock, p. 122.

108.   Epistola Wisigothica No. 18, MGH, p. 687, was
written by a monk, Mauricius, who was accused of being
a wanderer. See also, IV Tolet LIII, for legislation
forbidding monks from wandering.

109.   Brown, p. 87.   "The miracle...was merely a
proof of power - like good coin, summarily minted and
passed into circulation to demonstrate the untapped
bullion of power at the disposal of the holy man."

110.   Ward, p. 14.

111.   Braulio, pp. 125-29. Valerius also described
miracle cures in Aherne, pp. 138 and 140, and
Fructuosus' miracles are found in Nock, pp. 104-08.

112.   Braulio, p. 130.

113.   Nock, pp. 114, 110.

114.   Aherne, p. 140.

115.   Braulio, pp. 126 and 131.

116.   Ibid., p. 123.

117.   Ibid., p. 124.

118. Aherne, p. 82.
119. Nock, p. 122.

OFFICIAL REACTION — SAINTS AND MONASTERIES

Popular respect for the charismatic individualism of holy men and women was always potentially threatening to the religious uniformity that defined and perpetuated the official church. However, since people were unwilling to renounce the protection gained by venerating a holy person, the Church could not merely legislate such veneration out of existence. Nor could bishops who were structuring the kingdom's religious administrative order simply by-pass these holy men and women; they were too important. The Church attempted to resolve the continuing tension between administrative and charismatic authority in two ways: on the one hand, it accepted cults of dead virgins and hermits, encouraging these cults at the expense of the veneration of living holy people, and on the other, it forced holy men and women into monasteries and concentrated on regulating the collective units, which were more easily controlled than individuals personally in touch with God.

The earliest Christian holy men and women were martyrs. While their cults developed largely due to popular reverence, the official Church quickly recognized the value of encouraging the veneration of martyrs to promote orthodoxy. In the early fifth century, Pope Vigilius urged Gallegan bishops to encourage their parishioners to venerate saints as examples of a Christian life.[1] Early in the sixth century, Martin of Braga also encouraged "rustics" to visit sites where saints were venerated.[2] This encouragement came at a time when the Church was

actively fighting paganism, and martyrs were the early
heroes and heroines of that struggle. However,
veneration of martyrs led indirectly to a new threat to
official homogeneity, that of holy men and women
choosing to live in martyrdom, rather than to die for
it.

In the seventh century, as part of a general
effort to consolidate its organization and standardize
worship, the Church actively worked to bring the
veneration of holy people into the ecclesiastical
administrative order of the kingdom. In 633, the
Fourth Council of Toledo in a series of liturgical
reform canons[3] incorporated veneration of saints into
official worship. Several of Prudentius' hymns to
martyrs were included in the newly adopted breviary.[4]
Saint veneration was no longer to be a matter of
personal, private worship, because that would leave the
way open for private veneration of a local holy person.
On the contrary, it was to be a part of the structured
worship guided by the official Church.

Toward this end, the Fourth Council of Toledo
encouraged the writing of orthodox saints' lives which
were to be read in churches on feast days.[5] It was
after this that Braulio, who attended the Fourth
Council, wrote his Life of St. Emilian. It was also
during this century that the famous Passion of Vincent
of Saragossa was rewritten and expanded[6] and this
revised Passion became the prototype for other
narratives composed at this same time.[7] The
significance of the recording of the narratives was
that the Church could then make sure that the
veneration of the saint encouraged the faithful in
orthodox belief. Before the lives of the saints were
written down, people venerated a holy person for any

number   of   reasons   from   a   recalled   miracle   to   a
perceived   association   between   the   saint   and   a
pre-Christian deity.   By recording an official   version
of   a Passion, however, Churchmen made sure   that   each
saint presented a model of Christian, orthodox heroism.
When such a narrative was read in Church on the Saint's
feast   day,   official Churchmen were able   to   use   the
people's   respect for a popular saint to encourage   the
congregations   into orthodox belief.   By the   power   of
the pen, the Church took over popular cult figures   and
turned their veneration to   its own purposes.

In spite of this move to bring the saints into the
circle   of orthodoxy, the saints were never   completely
separated   from the popular images that had   surrounded
them long before their narratives were written down.

All the Lives recorded at this time, whether   they
were   based directly on the Vincent model,   or   written
independently   based on local traditions, continued   to
adhere   to   the   symbolism   that   represented   the
traditional   importance   of holy men and   women.   St.
Marcelo   of   Leon,   martyred   under   Diocletian   was   a
centurion   who laid down his Roman weapons and   claimed
henceforth   to be a soldier and centurion   of   Christ.[8]
The other martyrs continued either the soldier imagery,
or   were   the   purest   of   virgins   (like   Eulalia   and
Leocadia),   satisfying the conditions that   would   make
them   familiar intermediaries between peasants and   God
for aid in controlling nature.

Not only did official churchmen revise and attempt
to   channel the veneration of popular cult figures;   at
times   they   apparently encouraged veneration   of   new
saints to serve official purposes.   The most obvious of
the saints who received official support were confessor
saints, great bishops like Martin of Braga and Turibius

of Palencia. These men represented the ideal of
official Christendom, fully living up to the
responsibilities imperfectly fulfilled on a local level
by parish priests. Despite official references to
these men as "blessed" and the recording of their
lives, there is no evidence that veneration of bishops
became popular during the Visigothic years.[9]

An example of a widely-venerated saint who does
seem to have been a creation of the official Church was
Leocadia of Toledo. There is no evidence of her cult,
or even of her existence, before the seventh century,
when a Life was written based on the Saint Vincent
model. According to her Vita, Leocadia was a virgin
who was arrested by Dacianus, interrogated, and who
died as a result of her ordeal. According to the
hagiographer, Leocadia had been inspired by the
accounts of Eulalia of Merida (discussed in Chapter IV)
and desired to be martyred as Eulalia had been. King
Sisebutus dedicated a basilica to Leocadia in Toledo in
the year 618[10] and her cult became very popular in the
region of Toledo, to which her virgin martyrdom was
believed to have brought prosperity to rival the
blessings bestowed by Eulalia in the West. Since
Toledo was the royal city of the Visigothic kings, it
is not surprising that it was felt appropriate that it,
too, should have the protection of a fertility saint.
In this context, it is clear how closely tied were the
political and religious goals of official churchmen,
but the success of Leocadia's cult in contrast to the
early failure of bishop saints demonstrated that the
official Church had to bow to the religious
requirements of peasants even in the encouragement of
official cults. Brides and soldiers of Christ were
seemingly consistent with popular perceptions of
sanctity. Priests were not.

While the newly written and revised saints' lives were the official Church's means to regulate the lessons of sanctity, the concrete basis for this veneration popularly remained relics, magical, tangible, repositories of divine power. From the earliest sources, it is evident that martyr's relics were always recognized as powerful. For example, in Prudentius' fifth-century account, after Vincent's initial torture, people came to seem him and "...many moisten linen cloths with blood that oozes from his wounds to keep as relics in their homes for generations yet to come."[11]

The importance of relics was also stressed in the Passion of Fructuosus of Tarragona. After Fructuosus' martyrdom, two brothers saved his relics. Fructuosus appeared to the brothers and urged them carefully to guard the valuable relics.[12] Thus, from the moment of a holy person's death, relics were seen to contain his or her power. Yet, the official Church felt that relics were to be used carefully so that their power would benefit the community and not enhance the power of an individual. A canon of the Third Council of Braga clearly illustrates this point. During martyrs' processions, bishops were forbidden to wear the relics around their necks, but were to allow a deacon to carry them on a small chain. If a bishop wore the relics, the canon explained, he would be taking too much honor for himself.[13] Such legislation reflects the official Church's desire to limit the charismatic individualism that originally had given the relics such power.

Relics imbued with divine power had to be suitably housed, and from the earliest centuries, they were placed in separate religious buildings, centers of saintly magic, rather than in parish churches, centers of social worship. In 410 Pope Vigilius distinguished between these two main types of churches in his letter to the Gallegan bishop, Profuturus, by noting that some churches had relics (sanctuaria) and some did not.[14]

Churches with relics were originally centers of local piety. These buildings, called not only sanctuaria, but basilicae or oratoria were erected on the site of a saint's grave, or to house his or her relics, and since they were used only for prayer and veneration of the saint, there were no baptistries or cemeteries attached to them. Since basilicae were built in response to regional piety, they were frequently built by laymen. A lord would raise a building to house venerated relics, and these, not parish churches, were principally the Spanish proprietary churches about which so much has been written.[15] It was not unusual for a basilica to be located near, or even in, the same village as a parish church (parochia), for the two structures filled two completely different functions.[16] A basilica grew out of the religious needs and impulses of the village and was a visible symbol of the micro-space of parish religiosity. The parish church, on the other hand, was erected to satisfy the desire of official churchmen to join the kingdom in a homogeneous religious unit. As such, in the village the parish church represented the macro-space of the official Church.

Coinciding with other official efforts to control popular cults, in the seventh century proprietary basilicas began to be regulated. Basilicas were slowly converted to parish churches.[17] For example, all newly constructed basilicas were to be placed under the jurisdiction of a local bishop[18] and each religious building served by an appropriately ordained priest.[19]

Relics also increasingly began to be translated to parish churches, blurring the functional difference between a priest in his parish and a saint in his basilica. In this way, popular veneration of powerful holy people was further brought within the sphere of official religiosity as it widened to accommodate popular religiosity. The slow fusion of basilica with parish church vividly demonstrated the incorporation of the religious micro-space of the village into the larger religious unit of the kingdom.

The search for relics expanded as they became important as a basis for worship and increasingly translated to parish churches.[20] Bishop Braulio, responding to a request for relics from his priest Iactatus, poignantly described the confused state of seventh-century remains:

> As for the relics of the most
> revered apostles, which you
> have asked me to send, I
> truthfully reply that I have
> not a single martyr's relics
> so preserved that I can know
> whose they are. My lords and
> predecessors were of the
> opinion that the labels should
> be removed from all of them to
> make them indistinguishable,
> and that they should all be
> put in a single room, since,
> in many ways, either by theft
> or against their wills or by
> the coercion of the piety of
> many, they were being forced
> either to give away or to lose

what   they had.   Some   seventy
were   set apart,   however,   and
are   in common use, but   among
them   are to be found none   of
those which you requested.[21]

Regardless   of   the   problems   involved,   saint
veneration   flourished in Visigothic Spain   because   of
the   needs   of peasants for concrete magic   and   closer
intermediaries   between themselves and a   distant   God.
Cults   received   considerable impetus   in   the   seventh
century   from   the   official   Church,   which   not   only
recognized   the   tremendous   importance   of   local
veneration,   but   encouraged the   popularity   of   local
saints,   transforming   their   examples   of   highly
individual piety into examples of heroic orthodoxy.

During   the   seventh   century,   the   Church   also
encouraged   and   regulated   monastic   development.
Powerful   monastic   houses   were   founded   that   would
dominate the Gallegan hills throughout the Middle Ages.
The   strength of these houses rested upon both   popular
veneration   and   official encouragement.   Monasteries
represented   the   collectivization   of   the   power   of
traditional   holy   men   and women, and   as   such,   were
extremely   influential.   Their impact was   particularly
strong in Galicia where there were approximately   twice
as   many monasteries as in any of the other   provinces.
Furthermore,   the   density of monasteries   relative   to
both   the population and area is significantly   greater
in   Galicia   than in the rest of Iberia as   a   whole.[22]
(See map on p. 169).   Monasteries were stopping places
for   travelers   between cities, served as   conduits   of
communication   between members of the nobility, and   as
important media of religious exchange between elite and
peasants.   Although   many   aspects   of   Visigothic

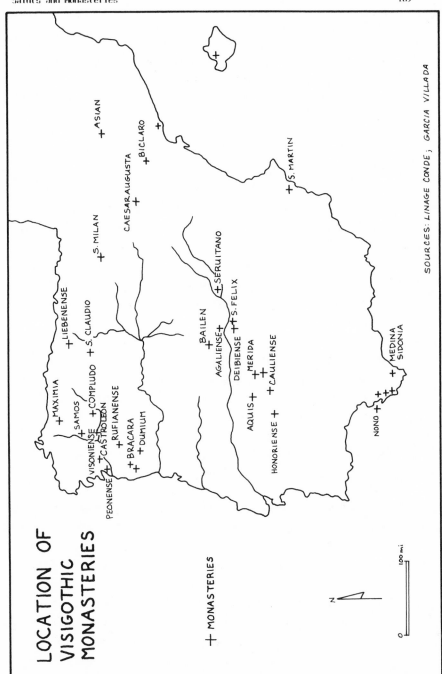

LOCATION OF
VISIGOTHIC
MONASTERIES

+ MONASTERIES

SOURCES: LINAGE CONDE; GARCIA VILLADA

monasticism have been studied,[23] many questions remain
unexplored.   Here I shall examine only   the   mediating
role of Visigothic monasteries.

An   analysis of the position of monasteries   in
relation   to   the   peasant   and   ruling   cultures   of
Visigothic   society properly begins with a   description
of the official Church's efforts   to   institutionalize
holy individuals and create and regulate the   monastic
institutions   themselves.   Forcing individual holy   men
and   women into monasteries was only the   beginning   of
institutionalization.   The next problem was to   insure
that the collective units themselves remained   orthodox
and   under   the   control of the hierarchy.   This   was
difficult because Iberian monasteries customarily   used
a Codex Regularum instead of an established Rule.   One
fairly   representative   example of such a Codex is
Escorial   manuscript a I 13.   Part of   this   Visigothic
codex   was   copied from an earlier   collection   in   the
ninth   century   by Leodegundia, a nun   of   the   convent
Bobatelle[24]   probably adjoining the monastery of   Samos
in Galicia.[25]   After two missing folios, the manuscript
begins   with   a signed pact between an   abbot   and   his
monks   (such   pacts are discussed   more   fully   below),
followed by the rules of Benedict, Fructuosus, Isidore,
Pacomius,   Leander and Augustine.   There are also   five
saints'   lives   to be read as   exemplars,   and   various
letters   and   tracts, most attributed   to   St.   Jerome.
These   epistles dealt with several topics,   among   them
virginity,   widowhood,[26] anger,[27] and health.[28]   These
would   likely   have been presented and   read   when   the
abbess   felt   they were particularly   relevant   to
circumstances that arose during the course of   monastic
life.   From   the varied documents   in   what   was   the
governing   collection of a monastery, it becomes   clear

that abbots and abbesses could choose which to use in
establishing the routine of daily life, which to stress
during public readings, and they could interpret these
items with a good deal of latitude.[29]

Along with abbots' and abbesses' considerable
discretionary powers there was an unusual relationship
between Gallegan monastery heads and the monks and
nuns. Instead of being bound by a Rule, monks and nuns
were bound in a personal contractural relationship to
their abbot or abbess. By the seventh century,
Gallegan monks signed a _pactum_ in which they agreed to
obey the abbot, not conspire against him with other
monks or relatives outside the monastery, and granted
the abbot power to return fugitive monks to the
monastery by force.[30] It is not surprising that the
pact focused on the problem of fugitive monks, since
the Church considered wandering holy people to be a
threat to orthodox uniformity.

The practice of pact-making was clearly a creation
of Gallegan official culture which was consistently
interested in making religious sentiments the subject
of jurisprudence. Pacts were one of several ways to
institutionalize and control the individualism of holy
people, but they also served to increase the power of
abbots and abbesses, so that there was still a problem
of the heterodoxy of the collective units. This
problem was addressed in the seventh-century reform
movement of Fructuosus of Braga.

The principal writings of this reform movement
were three monastic rules that were to supplement the
Codeces Regularum. One was written by Isidore of
Seville and two by Fructuosus of Braga, the _Regula
Monachorum_ and the _Regula Communis_. Fructuosus' Rules
were written specifically for monasteries in Galicia,

and thus, for the purposes of my regional analysis, are the most important. These Rules were intended to regulate both life within a monastery (particularly the Regula Monachorum) and the position of each monastery within the regional hierarchical structure, the primary interest of the Regula Communis.

The Regula Communis established in Galicia a system of federated monasteries headed by Dumium, near Braga, which was founded by Martin in the sixth century. This provided a structure that could control the individual houses.[31] Just as official legislation was intended to control the individualism of holy men by urging them into monasteries, the federated system reduced the discretion of abbots by placing them under the control of the Abbot of Dumium, who, from the time of Martin, had also held the Episcopal Chair of Dumium.

The Iberian Origins of this "Episcopus sub Regula" are unclear. Orlandis and Linage Conde attributed it to Irish/Celtic influences[32] and this is certainly possible, since an Irish colony with an adjacent monastery (Maximium) was established in a Gallegan town, Britonium, and this monastery periodically was governed by a bishop-abbot. Probably, however, the simplest explanation is the most accurate: the example of Martin of Braga, who founded Dumium, served as its abbot and was named bishop of Braga, could well have been strong enough to set a precedent that continued long after the coincidence of Martin's dual appointment. Regardless of the origins of the peculiarly Gallegan institution, a bishop-abbot, as head of Galicia's federated system of monasteries formed the perfect link to attach Gallegan holy men and women to the official Church structure.

A bishop under rule at Dumium had the sole

authority   to   authorize   the   establishment   of   new
monasteries.[33]   He also had the right to intervene   in
the   internal   affairs   of Galicia's   federated   houses,
since the Pactum, all monks had the right to appeal   to
a   "certain" bishop "...qui sub regula vivit"   if   they
had   a   grievance   against their   own   abbot.[34]   This
powerful   abbot-bishop   of   Dumium   could   not   act
completely independently, however.   As a bishop, he had
to   answer   to the king and to the bishops   sitting   in
council in Toledo.[35]   In his episcopal role, the   Abbot
of   Dumium   represented   the   federated   Gallegan
monasteries   at the councils of Toledo, completing   the
ligature between holy people and Visigothic rulers.[36]

The   Bishop   of Dumium's   control   over   Galicia's
monasteries   was part of a seventh-century tendency   in
Iberia to place monks and nuns under episcopal control.
Bishops   at   the Seventh Council   of   Toledo   expressed
clearly   the need for this control, writing that   since
it   was difficult to determine whether an   ascetic   was
honest or sinful, it was up to the bishop to   determine
his   orthodoxy.[37]   This canon   simply   restated   more
strongly what had been professed repeatedly in the late
sixth century, that bishops had authority over monks.[38]
By the seventh century, this process seems to have been
sufficiently   developed that it is likely that   bishops
appointed   the   abbots   in   the   monasteries   of   their
diocese.[39]   Episcopal control also extended   to   women
taking   vows.   For example, widows wishing   to   dedicate
themselves were to come before a priest, sign a written
profession of vows, and accept from the priest   special
religious clothing.[40]

By   this   combination   of   organization   and
legislation,   seventh-century monasteries were   brought
well   within   the control of   the   official   hierarchy.

There always continued to be individual holy men and
women who lived informally, but monasteries had become
influential as units in themselves and as part of
Galicia's communication network, both within the elite
culture and between elite and peasant cultures.

Like the holy men who preceded them, most of
Galicia's monasteries were located high in the hills.
The few descriptions in the sources make these
monasteries sound forbidding and inaccessible.
Valerius wrote "...below this monastery there yawned a
very deep and precipitous chasm which was fearful for a
man to look into."[41] Morales in the sixteenth century
visited the site of a Visigothic monastery "...in a
location so steep and with so many mountains that it is
difficult to imagine it."[42] But while monasteries were
indeed on top of hills or halfway up higher peaks,
their chosen mountains bordered wide valleys, usually
river valleys, which were main passes through the
Gallegan hills. Perhaps the most dramatic example of
this combination of precarious remoteness and
accessibility is the Liebanense monastery (now St.
Toribio de Liebano). This monastery is located in the
Picos de Europa, the highest peaks of the Cantabrians
on the eastern fringe of the medieval province of
Galicia. The monastery is on top of a mountain,
exposed to the storms and aloof from small stone
villages sheltered lower in the protected valley.
Liebanense, however, is not located deep within the
Picos, but on the top of a hill that borders the deep
valley of the Deva River. This valley is a
particularly fertile area of the Cantabrians, which
provides access to the interior of the range, and the
monastery's location at the point where the Deva
branches to the interior of the peaks made it an ideal

stopping place for travelers either entering into the range, or continuing around these peaks further south at the San Glorio pass.

This pattern was repeated throughout Galicia, for example in the region surrounding Braga, which was the location of three Visigothic monasteries. The precise location of these has not yet been discovered, but the region near Braga is known for mountains long considered "sacred" and crowned with shrines. (Bom Jesus, Ste. Lucia and Mount Sameiro are the best known.) It is probable that these same mountains with their impressive view of the important Braga valley housed the famous old monasteries. Similarly, Fructuosus' first foundation was located overlooking the valley of the Sil between the mountain range of Bierzo and the foothills of the Cantabrians, a convenient stopping place between the important Visigothic towns of Astorga and Lugo. The rest of Galicia's monasteries repeat the pattern of these important houses. In such a remote region, official foundations combined the two functions of Gallegan monasteries, conquering the inhospitable peaks with holy people, and unifying the province by a network of holy mediators.

Visigothic monastic rules confirm what is suggested by the locations of monasteries, that they served as important stopping places for travelers. Both Isidore's and Fructuosus' rules stressed the importance of hospitality towards travelers, making provisions for their comfort. Isidore ordered that bread served to visitors should be baked by skilled laymen, not by monks.[43] Fructuosus, too, showed much concern for hospitality. He said travelers should be received with the "most reverential charity" and

"offered gracious ministrations." The monks should
wash travelers' feet in the evening, provide soft straw
for them to sleep on and, upon their departure, give
them money to ease their travels.[44] It seems clear,
then, that monasteries served as necessary refuges for
travelers, and it is likely that most of the travelers
received so graciously were nobles, lay or
ecclesiastic. It is important to note that they were
not given hospitality in isolation, but sat at the
common table with the rest of the monks,[45] thus
providing a perfect opportunity to discuss peninsular
and provincial events. In this way, information passed
to the most remote regions of Galicia.

Not only were monasteries connected to the world
by travelers, but their lack of economic
self-sufficiency forced them to trade with cities.
Both Isidore's and Fructuosus' rules provided for ways
to establish this needed economic interaction. Isidore
recommended that a cella be established in the nearest
city where an older monk and two younger ones would
reside to handle monastic business.[46] Fructuosus
wanted to keep all his monks from the cities'
corrupting influence, and suggested that secular
affairs be entrusted to a pious layman.[47] In both
cases, surely ideas along with goods would have been
transferred from city to rural monastery.

All these points of contact demonstrate the
importance of monasteries in the elite communication
network, but the monasteries' function as mediators of
religious information between elite and peasants
derived from their contacts with villagers. The most
obvious potential for contact between monk and peasant
was the proximity of monasteries to villages. Since
many monasteries were located near Galicia's more

fertile valleys, that automatically placed them overlooking villages. Furthermore, monasteries stimulated the growth of nearby villages because monastic lands were frequently more extensive than could be cultivated by the monks themselves. Therefore, abbots paid peasants a fifth of their crop to cultivate surplus land.[48] Thus, by the seventh century an increasingly common settlement pattern was an austere, stone monastery high on a hill served by clusters of Gallegan stone houses lower on the slopes. The old informal relationship between peasants and a magic holy man had been expanded by a new economic interdependence between the two.

Along with simple proximity, there were other reasons for frequent interaction between peasants and monks. In some areas, a mill was located at the local monastery and run by monks; in other regions, monasteries controlled the local blacksmith forge and made items for local use.[49] Peasants coming to monastic mills or forges would no doubt have spoken to and passed some time with monks there.

Gallegan environmental circumstances also forced monks out into the countryside as shepherds entering into the small-scale transhumance of this region. Fructuosus wrote that monks were forced to become shepherds or "...most monasteries would scarcely have enough food for three months if there existed only the daily bread in this province, which requires more work on the soil than any other land."[50] Thus, whether in the fields, out among the flocks, at the mill or the forge, there were possibilities for frequent interaction between peasants and monks.[51]

For monasteries to be defined as true mediators between peasants and elite, however, they must have

embodied   some values of both and belonged   totally   to
neither.   Parish   priests,   combining   their   village
origins   and   elite   education,   fulfilled   this
requirement.   While a particular monk may not have   so
clearly   combined   the two value systems,   a   monastery
itself   as   a   collective   certainly   did.   Within   a
monastery,   there were both peasants and nobility,   and
while   theoretically there was equality between   monks,
in   practice   the   monastic   hierarchical   structure
continued   to   parallel roughly that of   society,   with
nobles   ruling   as abbots and   abbesses,   and   peasants
doing   much   of   the physical labor.   For   as   Isidore
wrote,   "men come also from rustic life...with so   much
more   advantage as they are better inured to   labor."[52]
There   seem   to   have   been   considerable   numbers   of
peasants   and   freed   slaves   recruited   from   several
sources and coexisting within a monastery.   Some nobles
probably followed the example of Fructuosus, who filled
his   first monastery "...to overflowing with a band   of
monks,   as many from his own   household...[as   gathered
from other parts of Spain],"[53] and a noble who felt the
call   to   a   religious   life   could   also   have   brought
several   servants   who   took   vows.   Sometimes   rural
monasteries   had   difficulty   finding   enough   people.
Since   it was to the advantage of a nobleman to have   a
monastery   upon   his   lands, for he   could   thus   avoid
paying ecclesiastical taxes on that portion,[54] a   local
lord   frequently   forced   peasants   to   become   monks.
Valerius   of Bierzo, condemned this practice,   writing,
"The...monasteries   are   corrupted   by   swineherds   and
shepherds   who are torn from their families and   forced
to   enter   the   monastery   and   take   the   false   name,
monk."[55]   It is also probable that during   particularly
difficult   times,   peasants   would   rather   enter   a
monastery that had food and an income than starve.

Both the economic desirability for poorer peasants
of entering a monastery and forced recruitment (often
of whole families) led to the proliferation in Galicia
of family monasteries.[56] Fructuosus described these
social-religious institutions: "...some [persons] are
accustomed...to found monasteries within their own
homes, and to join...under the terms of an oath with
their wives and children and slaves and neighbors...and
falsely to call such establishments monasteries."[57] By
including paragraphs to regulate these family houses,
Fructuosus combined official monastic requirements with
several concessions to family social structures that
were a hallmark of family monasteries. The buildings
of the family monasteries remained adjoining, but men
and women were to be separated. When families entered
the community, a husband and wife parted and children
were given to the care of nuns to be raised "properly"
into the religious life.[58] Fructuosus, however, showed
a concern for the needs of children by permitting them
to visit their parents whenever they wished.[59] Some
very pious monks were permitted to dwell in the nuns'
convent to do manual labor, and assist in regulating
the interaction between the two houses, such as
visitations and communal hymn singing.[60] Monks and
nuns worked together in the fields, but Fructuosus
insisted on strict precautions against too much
familiarity during these times.[61] In these ways,
monastic communities grew in the Gallegan mountains
approximating, as closely as possible within the
broadest limits of orthodoxy, the village life from
which many of the new coenobites had been wrenched.
Men and women worked together, celebrated festivals by
singing together and were surrounded by children born
before, and often after, monastic vows had been taken.

Thus the collective monastic units, while representing supernatural power in the countryside, combined elite, literate, legalistic religiosity with village social cohesiveness. During moments of contact with either elite or peasant cultures, monks had enough in common to be able to interact, but they also had enough familiarity with the other culture to mediate information from one group to the other.

As collective units, monasteries were more effective mediators of religious experience than their predecessors, individual holy men and women. Monasteries could transmit a broader range of information than could a single hermit or virgin. A holy shepherd like Emilian, with village values would, when preaching, probably have accented those elements made important by his personal experience. In the same way, villagers listening to the educated Valerius probably learned of elite values as they were filtered by Valerius' perception of his experiences. Monasteries, on the other hand, contained a broader representation of peasant and elite values, which acted as a counterweight to individual experience. Also contributing to their effectiveness as mediators was the location of monasteries in space and their position in society. While a holy man was effective when he was in a region, he frequently moved, nor did he have as direct access as abbots to church legislation. The network of Gallegan monasteries, on the other hand, was a peripheral but permanent part of Galicia's structure, and interaction between peasants and monks became as much a part of the seasonal rhythms of life as spring wildflowers and Sunday churchbells.

From the point of view of the official Church, a monastery was preferable to an individual holy person.

This was true both because a monastery was more controllable, and because it was more effective as a locus of communication between groups in society. A collective unit can be regulated by rules and placed under official jurisdiction in a way that personal supernatural charisma cannot, which, of course, was why the Church was so eager to institutionalize holy people.

There was a danger, however, in too effective control of holy men and women. The official Church could not afford to forget that the foundation of monastic influence was popular respect for the supernatural power of a monastery's inhabitants. The same frequency of interaction and monastic obedience that made monasteries good mediators from the viewpoint of official religiosity contributed to reducing people's awe of monks. This was more true with respect to monks who had to be heroic to be holy than with virgins who simply had to remain chaste. Familiarity made it more difficult for a monk to sustain his reputation as one who was in touch with God. In spite of regulation, the supernatural, magical quality of monasteries was preserved in two main ways. The first was the monastic vocation itself. An individual monk may not have struggled enough to personally perform miracles, but his renunciation would have earned him some supernatural merit, and the monastery itself acquired the sum total of all the monks' efforts.

Second, saints' relics were frequently translated from basilicas to rural monasteries in the seventh century. The relics were repositories of holiness from powerful holy men and women, and by placing them in monasteries, the Church insured that these collective units maintained a high level of holy power. In these

ways, monasteries retained the supernatural power   that
had   always permitted holy men and women   to   intercede
for local villagers against natural disasters.

By   the end of the seventh century,   the   official
Church had established the means to bring saints' cults
and   holy men and women into the control of the   Church
hierarchy.   Thus, the Church had   virtually   completed
the   establishment   of   an   administrative   structure
through   which it would continue its efforts   to   bring
the   kingdom   into   religious   uniformity,   thereby
validating its power as the ruling religion.

Notes

1. Pope Vigilius, "Epistola Episcopi Profuturo" PL 84:832 "...praesumentes fidem vestram eorum deinceps plenius esse meritis adjuvandam."

2. Claude W. Barlow, ed., Martini Episcopi Bracarensis Opera Omnia (New Haven, 1950), "De Correctione Rusticorum," ch. 18, p. 202.

3. IV Tolet, PL 84:370-72.

4. M. Clement Eagen, trans. The Poems of Prudentius (Washington, 1962), p. xxi. The hymns that were included were those of Emeterius and Chelidonius, Eulalia, Agnes and Fructuosus (the martyr, not the monastic founder).

5. Angel Fábrega Grau, Pasionario Hispánico (Madrid, 1953), p. 255. "Doble impulso dado al culto de los santos en España hacia mediados del s. vii..." Also, on p. 261, see the discussion of the upsurge of hagiographic hymn composing.

6. See Joyce Salisbury, "The Origin of the Power of Vincent the Martyr," PMR Conference Proceedings (1984) for an analysis of the changes in St. Vincent's Passion that brought it into conformity with orthodoxy.

7. The saints whose passions were composed in the seventh century were Leocadia, Justus and Pastor, Eulalia of Barcelona, Felix of Gerona, Cucufate, and Vincent, Sabina and Cristoba.

8. "Passio Marcelli," B.N. Ms. 494, Fol. 114v.

9. Since it is difficult to determine actual cult activity during such an early period, it is necessary to explain the method I have followed to determine the success of officially encouraged cults. To understand the actual patterns of rural worship, I found it necessary to go beyond the written lives, and place

them in a larger context. I could not assume that all
the saints in the calendar who died prior to the
seventh century were venerated during the Visigothic
years, since many of their cults only developed later.
I used only those saints for whom I could prove early
cult activity by sources other than the existence of a
Vita.   Some cults were referred to in other
contemporary documents (i.e., Valerius' works mention
several).   I also checked saints against the earliest
Visigothic calendars, considering a continuing record
of a feast day to be a fairly reliable indication of
cult activity, or at least that the absence of a feast
day, especially in the local calendar of a presumed
saint's region, is fairly reliable evidence of the
absence of a cult. The standard analysis of Visigothic
calendars is J. Vives, "Santoral visigodo en
calendarios e inscripciones," Analecta Sacra
Tarraconensis, 14 (1941), pp. 31-58. More current and
very thorough is C. García Rodriguez, pp. 77-94.
Furthermore, I accepted archeological evidence, for
example, an early inscription dedicating a basilica or
church to a saint, as strong evidence of cult activity.
I also limited my analysis geographically, choosing
only those saints either wholly of the Iberian
northwest, or in the case of very popular national
saints (like St. Vincent) whose cult can be
demonstrated to have been observed in the northwest.
By this method, I may have eliminated several saints
who were worshipped, but I can be fairly certain that
the saints I am analyzing are an accurate indicator of
Gallegan popular religion. From this analysis, it
appears that official encouragement of saints who
corresponded roughly to soldiers and brides of Christ
was largely successful, and official encouragement of

bishops was, at least in the Visigothic years, unsuccessful.

10. J. Vives, Inscripciones cristianas de la España romana y visigoda (Barcelona, 1962), p. 265: "...In hoc tempore... Sisebutus, Toleto regale culmen obtinuit...Toleto quoque beatae Leocadiae aula miro opera, iubente praedicto principe, culmine alto extenditur."

11. Eagen, p. 159.

12. "Acta Sancti Fructuosi," Actas de Los Martires, ed. Daniel Ruiz Bueno (Madrid, 1962), p. 793.

13. III Bracara, V PL 84:589.

14. "Epistola Vigilii Papae ad Profuturum Episcopum," sec. IV, PL 84:832.

15. Manuel Torres Lopez "La doctrina de las 'Iglesias Proprias' en los autores Espanoles," Anuario del Historia del Derecho Español 2 (1925), pp. 402-61 provides an extensive historiographic analysis of the study of Spanish proprietary churches with a complete biliography.

16. Ambrosio de Morales, Viage por orden del Rey D. Phelipe II a los reynos de Leon y Galicia y principado de Asturias, ed. H. Flórez (Madrid, 1765), p. 102, describes two small Visigothic churches in Galicia north of Oviedo, located very close together, which can probably best be explained by recognizing that one was a basilica and the other a parochia.

17. Pierre David, Etudes historiques sur la Galice et le Portugal du VI au XII siecle (Lisbon, 1947), pp. 9-10 contains an excellent analysis of the development of rural parishes during this time.

18. IV Tolet, XXXV, PL 84:376.

19. IX Tolet, II, PL 84:435.

20. See García Rodriguez, p. 108, for a discussion

of the rapidly spreading traffic in relics in
Visigothic Spain.

21. "Braulio of Saragossa," The Fathers of the
Church: Iberian Fathers, vol. 2, ed. Claude W. Barlow
(Washington, 1969), pp. 27-28.

22. There were twelve monasteries in Galicia, a
province of approximately 38,000 square miles, with a
population of approximately 700,000. In the rest of
the peninsula, an area of approximately 192,000 square
miles, there were twenty-two monasteries for a
population of approximately 5,300,000. [The population
estimates were prepared by P. Bosch Gimpera, El
Poblamiento Antiguo y la Formación de los Pueblos de
España (Mexico, 1944), p. 260, and Jose Maria Lacarra,
Estudios de Alta Edad Media Española (Valencia, 1971),
p. 32.] From these figures, one can calculate the
density of monasteries per 10,000 square miles in
Galicia to be 3.2 and the density of monasteries per
100,000 people was 1.7. For the rest of the peninsula,
the density of monasteries per 10,000 square miles was
1.2 and the density of monasteries per 100,000 people
was .42. These calculations show that there were over
twice as many monasteries per unit area in Galicia as
in the rest of Spain, 2.7 to be precise. There were
four times as many monasteries per unit population in
Galicia as in the rest of Spain.

23. Antonio Linage Conde, Los Orígenes del
monacato Benedictino en la Peninsula Iberica, vols. I,
II and III, (Leon, 1973), is an impressively complete
study. Older, but still valuable, is Justo Perez de
Urbel, Los monjes españoles en la edad media, vols. 1
and 2 (Madrid, 1933).

24. Ms. Esc. a I 13 Fol. 186. "O vos omnes qui
legeritis hunc codicem mementole clientula et exiqua

leodegundia qui hunc scripsi in monasterio bobatelli..."

25. M.C. Diaz y Diaz, "El Codice monástico de Leodegundia," La Ciudad de Dios 181 (1968), p. 570 argues convincingly for the Gallegan origin of this manuscript, specifically associating it with Samos.

26. Ms. Esc. a I 13, Fols. 145v, 158v, 168 and 180.

27. Ibid., Fol. 170.

28. Ibid., Fol. 175v.

29. Andres Manrique, "La Regla de S. Agustín en España durante los primeros siglos de su exitencia," in La Ciudad de Dios 182 (1969), p. 503, discusses the early evolution of collections of rules, pointing to Martin of Braga as an early originator of the form, because Martin "...reunió una serie de máximas de los monjes orientales, bajo el título de Sententiae Patrum. Este librito junto con el de 'Verba Seniorum'...sirvieron a modo de Regla a los monjes de S. Martín."

30. The geographic limits of this peculiar monastic form was noted both by Linage Conde, p. 37, and Bishko, "Salvius of Albelda and Frontier Monasticism in Tenth Century Navarre," Speculum 23 (1948), p. 580.

31. Jose Orlandis, "Las congregaciones monásticas en la tradición suevo-visigótica" Anuario de Estudios Medievales I (1964), pp. 97-119, contains a thorough analysis of Fructuosus' federated system of monasteries.

32. Linage Conde, i:242.

33. Fructuosus, "Regula Monastica Communis" Caput Primum, PL 87:1111.

34. Fructuosus, "Pactum" PL 87:1129.

35. For example, Potamius, bishop of Braga, was tried at the Tenth Council of Toledo for being too generous with church funds. While Potamius was from Braga, not the neighboring Dumium, it is equally likely that bishops would have censured the bishop-abbot of Dumium, too, if he had deviated too far from expected behavior. See Addendum to X Tolet, <u>PL</u> 84:448-49.

36. Based on the signatures on the Toledan councils, the Bishop of Dumium (or in one case his representative) attended the III, IV, VII, XIII, XV, and XVI Councils of Toledo.

37. VII Tolet, V <u>PL</u> 84:408.

38. IV Tolet, LI <u>PL</u> 84:378, "De discretione potestatis episcoporum quam in monasterium habere possunt." See also III Tolet, IV <u>PL</u> 84:352, "ut liceat episcopo unam ex parochiis basilicam monasterium facere."

39. W.S. Porter, "Early Spanish Monasticism," <u>Laudate</u> Vol. X (1932), p. 73.

40. X Tolet, IV <u>PL</u> 84:442-43: "...ut vidua quae sanctae religionis obtinere propositum voluerit, sacerdote vel ministro ad quem...scriptis professionem faciat a se aut signo aut subscriptione notatem...ac tunc accepta a sacerdote vel ministro apta religionis usui vesta..."

41. Consuelo Maria Aherne, Ed., <u>Valerio of Bierzo - An Ascetic of the Late Visigothic Period</u> (Washington, 1949), p. 104.

42. Morales, p. 161.

43. Isidori Episcopi Hispalensis, "Regula Monachorum," <u>PL</u> 83:568.

44. Fructuosus "Regula Monachorum," ch. X, <u>PL</u> 87:1105, "...cum summa reverentia charitatis et ministrationis obsequia sunt praebenda, et ad vesperum

lavandi pedes: ...et stramina mollia exhibenda...viaticum imponendu."

45. Fructuosus, "Regula Monastica Communis," PL 87:1119, "...cum fratribus advenientibus hospitibus et peregrinis in una mensa communiter vivant..."

46. Isidori, "Regula Monachorum," PL 83:568.

47. "Fructuosus' General Rule," in Barlow, Fathers of the Church, p. 182.

48. Agustín Diez Gonzales Florentino, et al., San Fructuoso y Su tiempo (Leon, 1966), p. 60.

49. The Visigothic forge of the monastery of Compludo, for example, is still in remarkably good shape. Its function is fully described in Ibid., pp. 44-6.

50. "Fructuosus' General Rule" in Barlow, Fathers of the Church, pp. 117-18.

51. Much has been written describing monastic daily life. Here I have limited my discussion only to those elements directly contributing to monastic mediating functions. For more detailed descriptions, see C.W. Porter; Mario Martins, "A vida economica dos monges de S. Fructuosus," Broteria 44 (1947), pp. 391-400, and Mario Martins, "A vida cultural de S. Fructuosus e seus monges," Broteria 45 (1947), pp. 58-69.

52. Isidori, PL 83:867.

53. Frances Clare Nock, ed., The Vita Sancti Fructuosi, (Washington, 1946), p. 90.

54. The canon insisting that monasteries must be full if they are to be exempt from bishop's exaction of temporalities is in "Concilium Ilerdense," III, PL 84:323.

55. Valerius of Bierzo, "De Genera Monachorum," PL 87:457, "Et ne monasteria...tolluntur ex familiis sibi

pertinentibus subulci, de diversisque gregibus dorsini, atque de possessionibus parvuli, qui pro officio supplendo inviti tondentur et nutriuntur per monasteria, atque falso nomine monachi nuncupatur."

56. A good analysis of family monasteries in Spain is Jose Orlandis, "Tradition corporis et Animae: La 'Familiaritas' en las Iglesias y monasterios españoles de la Alta Edad Media," Anuario de Historia del Derecho Español 24 (1954), pp. 95-279. For a discussion of family monasteries throughout Europe, see Mary Bateson, "Origin and early history of double Monasteries," Transaction of Royal Historical Society New Series, XIII (1899).

57. Fructuosus, "General Rule," pp. 177-78.

58. Ibid., p. 185.

59. Ibid., p. 186.

60. Ibid., p. 200.

61. Ibid., p. 199.

PRISCILLIANISM

Throughout the sixth and seventh centuries, the Visigothic official Church was establishing its hierarchical network that would ultimately accommodate the religious needs of peasants. In the late fourth century, however, a comparable and temporarily successful combination of peasant and elite religious views was effected by the heresiarch, Priscillian. This syncretic heresy was popular enough to cause a serious Gallegan regional schism in the Iberian Church for almost 200 years.[1]

Priscillian himself seems to have had considerable personal magnetism. Sulpicius Severus, in about 420, wrote, "[Priscillian] drew into its [the heresy's] acceptance many persons of noble rank and multitudes of the common people by the arts of persuasion and flattery which he possessed."[2] Priscillian's success was not only due to his charismatic qualities. His success was also due to his genius for integrating peasant beliefs with a theoretical and ethical cosmography that appealed to the Hispano-Roman elite.

One of the primary concerns of rural religion was to try to control nature by ritual. The official Church defined these efforts as magic. Priscillian, however, did not share the Church's disdain and was reputed to have "...practiced magical arts from his boyhood."[3] He presumably learned some of the rituals that remained widespread in the Gallegan hills. This dabbling in local magic did not bring him to the attention of the Church hierarchy, but his anonymity ended shortly after Priscillian was introduced to a

form of Gnostic theology from the East. According to
Sulpicius, a traveler from Memphis named Marcus brought
Gnostic heresy to Galicia, where "his pupils were a
certain Agape, a woman of no mean origin, and a
rhetorician named Helpidius." By these "...Priscillian
was instructed, a man of noble birth, of great riches,
bold, restless, eloquent, learned through much reading,
very ready at debate and discussion..."[4] Priscillian
accepted the "secret knowledge" of the Gnostics and
constructed a theology based upon a dualist cosmology
combined with traditional Gallegan beliefs. Both the
appeal of Priscillian's ideas and their threat to the
official Church rested upon his combination of peasant
and elite religiosity.

Since the principal purpose of peasant ritual was
to persuade the land to be fertile, it is not
surprising that many of the magical practices to which
Priscillian admitted at his trial were traditional
fertility rituals.[5] Priscillian and his followers
chanted "...magical incantations over the first fruits
[of the harvest]"[6] and seemingingly increased the
efficacy of these prayers by walking the fields with
bare feet pressed to the earth. Bareness was ritually
significant in Celtic and Roman cultures,[7] the Council
of Saragossa, as early as 380, forbade faithful
Christians to "walk with unshod feet."[8]

The efficacy of magic apparently increased with
the degree of nudity, for Priscillian also confessed to
praying naked.[9] Priscillian also admitted to having
held nocturnal meetings with women and the sources
imply that these meetings may have been conducted in
the nude. Priscillian did not elaborate on the motives
behind these nocturnal meetings (or, if he did, they
were expunged from his surviving works) but the strong

tradition tying women to fertility rites may suggest a
reason for those convocations. One might imagine women
imitating the Light Virgin who coaxed fertility from
the groaning Prince of Darkness[10] (see Chapter IV), and
it is interesting to note that even today it is not
unheard of for Gallegan women to increase their own
fecundity by standing nude at an open window to be
bathed by the light of a full moon.[11] It is likely
that Priscillian presided over an old lunar fertility
rite during some nights of the full moon.

For Priscillian, women's ritual importance was not
limited to fertility rituals. He believed that women,
as well as men, possessed the capacity to be filled
with the Holy Spirit,[12] and he implemented this
theoretical stand by having women participate fully in
the religious life. Women taught, indulged in
theological disputes, and performed exorcisms.[13] Ramon
Lopez Caneda traced the special position of women in
the Priscillianist heresy to Galicia's Celtic
background which recalled priestesses serving the old
Gods.[14] While this parallel is certainly evident, it
may not be really necessary to look further than
Galicia's villages for the origins of Priscillianist
priestesses. In a region where division of labor by
sex was blurred, and women plowed fields beside men or
alone, it would have been reasonable for women also to
share spiritual labor. Needless to say, women were
attracted to a sect that permitted them to participate
so fully in the religious life. Sulpicius Severus,
while ignoring the appeal of Priscillianism to women
and dismissing it as feminine frailty, did acknowledge
the attraction: "Women who were fond of novelties and
of unstable faith, as well as of a prurient curiosity
in all things, flocked to him in crowds."[15] Even

Jerome had heard of Priscillian's appeal to women, and
warned a newly widowed Spanish woman not to fall prey
to this heresy in her solitary life.[16] As part of
sharing religious responsibility, Priscillianist holy
men and women apparently frequently lived together, for
the First Council of Braga pronounced anathema upon
monks or clergy living with women since it was a
practice "taught by the Priscillianist sect."[17] While
this sort of cohabitation was fairly common in Galicia
even where there was no hint of heresy, it appears also
to have been an important element of Priscillianist
sexual egalitarianism.

Apparently, Priscillian was accustomed to traveling
in the company of a number of women, and he did so even
when he went to Rome to attempt to prove his orthodoxy
to Pope Damasus in the face of increasing pressure from
bishops in southern Iberia.[18] Priscillian may have
found the mixed company of his traveling companions
theologically sound, but it was hardly sensible to
flout established morality on the way to the Holy City,
and Severus was harsh in his description of the
journey: "They then pursued the journey on which they
had entered, attended by a base and shameful company,
among whom were their wives and even strange women. In
the number of these was Euchrotia and her daughter
Procula..." To compound the scandal, Procula became
pregnant, and "...when pregnant through adultery with
Priscillian, she procured abortion by the use of
certain plants"[19] that she gathered. Rumors of
Procula's abortion traveled widely, and while they
undoubtedly hurt Priscillian's appeal to Rome (Pope
Damasus refused to hear Priscillian's case), they did
not necessarily hurt Priscillian's reputation in the
countryside. The knowledge of how to induce an

abortion was a natural corollary to the knowledge of magic fertility rituals, and Priscillianists were renowned for both.

While fertility magic was a large part of the country rituals adopted by Priscillian, it was not the only form of magical practices acquired by the heretics. Priscillian's main accuser, Ithacius, charged him and his followers with "consecrating an unguent with curses to the sun and moon...."[20] Chadwick suggests that the unguent was then poured over some sacred stone in the countryside,[21] an act consistent with traditional Celtic reverence for particular stones. Working magic with another sacred stone, an amulet, was also staunchly defended by the Priscillianist author of the _Tractates_.[22] In fact, so closely has Priscillianism been associated with magic in the historiography of Spain's northwest province, that Stephen McKenna was led to claim that "Priscillianism inculcated among the people a belief in the efficacy of magic..."[23] This is not so. Magical practices had always been a part of Galicia's rural religion, and Priscillian merely incorporated them into his heresy.

Priscillian not only adopted traditional magical practices, but he also wove elements of a traditional Gallegan world view into the much more intricate pattern of Marcus' dualism. The Gnostics believed that the world was created by an evil God, and that man's spirit was separated from the true God by worlds and circles of demons, not only demons of nature and flesh, but of time and space, which separated spirit from its pre-cosmic unity with God. A gnostic writer mourned, "...through how many bodies, how many ranks of demons, how many concatenations and revolutions of stars, we have to work our way in order to hasten to the one and only God."[24] Galicia's demons of trees, mountains and streams, traditionally feared and placated with candles and offerings, became, in Priscillian's hands, part of a larger company of demons with a universal purpose to keep mankind trapped in suffering.

Priscillian, undoubtedly influenced by tales of spirits that lived in the dark woods and storm-swept peaks of Galicia, stressed the threat of nearby nature demons. He devoted a disproportionate amount of space in the "First Tractate" to warning against demons and censuring those who interpreted biblical references to beasts as symbols of proper religious worship, when, in fact, they were dangerous demons that must not be underestimated.[25] Chadwick suggests that this demonic preoccupation was "...a private obsession of a theological autodictat with a lonely mind and an axe to grind...."[26] While this may be true, it seems more important to understand such interest within the context of Priscillian's early experiences in Galicia's hills which, as far back as our knowledge extends, had been believed to be inhabited by demons. So complete was Priscillian's incorporation of traditional demonology into his thought that bishops at the First Council of Braga equated power with the heresy of Priscillianism.[27] Thus, Priscillian's dualistic theology provided a way to incorporate Galicia's pantheon of demons into a more unified cosmography that also appealed to elite questions regarding the origin of good and evil.

Chadwick raised the question of whether Priscillian was actually a dualist and suggested that the charge of Manichaeanism was raised by Ithacius at Priscillian's trial to make the accusation stronger.[28]

Chadwick came to this conclusion mainly from the strong
denials of Manichaeanism in the Tractates, written by
Priscillian or one of his followers.[29] This evidence
alone, however, cannot absolve Priscillian of the
charge of dualism, since the Tractates themselves are
problematic as an historical source. First of all,
they had been written to answer the charges brought
against the Priscillianists; to prove Priscillianist
orthodoxy, not to circulate among the initiated. The
Tractates thus can hardly be expected to be blatantly
heretical. The other major source of Priscillianist
thought is a collection of canons on the Pauline
epistles. These, however, survive only in a recension
prepared by "Bishop Peregrinus," who claimed to have
corrected any heretical language.[30] Again, this is a
source that would hardly reveal Priscillian's heresy.

Official sources, on the other hand, unreservedly
accused Priscillian of dualism. Gallegan churchmen who
could have observed the heresy described it in terms of
Manichaeanism. Hydatius described "hidden
Manichaeas,"[31] while Orosius traveled to Africa from
Galicia and wrote for Augustine in 414, a Commonitorium
de errore Priscillianistarum et Origenistarum.[32]
Augustine saw so many dualist elements in Orosius'
description that he did not feel he had to argue any
further against Priscillianism, but instead just
referred Orosius to Augustine's many anti-Manichaean
tracts. Jerome, too, used Priscillianism to exemplify
ideas of the fall of the soul.[33] With all this
testimony, along with passages in the Tractates which
come very close to crossing the sometimes blurred line
of orthodoxy,[34] it is hard to believe that Priscillian
was innocent of a dualistic world view with a related
rejection of the flesh.

The question of Priscillian's dualism is important
for an understanding of Galicia's heresy, but it cannot
explain the appeal of the heresy in rural areas, and
Galicia was predominantly rural.[35] The peasants' view
of the world was not the Gnostic. Gnostics made an
essential differentiation between good and evil; the
world, matter and flesh, were ontologically evil; any
appearance of good within the world was false. The
spirit was good; any appearance of spiritual evil was
also false, caused by the flesh in which the spirit was
trapped. In the countryside, however, the distinction
between good and evil seems not to have been so sharply
defined. Peasant religiosity is basically
materialistic[36] so it seems likely that villagers would
have drawn notions of good and evil from the practical
world, not from the world in contrast to a pre-cosmic
perfect state of light. Thus, good and evil were
potential or temporary states, not essential or
absolute. For example, rain could be good or bad,
depending on whether it moistened seeds or damaged a
harvest. The same potential for good as well as evil
existed in everything worldly, from the earth to wine
to sex. While it is impossible to say with certainty
how Gallegan peasants received the prophecies of
Priscillianist holy men bringing dualism to the
countryside, it seems likely that peasants listening to
abstract notions of good and evil would have translated
the ideas into a concrete frame of reference with which
they were familiar. Thus, when one eliminates the
abstract spheres as the only source of good, good is
once more returned to the world, automatically
converting radical into relative dualism. While "pure"
dualism may not have been particularly attractive to
peasants, it could have been either ignored or

reinterpreted in a countryside adhering to the heresy for other reasons. In fact, when the sources refer to Priscillian's popularity in the countryside, the references are usually juxtaposed with references to magic rather than to dualism. A dualist theology did, however, make it easier for peasant beliefs to fit into an elite religiosity, permitting both peasants and rulers to share a religious structure more readily. This was something the fourth-century orthodox Church was still unable to do.

Along with dualism, Priscillianism offered another set of beliefs that permitted a smooth accommodation of traditional peasant beliefs with elite sensibilities. This was a profound and highly elaborated belief in astrology.[37] Lopez Caneda attributed part of the attraction of Priscillianism in Galicia to the emphasis on astrology, a more complex version of the old lunar cult.[38] However, it would be an oversimplification to draw too direct a line from lunar cults to as complicated an astrological system as that of Priscillian. It is perhaps more useful to approach the topic as Theodore Wedel has done, noting in effect that "The pagan worship of sun and moon...though they cannot yet be called astrology, constitute a foundation upon which it can build."[39] Essentially, Gallegan peasants had traditionally understood that the moon's movement through the sky and through its phases had an immediate influence on their lives. The Priscillianists did not deny this long-held belief, but claimed that the moon's movements were more complex than they appeared. Knowledge of the moon's movements through the complicated zodiac signs as well as those of planets and other celestial objects increased the possibility of accurate prediction of the moon's influence. In

this way, instead of trying to eradicate an old belief,
Priscillian claimed to have refined and improved upon
ancient wisdom.

Furthermore, Priscillian's advocacy of astrology
as a respectable theological tool also made him popular
with many Hispano-Roman townspeople and nobles.
Astrology had spread widely during the late Empire, and
although its practice was strongly censured by the
Church as "divination," undoubtedly many townspeople
privately consulted astrologers. Thus even for the
elite, Priscillian legitimized popularly held beliefs.
The First Council of Braga considered the practice of
astrology as both pagan and Priscillianist,[40] and
Turibius, in his letter to Pope Leo, described
astrology, part of the "vain lies in mathematics," as
one of Priscillian's chief attractions.[41]

The heresy's popularity was not due solely to the
skillful molding of its theology to suit regional
values. As important as the actual beliefs that
Priscillian wove together, was the structure he
advocated to preserve and transmit those beliefs.
Priscillian never intended to stay aloof from the
established hierarchical structure of the official
Iberian Church. But he hoped to transform the Church
from within, thus co-opting the elite structure into
his own system, much as he accommodated to and absorbed
peasant religiosity. At the height of his popularity,
Priscillian became Bishop of Avila, solidly within the
official structure. Priscillianist infiltration of
Galicia's hierarchy did not end with the heresiarch's
death.[42] Symposius, Bishop of Astorga, was at least
sympathetic to Priscillianism, and his son, Dictinius,
who was raised by popular acclamation to the See of
Astorga, was an enthusiastic supporter of Priscillian.

Dictinius even wrote a book (now lost) defending
Priscillianist beliefs.[43] Paternus, the first known
Bishop of Braga, was also an acknowledged heretic.[44]
That Priscillianist sentiments in the clergy rested
upon solid popular support was clearly evident at the
First Council of Toledo, where four Gallegan bishops
feared to recant and condemn Priscillian, for "...if
they were to do so they would lose the support of all
their clergy and people."[45] So, through the late
fourth century and into the fifth, Gallegans who
believed in Priscillian's vision were not denied the
legitimacy afforded by the Church hierarchy.

Priscillian did more than simply adopt Catholic
organization for the transmission of his beliefs.
Recognizing the importance of virgins and hermits, he
gave traditional holy men and women (to whom the
official Church denied recognition) a legitimate and
prominent place in his movement, as a result of which
Priscillian's popularity among peasants increased.

The dualistic quality of Priscillian's theology
introduced a strong anti-carnal element into the
region's religious mosaic. If the Lord of Darkness
created all flesh, then fleshly contact weighed down a
soul, preventing its return to the Lord of Light. Such
carnal rejection was expressed both in a strong
vegetarianism,[46] not to consume spirit-killing flesh,
and in a strong advocacy of chastity, not to be
consumed by desires of the flesh. By combining high
respect for the spiritual benefits of virginity with
the recognition that women were equal to men as
vehicles of the Holy Spirit, Priscillian placed
traditionally respected virgins in the forefront of
veneration. Virgins lived on a higher spiritual plane
and, therefore, among the "perfect" here on earth,

closer to God and possessing considerable power. Thus,
by a complex theology, Priscillian and his followers
came to believe what Gallegan peasants had always
known, that virgins were deserving of awe and
reverence.

Undoubtedly, stories and Vitae of some of these
holy women circulated just as lives and passions of
Catholic saints and martyrs did. Unfortunately, most
were lost in the purging of all Priscillianist works,
but one probable example of such a work survived and
deserves special mention. This is the Life of St.
Helie, the eloquent virgin who staunchly defended her
vows in the face of parental pressure to marry. Due to
a repeated condemnation of marriage and the absence of
Helie's mention in any calendars, Garcia Villada argued
strongly for a Priscillianist origin of the text and
suggested that Helie was one of Priscillian's many
women followers.[47]

The structure of the tract in the manuscript also
suggests that this was a Priscillianist work that was
slightly revised for preservation in an orthodox codex.
The long Vita appears actually to have two
introductions. The first is entitled "incipit Prologas
de Vita Sancte Helie,"[48] in which the author with
formulaic modesty announced his intention to present
the Life of St. Helie. This prologue is followed by a
section opened by the words "Incipit Liber Primus de
Vita Sancte Helie,"[49] which is, in fact, another
prologue urging the reader to reject the material world
in favor of the spiritual and offering the Vita as an
example of the spiritual life. Helie's life actually
is introduced by the subheading "Igitur Sancte Helie
vitam dicturo hic jam si placet, sermo incipiat
aperiri."[50] I suggest that the original Priscillianist

life began with the "Liber Primus," and the prologue
was added when it was incorporated into the Codex of
the saints' lives, probably assembled in the sixth
century in the form that survives. Antolin suggested
that the Life was written by Pascasius of Dumium,
because the language of the prologue was similar to
Pascasius' in his collection Vitae Patrum.[51] If this
is the case, Pascasius probably wrote only the
prologue, and may have been the one who assembled the
Codex in the early sixth century. If this was indeed a
Priscillianist tract, it survived not because it
embodied a strong heretical theology, but because it
spoke to a deeper Gallegan religious sensibility. St.
Helie presented the same ideal of independent virginity
that characterized the other orthodox virgins' Lives in
the Codex, in the same way that Priscillianist views of
virginity blended with the region's traditional values.

Priscillianist dualistic rejection of the flesh
and elevation of the ideal of virginity raise the
question of why Priscillian's reputation for
inconstancy with Procula, not to mention his admitted
"nocturnal meetings" with other women, did not
appreciably damage his reputation with the heretical
faithful as an ascetic holy man. Consistent with their
theology, most dualist sects completely rejected sexual
contact by the initiated. However, there were
exceptions. The Massalians, for example, believed that
rigorous asceticism was required only until an
individual reached a state of perfection. At that time
sin was no longer possible, and as Dmitri Obolensky
noted, "this belief frequently drove them into the
worst sexual excesses...Extreme asceticism and extreme
immorality thus appear as equally characteristic of the
behavior of these heretics."[52] Due to the paucity of

Priscillianist documents, it is difficult to prove that Priscillian's relations with Procula sprang from a Massalian belief in the inability of a "perfect" to sin.

However, there are some parallels between Priscillianism and Massalianism that may at least suggest a theological relationship between the two sects, which perhaps could have led Priscillian to believe that as a perfect he could not sin "under the belt."[53]   Like Priscillianists, Massalians permitted women to take a leading role in the movement[54] which was the sort of spiritual egalitarianism that may have led Priscillian to travel with Procula in the first place.   Additionally, the First Council of Braga attributed to Priscillian a belief that the conception of a child in the womb was the work of the devil.[55] This belief is similar to the Massalian notion that a demon dwells within each infant from the time of his conception.[56]

These similarities are not substantial enough to suggest a direct connection between Priscillianism and Massalianism.   It may be that Priscillian's sexual activities should be attributed less to antinomianism than to a traditional Gallegan belief in a kind of division of labor regarding sanctity. As I described in a previous chapter, women were made holy by virginity and men by heroic deeds of self-mortification.   As long as Priscillian did not falter in his fasts and his disregard of physical needs and comfort, his reputation for holiness remained intact.[57]   Procula, on the other hand, may have been held in awe for her knowledge of herbs, but she was never thought of as a Priscillianist saint.

Priscillian himself was not the only heretical spiritual athlete. Together with holy women, Priscillian's message was carried into the countryside by ascetic holy men, who, Turibius of Astorga complained to Pope Leo, wandered about the countryside "...under the name Prophet and Apostle..."[58] As Mario Martins noted, it was a rigorous asceticism on the part of the "perfect" that brought Gnostic heresy to the poor.[59]

For Priscillian and his followers, asceticism was a means to a very particular end, to free the spark of divinity[60] trapped in the flesh and thus to receive the gift of knowledge of God in a spiritual, not an intellectual sense.[61] This yearning of the individual soul for God was a search calling for private study and asceticism. Individual study of sacred texts was the starting point for a Priscillianist path to salvation.[62] The official Church was always suspicious of the possibility of unorthodox interpretations in private Bible study. For example, priests were to use prepared homiles rather than their own exegeses, as described above in Chapter III. Priscillian went even further, favoring the reading of apocryphal texts as useful to salvation.[63] The apocryphal books favored by the Priscillianists were the Acts of Andrew, John and Thomas[64] and the Memoria Apostolorum. These books were probably popular with Priscillian because of their strong stand on celibacy, as well as their tales of wandering apostles,[65] both Priscillianist values.

The main threat embodied in the reading of apocrypha, however, lay less in the specific content of the texts than in the fact that these books symbolized the individualism inherent in Priscillianist thought. If, as Priscillian claimed, divine truth could be found

outside   the   covers   of   official   books,   then   an
individual   could   also   find   salvation   outside   the
established   ecclesiastical   hierarchy.   In   fact,   this
was Priscillian's message.   He stressed the role of the
laity   as   individuals[66]   but   added   a   strong
responsibility for study on the part of his   followers.
A follower of Priscillian's path could gain "knowledge"
and   thus   salvation by diligent   study   combined with
ascetic rejection of the flesh.

     To   pursue this private quest,   Priscillian   urged
believers   to   withdraw   to   the hills   and   other   rural
retreats, to return to Galicia's countryside which   had
been   an early source of   Priscillian's   inspiration.[67]
The practical result of this religious belief was   that
the   Gallegan heights were again conquered by holy   men
tapping   supernatural   sources   of   power.   These
individual   ascetics brought protection to   neighboring
villages.   Furthermore, since one result of   acquiring
knowledge of God was to prophesy,[68] heretical holy   men
spoke of their wisdom to local people, thus serving   to
transmit Priscillian's beliefs to the countryside.

     Priscillian's   combination   of   rural   magic   with
Gnostic   theology   made his   heresy   particularly   well
adapted to Galicia.   Since Priscillianism appealed both
to   peasants   and to the educated elite,   it   was   in   a
position   to   give religious unity to the   region   long
before   Catholicism.   Nevertheless, it was to   collapse
under   the pressure of the Catholic Church which   would
insist   on   a universal rather than a   regional   unity.
Even though Priscillianism was well established   within
the   structure   of the Gallegan Church,   bishops   from
other   provinces brought pressure to uproot the   heresy
and   bring Galicia back into religious conformity   with
the rest of the peninsula.

After the Pope refused to grant Priscillian an
audience, Ithacius and Hydatius, two strong Spanish
bishops, brought pressure to try Priscillian before an
episcopal synod in Bordeaux. Priscillian apparently
felt that he would not do well in Bordeaux and demanded
to be tried in Trier by the new emperor Maximus.[69]
Priscillian misjudged the sympathy of the secular
authorities. Found guilty of sorcery and
Manichaeanism, he was executed in Trier in 385. As
Sulpicius Severus relates, "The bodies of those who had
been put to death were conveyed to Spain, and their
funerals were celebrated with great pomp. Nay, it came
to be thought the highest exercise of religion to swear
by Priscillian."[70]

Sorcery and Manichaeanism, the charges on which
Priscillian was convicted, were designed to inspire
revulsion in the hearts of the fourth-century orthodox.
No doubt, to some degree, both charges were accurate,
but Priscillian did not die because he had walked
barefoot in a field to help crops grow, nor because he
had believed that the earth he trod was created by an
evil God to torment the spark of divinity trapped in
mankind. Priscillian died because his movement was so
popular locally that it impeded the spread of orthodox
Christianity. Not only did Priscillian encourage
individuals to find their own paths to salvation
outside the narrow path of hierarchical obedience, but
in the countryside, Priscillianism spoke to an age-old
Gallegan religiosity in a way that the nascent Catholic
Church was as yet unable to do.

With Priscillian dead, the Church was left with
the problem of the popularity of his beliefs in
Galicia's countryside and towns and among the
priesthood itself. As Sulpicius Severus wrote, "...not

only was the heresy not suppressed, which, under him,
as its author, had burst forth, but acquiring strength
it became more widely spread. For his followers who
had previously honored him as a saint, subsequently
began to reverence him as a martyr."[71]   Before the
Iberian Church could be unified throughout the kingdom,
it had to transfer the allegiance of the people from
Priscillianism to orthodox Christianity.

Bishops from Braga to Rome were aware of the
threat to ecclesiastical homogeneity posed by this
popular heresy set firmly in Gallegan religiosity.
Spanish bishops tried to eradicate the heresy by
legislation at the First Council of Saragossa and again
at the First Councils of Toledo and Braga. Popes Leo
and Vigilius wrote to Spanish bishops urging them to
battle the heresy. In all these sources, bishops wrote
of Priscillianism as a monolithic entity. They felt
that anyone practicing any of the rites listed as
heretical was a Priscillianist. This was because the
official Church was primarily interested in
demonstrating its power by imposing religious
uniformity over the kingdom; it was less concerned with
distinguishing between practice and commitment to, or
belief in, heresy. To understand the eventual
elimination of Priscillianism in Galicia, it is
necessary to keep in mind the distinction between
commitment and practice. Obviously, every peasant who
performed fertility rites over his crops or carried an
amulet to ward off evil did not necessarily consider
himself a Priscillianist. Villagers had been doing
these things long before Priscillian. Nor was every
hermit who retired to a mountain cell committed to a
dualist theology. The official Church actually had two
problems, first, to convert avowed Priscillianists, and

second, to eliminate practices that had been defined as Priscillianist. Since Priscillian had not acquired his rituals from one source only, there were two broad categories of practices that had to be controlled, those stemming from Marcus' Gnosticism and those assimilated from rural religiosity. Thus before the appearance of religious homogeneity could be restored to the kingdom, Iberian churchmen were faced with three main tasks in an ascending order of difficulty. First, they had to force proclaimed Priscillianists to recant. Second, they had to educate elite orthodox Christians who had unknowingly acquired Priscillianist practices. Finally, they had to win country people back from their respect for the heretic who had surrounded their traditional beliefs and practices with the formality of theology and organization.

Shortly after Priscillian's death, Iberian churchmen assembled in Toledo (ca. 400) to begin the struggle against the remnants of Priscillianism[72] and to address the immediate problem of heretical Gallegan bishops. To begin with, in the interests of reestablishing orthodoxy in the North, the bishops reinstated the orthodox Bishop Ortygius at Celenius, who had been expelled by Priscillian bishops during their ascendancy.[73] The Council then called on suspect bishops to recant. The most prominent churchmen of the northwest called before the Council were three from Astorga: Bishop Symposius, his son Dictinius, and the priest Comasius. Chadwick notes that these three did not want a separate church in Galicia, so they "...solemnly abjured anything wrong that Priscillian had written, together with Priscillian personally."[74] The bishops at Toledo sensibly decided to accept the heretical priests' recantation as sufficient for their

reacceptance into Iberia's Church. To expel the
popular Astorgans would have undoubtedly prolonged
resentment in the North, and the heretics had conformed
to the most important requirement of official
religiosity, obedience to hierarchical authority. Pope
Innocent I approved of this conciliatory action, noting
that the result of any action should be "...that the
church may be whole and not split by scandal."[75]

The First Council made a good beginning in its
struggle against heresy by forcing orthodoxy upon
Priscillian's most visible and vocal supporters. The
Iberian Church, however, was unable to consolidate its
victory, for in 411 Galicia was invaded by the pagan
Sueves. The resulting political instability permitted
heresy to flourish once again.[76] In 457, Turibius,
bishop of the reformed see of Astorga, wrote to Pope
Leo asking for advice on combating the newly
strengthened heresy. But lacking the support of the
Suevian rulers, Galicia's orthodox church was unable to
take direct measures against the heretics.

During this period, the battle for Gallegan
orthodoxy was limited to polemical writings mainly from
North Africa, where Orosius had presented the threat of
Priscillianism to Augustine. Augustine wrote a number
of tracts and sermons against Priscillianism.[78] The
great Church father brought all his eloquence and
persuasive skill to the task of undermining the Spanish
heresy. For example, Augustine's long tract, "Contra
Mendacium," argued that Priscillianists hid their
heresy by deliberately lying.[79] Thus, Augustine
provided an explanation for how orthodox Christians
could have been seduced into inadvertently acquiring
Priscillianist practices, and his writings provided
powerful authority for the Iberian Church when the

political situation again permitted it to reassert itself against Priscillianism.

In the sixth century, when the Suevian king was converted to Catholicism, the Gallegan Church was able to undertake a final campaign against Priscillianism. The First Council of Braga convened in 561 to strengthen the organization of the Church in Galicia, eliminate Priscillianism, and reestablish orthodoxy in the kingdom of the northwest.[80] Apparently, the principal problem was not that of professed Priscillianists in the Church, for unlike at the First Council of Toledo, at Braga no churchmen were called to recant and proclaim their orthodoxy. Galicia's Church was actually faced with Priscillianist practices that persisted in the region and that were performed by orthodox and heretics alike. The first order of business, then, was to educate the faithful who, "by their ignorance" had slipped into heterodoxy.[81] If education was to be the main weapon in bringing the religious rituals of Galicia's faithful into conformity with accepted orthodox practices, churchmen first had to list and pronounce anathema upon those practices that were defined as Priscillianist.

The Council listed seventeen canons proclaiming Priscillianist errors. Most were directed against Gnostic/dualist errors that essentially comprised the elite theology of Priscillian's system of belief. Several canons (I, II, III, IV) condemned dualist views of the Trinity and the nature of Christ; others (V, VI) corrected the Gnostic view of a pre-cosmic fall and the entrapment of god's substance in man; three (VII, VIII, XIII) condemned dualist elevation of the devil and pronounced anathema upon those who believed the devil to be uncreated and the creator of the world; and three canons (XI, XII, XIV), condemned the anti-carnal views and concomitant vegetarianism growing out of the dualist perception of the world. The remaining three canons condemned other Priscillianist practices which grew out of elite religiosity: 1) cohabitation with women (XV); 2) breaking the Holy Week fast on Maunday Thursday (XVI)[82] and 3) reading forbidden or apocryphal texts (XVII).[83] These prohibitions were strengthened by linking Priscillianist beliefs to other Eastern heresies (Manichaeanism, Sabellianism, Marcionism) which Church authority had previously condemned.

It is important to note that none of these canons dealt with the country magic that had contributed to Priscillian's death sentence. Nowhere did the First Council of Braga mention ritually walking barefoot, or magic amulets, or even the "nocturnal meetings" that had scandalized the fourth-century churchmen at Priscillian's trial. There are several possible reasons for the Church's focus on only one part of Priscillian's theology. The elitist bishops sitting in Council were more interested in the theoretical structure of the heresy once the immediate threat of the presence of a heretical magician had been removed. It is also possible that the bishops attacked those ideas and practices that were most apparent to them. Since most of the bishops were from cities, they would not have had the opportunity to see heretical holy men and women performing fertility rites in the hills. Finally, it is possible that Martin of Braga, who was an influential participant at the First Council of Braga, and who was well acquainted with Gallegan rural practices, may have realized that country magic represented a problem different from the intellectual Priscillianism practiced either consciously or accidentally by the Gallegan nobility.

The First Council of Braga was probably successful
in eliminating the heresy, for by the Second Council of
Braga, just ten years later, bishops did not feel they
had to bring up the problem of Priscillianism. This
victory over the heresy, however, was partly
definitional. Priscillianism had been defined as a
Gnostic heresy centered in cities, which could be
successfully cured by education and legislation. The
First Council of Braga attacked and largely eliminated
the heresy of Marcus of Egypt, but the heresy of the
Gallegan countryside remained and required a
considerably different approach.

Along with elite churchmen's interest in
establishing orthodoxy in their own culture, they also
were particularly concerned with promoting orthodoxy
among the all-important mediators between elite and
peasants. The official Church was always fearful of
the individualism and power of holy men and women
existing on the periphery of established hierarchy, a
fear exacerbated in the late fourth century when
asceticism in all its forms was associated with
Priscillianism. Sulpicius Severus was afraid that
orthodox asceticism would be condemned during the
anti-Priscillianist fervor that was stirred at
Priscillian's trial. Severus wrote that Ithacius,
Priscillian's main accuser, "...went even so far that
he denounced as accomplices and disciples of
Priscillian all men, even holy ones, who had a taste
for sacred reading or a firm disposition toward
frequent fasting."[84] Around 400 A.D., one such
orthodox Gallegan holy man, Bachiarius, was called upon
to prove the orthodoxy of his asceticism. Bachiarius
left Galicia to go on a pilgrimage to Rome.[85] In Rome,
he was summoned to defend his orthodoxy. The Gallegan

holy man eloquently complained of the injustice: "For
the   fault   of   one   man,   the   whole   province   is
anathematized..."[86]   Bachiarius' profession of faith
did   much   to   help   Iberian   asceticism   overcome   its
association with Priscillianism.[87]

While the circulation of orthodox monastic   tracts
like Bachiarius' helped establish the dependability   of
holy men as mediators of Orthodox Christianity, equally
important   were the monastic reforms of the   sixth   and
seventh   centuries described in the   previous   chapter.
By placing monasteries under the control of bishops   in
the official hierarchy and by providing mechanisms   for
checking and controlling institutionalized holy men and
women,   the   Church no longer had to worry   that   these
important   mediators   would cultivate the   heresy   that
Priscillian had planted in the countryside.

These   measures   of   education   and   organization
satisfied   the official Church of the orthodoxy of   the
elite   and their mediators.   The remaining problem   was
bringing   peasants   into   conformity with   official
religiosity.   Since rural magic and   demonology   were
removed from association with Priscillianism, the   only
remaining   visible   Priscillianist   practice   was   the
continued   popular   worship   of   Priscillian's   relics
buried   deep   in   the Gallegan   hills.[89]   The   Church
probably hoped that official encouragement of   powerful
approved   cults   would persuade tenacious   peasants   to
abandon the shrine of their holy martyr.   The   official
Church   tried   with   little   success   to   encourage
veneration   of great bishops, and at the First   Council
of Braga, Lucretius, Archbishop of Braga, seems to have
begun   to   present Turibius of Astorga, known   for   his
anti-Priscillianist efforts, as a saint;[89] but there is
no   evidence of cult activity for St.   Turibius   before

the Reconquest, when his power for fighting heresy was
brought forth to fight the infidel.

It is very likely that the official Church never
really succeeded in secularizing the site of
Priscillian's burial. I concur with Chadwick's
speculation that the powerful holy man buried at
Santiago de Compostella identified as St. James was
Priscillian.[90] If this were the case, the official
Church only eradicated the final Priscillianist
practice indentified in the countryside by co-opting
the heretical martyr's shrine and making of it a great
center of orthodoxy.

While the Church's co-optation of Priscillian's
shrine must remain speculative, it is possible to
document the official Church's ultimate acceptance of
the fundamental elements of rural religiosity that
Priscillian first incorporated into a comprehensive
theology. Whether the Church's removal of the popular
religious elements from the definition of
Priscillianism was a conscious decision on the part of
perceptive churchmen, or pragmatic, growing out of the
interests of elite churchmen, it was very useful for
its final assimilation of peasant religiosity. Once
the Gnostic elements of the heresy had been eradicated,
Gallegan rural religiosity retreated to the hills. The
official Church, no longer threatened by a competing
elite religion, could slowly expand to the countryside,
incorporating peasant religion as it brought the
fiercely traditionalist Gallegans into the orthodox
Church.

SANTIAGO DE CAMPOSTELLA -
STATUE OF ST. JAMES

STONE SARCOPHAGUS BURIED UNDER
THE CATHEDRAL IN WHICH THE
RELICS WERE DISCOVERED

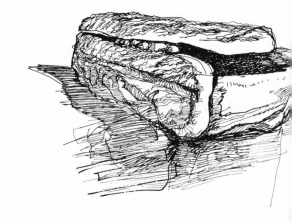

Notes

1. Ramón Lopez Caneda, Prisciliano; su pensamiento y su problema historico (Santiago de Compostela, 1966), p. 71, provides a detailed discussion of the evidence for Priscillian's Gallegan origins. The heresy itself was strongly identified with Galicia regardless of the question of Priscillian's region of birth. As Lopez Caneda expressed, "La...intensa identificación del priscilianismo con Galicia es la más acusada característica de todo su historia a partir del año 385. Porque, además, se restringe exclusivamente a esta región."

2. Sulpicius Severus "Sacred History," Book II, ch. XLVI, in A Select Library of Nicene and Post-Nicene Fathers of the Christian Church, second series, (New York, 1894), XI:119.

3. Loc. cit.

4. Loc. cit.

5. Ibid., Book II, ch. L, p. 121.

6. Priscillian, "Tractatus," i, p. 24, PL Supp ii, c. 1427.

7. Henry Chadwick, Priscillian of Avila (Oxford, 1976), discussed in detail the classical precedents for bare feet as part of prayer rituals. For example, he wrote: "Romans felt bare feet were a special requirement for efficacy of prayer against drought," (p. 18). The Celts, too, held similar beliefs, as Pliny the Elder wrote in regard to the gathering of special herbs by Druids, "...the worshipper must be dressed in white, with feet washed and bare..." [Alexander McBain, Celtic Mythology and Religion (Stirling, 1917), p. 76.]

8. Caesaraugustanum IV, <u>PL</u> 84:316, "...nec nudis
pedibus incedere...."

9. Sulpicius Severus, p. 121.

10. Lopez Caneda, p. 178, argues that Priscillian
is suspiciously overzealous in denying lunar worship in
his first <u>Tractate</u> (refuting it six times).

11. <u>Ibid.</u>, p. 172.

12. Priscillian, "Tractatus," i, p. 28, c. 1431,
"nobis autem et in masculis et in feminis dei spiritus
est."

13. Mario Martins, <u>Correntes   da   Filosofia
Religiosa em Braga dos sec. IV a VII</u> (Porto, 1950), p.
47.

14. Lopez Caneda, pp. 167-68.

15. Sulpicius Severus, p. 119.

16. Sancti Hieronymi "Epistola 75," <u>PL</u> 22:687-88.

17. I Bracara XV, <u>PL</u> 84:564.

18. Priscillianus "Tractatus ii, Liber ad Damasum
Episcopus," <u>PL</u>, Supp. ii, c. 1434.

19. Sulpicius Severus, p. 120. For an excellent
discussion of medieval use of abortive herbs, see
B.D.H. Miller, "She Who Hath Drunk Any Potion," <u>Medium
Aevum</u> 31 (1962), pp. 188-93. Conciliar legislation in
Galicia prohibited women from procuring abortions, so
apparently it was recognized that there were those who
knew how to produce an abortion.   See, "Canoni
Martini," LXVII, <u>PL</u> 84:584. See also, S.P. Scott, ed.,
<u>The Visigothic Code</u>, Book VI, Title III, chs. I-VII,
pp. 206-7, for civil prohibitions of performing
abortions.

20. Priscillianus, "Tractatus," ii, p. 24, c.
1427, "...consecrari oportere gustatus unguentumque
maledicti Soli et Lunae..."

21. Chadwick, p. 51.

22.   Priscillianus, "Tractatus," i. p. 26, c. 1429.

23.   Stephen McKenna, "Paganism and Pagan Survivals in Spain up to the Fall of the Visigothic Kingdom," The Catholic University of America Studies in Medieval History, New Series, vol. I (Washington, 1938), p. 151.

24.   Hans Jonas, The Gnostic Religion, (Boston, 1958), p. 52. See also, pages 51 through 56 for an excellent discussion of Gnostic imagery of demons, worlds and aeons.

25.   Priscillianus, "Tractatus," i, pp. 7-8, c. 1416: "Anathema sit qui legens grifos aquilas asinos elefantos serpentes et bestias superuacuas confusibilis obseruantiae uantitate captiuus velut mysterium divinae religionis adstruxerit, quorum opera et formarum detestabilitas natura daemoniorum non divinarum..."

26.   Chadwick, p. 91.

27.   I Bracara VIII, PL 84:564: "Si quis credit quia aliquantas in mundo creaturas diabolus fecerit, et tonitrua et fulgura et tempestates et siccitates ipse diabolus sua auctoritate faciat, sicut Priscillianus dixit, anathema sit."

28.   Chadwick, pp. 96-99, 126.

29.   For a discussion of the authorship of the Tractates, see D.G. Morin, "Pro Instantio--contre l'attribution a Priscillien des opuscules du manuscrit de Wurzburg," in Revue Benedictine, 30(1913), pp. 153-73. Chadwick, p. 64, also discusses this question. An example of the Tractates' denials of Manichaeanism can be found in Priscillianus, "Tractatus," i, c. 1426: "anathema sit qui Maneten et opera eius doctrinas adque instituta damnat...."

30.   Chadwick, p. 59.

31.   Idatii Episcopi "Chronicon," in Migne, PL LI:875, "In Asturicensi urbe Gallaicia, quidam ante

aliquot   annos   latentes Manichaei gestis   episcopalibus
deteguntur..."

32.   Roy J. Deferrari, ed., <u>Orosius, The Seven</u>
<u>Books of History against the Pagans</u>, Fathers of the
Church   series   (Washington,   1964),   has   a   good
description of Orosius' life and works in his
introduction.

33. Augustine, "Ad Orosium," <u>PL</u> XLII:669. Jerome,
"Epistola CXXVI," <u>PL</u> XX:1085.

34. Chadwick, p. 99, acknowledges that Priscillian
was "...genuinely vulnerable [in his similarities to
Manichaeanism]...to   orthodox   anxieties   about   his
position."   Lopez Caneda, pp. 86-88, unreservedly
accepts the validity of the charge of dualism against
Priscillian.

35.   Unlike Emmanuel LeRoy Ladurie, in <u>Montaillou</u>
(New York, 1978), I see no evidence that Gallegan
peasants   were particularly concerned with dualist
versus orthodox paths to individual salvation.

36.   Carlo Ginzburg, <u>The Cheese and the Worms</u> (New
York, 1982), describes the religious materialism of
traditional peasant culture. On p. 68 he writes: "His
[the   miller   protaganist's]   was   a   religious
materialism...This, in short, was a peasant religion
that had very little in common with that preached by
the priest from his pulpit."

37.   Chadwick, p. 191, has a thorough analysis of
the astrological elements in Priscillian's thought. He
compares Priscillian's views with astrological beliefs
of other contemporary sects.

38. Lopez Caneda, p. 182.

39.   Theodore Otto Wedel, <u>The Medieval Attitude</u>
<u>Toward Astrology</u> (New Haven, 1920), pp. 43-4.

40.   I Bracara IX, <u>PL</u> 84:564: "Si quis animas et

corpora humana fatalibus stellis credit astringi, sicut
pagani et Priscillianus dixerunt, anathema sit."

41.   "De Sancto Turibio, Episcopo Asturicensi   in
Hispania,"   Acta   Sanctorum,   Aprilis   II,   p.   422:
"...mathematicorum vana mendacia, religionis et effectu
fiderum   collocaret."   So   closely   was   astrology
associated with Priscillianism, that Pope Gregory,   ca.
600, specifically mentioned Priscillianism in a   homily
against astrology.   "Sancti Gregorii Magni.   Homiliarum
in Evangelia Lib. I. Homilia X." PL 76:1110-14.

42.   Chadwick, p. 152, discusses   in   detail   the
schism in the Spanish Church after Priscillian's death.

43.   See   E.C.   Babut,   Priscillien   et   le
priscillianisme   (Paris,   1909),   pp.   283-90,   and
Chadwick,   pp.   154-56, for a description   of   Dictinius
and his thought.

44.   Chadwick, p. 183.

45.   Ibid., p. 194.

46.   Priscillian defended   the   practice   of
vegetarianism for example, in "Canones Pauli," PL Supp.
ii,   c.   1400--canon XXXV.   Vegetarianism became
associated so solidly with heresy that abstaining   from
meat was considered sufficient grounds for   accusation.
See, "Epistola Vigilii Papae ad Profuturum   Episcopum,"
Migne,   PL 84:829-30.   For   further   prohibitions   of
vegetarianism,   see   I   Bracara   XIV,   PL   84:567,   and
"Canones Martini," PL 84:582.

47.   Garcia Villada, "La vida de St. Helia.   Un
tratado   priscillianista   contra   el   matrimonio?"
Estudios   Eclesiasticos   2 (1923), p.   272,   "...ni   el
autor   de   la obra, ni el que la mandó   redactar,   eran
francamente católicos.   Por todas partes   aparece   en
ella   una   marcadísima   tendencia   a   condenar   el
matrimonio.   Esto unido a otros various indicios,   nos

hace creer que esta vida es un tratado de orígen
priscillianista y que Santa Helia debe ser alguna de
aquellas mujeres que se adhirieron a su secta."

48. Ms. Esc. a II 9, Folio 72.

49. Ibid., Folio 72v.

50. Ibid., Folio 73.

51. Guillermo Antolin, "Vida de Santa Helia,"
Boletin de la Academia de la Historia 55 (1909), p.
122.

52. Dmitri Obolensky, The Bogomils (Cambridge,
1948), p. 50. See also, Obolensky's similar analyses
of the Boborites (p. 52) and the Euchitae (p. 186).
This explanation does not resolve the seeming
inconsistency between dualism and promiscuity. Milan
Loos, for example, could not reconcile the Massalian,
"...longing to comprehend mystical revelation through
sensual experience" with a dualistic rejection of the
flesh: "This strange movement was essentially alien to
the cosmological dualism of the Bogomils," [Milan Loos,
Dualist Heresy in the Middle Ages (Prague, 1974), p.
72]. Obolensky's examination of the sources, however,
leaves little doubt that the Massalians were dualists.

53. For a general discussion of the relationship
between heresy and fornication, not specifically
related to dualist sects, see Robert E. Lerner, The
Heresy of the Free Spirit in the Later Middle Ages
(Berkeley, 1972), pp. 10-34.

54. Obolensky, p. 50.

55. I Bracara XII, PL 84:564.

56. Obolensky, p. 49.

57. Sulpicius Severus, Book II, ch. XLVI, p. 119.
[Priscillian] "was able to spend much time in
watchfulness, and to endure both hunger and thirst; he
had little desire for amassing wealth..."

58. "De Sancto Turibio," p. 422 "...sub nominibus
Prophetarum et Apostolatorum..."

59. Martins, p. 59.

60. Priscillianus, "Tractatus," vi, c. 761-763.

61. For an excellent discussion of Gnostic
theology and the impulse of the spirit to experience
God, see Jonas, pp. 31-46.

62. Priscillianus, "Tractatus," i, p. 8, c. 1416.

63. "S. Turibii Asturicensis Epistola," PL
LIV:694: "...quantaeque blasphemiae apocryphis libris,
quos hi nostri vernaculi haeretici ad vicem sanctorum
Evangeliorum legunt." Priscillianus, "Tractatus III,"
c. 1442-51, contains Priscillian's strong defense of
Christians reading apocryphal texts.

64. G.G. King, Preromanesque Churches in Spain
(Pennsylvania, 1924), pp. 55-56, describes a carving in
S. Pedro de la Nave, of St. Thomas carrying the book of
his Actas.

65. Chadwick, p. 77.

66. Priscillianus, "Canones in Pauli," c. 1406,
"Quia bonae vitae quorundam laicorum et fidei atque
humanitate eorum testimonum reddat apostulus, quod
refecerint vel ipsum vel sanctorum pauperes."

67. This practice was condemned at the Council of
Saragossa as early as 380. "Concilium Caesaraugustanum
I," PL 84:315.

68. For Priscillian's views on prophesy, see
"Tractatus," i, p. 29, c. 1431, and "Tractatus," iii,
p. 54, c. 1449.

69. Chadwick, pp. 110-69, provides a complete
discussion of Priscillian's trial, the political
circumstances surrounding his execution and the
controversy arising out of the secular trial of the
ordained bishop of Avila.

70.   Idatii Episcopi, PL LI:872, and Sulpicius
Severus,   p. 122, both testify to Priscillian's
execution,   and   the   quotation   on   the   return   of
Priscillian's relics comes from Sulpicius Severus.

71.   Sulpicius Severus, p. 122.

72.   I Tolet, PL 84:328 "...isti sunt qui   et   in
aliis   gestis   adversus Priscillian sectatores   et
haeresem..." Chadwick, pp. 170-88, has a thorough
analysis of this Council.

73.   Chadwick, p. 171.

74.   Ibid., p. 181.

75.   Innocent I, "Epistola III," PL XX:486-87,
"...et status Catholicae fidei integer permaneret,   et
nullum   scandalum   concordiam   rebus   omnibus   utilem
corrupisset."

76.   "S. Leonis Magni Epistolae. Epistola XV--Ad
Turibium Asturicensem Episcopum, De Priscillianistarum
Erroribus," PL LV:680, "Ex quo inter   sacerdotes Dei
difficiles commeatus et rari coeperunt esse   conventus,
invenit   ob   publicam perturbationem   secreta   perfidia
libertatem,   et   ad multarum mentium   subversionem   his
malis est incitata, quibus debuit esse correcta."

77.   "De Sancto Turibio," p. 423.

78.   For example, see Augustine, "Contra   Mendacium
ad   Consentum" PL XL:517-48, and "De   Haeresibus," PL
XLII:44.

79.   Augustine, "Contra Mendacium," Caput   V,   PL
XL:523,   "Priscillianistan   tolerabilus   mentiri
occultando   haeresim   suam   quam   catholica   occultando
veritate."

80.   I Bracara, PL 84:562, the   long   introductory
statement   by   Lucretius, the   Metropolitan   of   Braga,
outlines these goals.

81.   Ibid.,   "...manifestius   ignaris   hominibus

declaretur qui in ipsa extremitate mundi,   et altimes
hujus provinciae regionibus constituti, aut exiguam,
aut   pene   nullam   rectae   eruditionis   notitia
contigenunt."

82.   Chadwick, p. 226, analyzes this unusual
prohibition.

83.   All the canons can be found in I Bracara, PL
84:563-4.   There is also a list of anti-Priscillian
canons appended to some recensions of the First Council
of Toledo.   These are similar to those of I Bracara,
but in less detail. I have not used them in this
analysis, because there is a problem of the dating.
They cannot have been drafted at the First Council of
Toledo in 400, because the preface says that it was
sent to Balconius, Bishop of Braga.   Balconius only
became Bishop in 415, so the canons were likely drafted
only after the Sueves invaded the Northwest.   Thus,
even if the canons were sent to Galicia, their impact
could not have been great until after the conversion of
the Sueves to Catholicism, by which time   their
importance would have been superseded by the canons of
the First council of Braga.

84.   Sulpicius Severus, p. 121.

85.   See Joseph M.-F. Manrique, ed., Leaders of the
Iberian Peninsula (Boston, 1962), p. 121, for a
description of Bachiarius and his travels.

86.   Bachiarius "Fides," PL XX:1023, "Si pro culpa
unius, totius provinciae anathemanda generatio est..."

87.   Martins, p. 136.

88.   Chadwick, p. 232: "In the seventh century
there may still have been country folk in the valleys
of Galicia who remembered how their fathers had sought
strength and healing and had sworn great oaths at
Priscillian's tomb in the northwest."

89. "De Sancto Turibio," p. 422: "Fuit enim in hoc sanctissimo viro, cujus diem veneramur..."

90. Chadwick, p. 233, proposes this hypothesis on the basis of a necropolis with graves of the fourth and fifth centuries excavated near the Cathedral. Further excavations at the Shrine have revealed three decapitated bodies, and these may be Priscillian and his followers who died at Trier.

CHRISTIAN VILLAGE: NATURAL ORDER

The Church's process of expanding the limits of orthodoxy to incorporate elements of peasant religiosity was a slow one. The sources are not sufficiently detailed to permit an exact identification of the chronology of this slow expansion, but it is possible to analyze and describe the religiosity of Gallegan Christian villagers on the eve of the Moslim invasions. A comparison of late seventh-century village religiosity with that of the traditional village described in Chapter I makes it very clear that the process of expansion of orthodoxy did occur. The official Church made it easy for peasants to retain many of their traditional views while remaining orthodox.

The religion of pre-Christian villagers ritually ordered peasants' relations with nature and with each other. The religion of the Christian villagers did the same thing. The basic element of pre-Christian relations with nature was defined by official churchmen as idolatry. Idolatry was too visible and flagrant a violation of orthodox power for the Church to overlook. Beginning as early as the first Iberian church council held at Elvira in 306, churchmen forbade idolatry and established penalties in order to force pagans into orthodox practice,[1] if not orthodox belief. However, peasants did not easily abandon the worship of ancient nature deities. The Third Council of Toledo in 589 observed that the "...sacrilege of idolatry is firmly implanted throughout almost the whole of Spain...."[2] In the northwest, archeological evidence reveals an

altar dedicated to a local god Erundino in 399, nearly
a century after the first prohibition at Elvira.[3]
Through the seventh century (in 681 and again in 693)
councils revived legislation against worshipping
fountains, trees and stones. Official canons called on
lay and spiritual authorities (judges and bishops) to
work together against rural idolators.[4] In spite of
official impatience with the persistent idolatry, the
legislation from Iberian centers of power was seldom
effective in persuading peasants to change their
traditional practices.

Therefore, together with establishing punishments
for offenders, the Church tried persuasion. At the
Second Council of Braga, bishops were told to summon
the people and warn them against idolatry.[5] Martin of
Braga (who presided over that Council) wrote a
fascinating sermon, "De Correctione Rusticorum,"[6] at
expressed the official position on idols and old gods.
In "everyday language" Martin described the fall of
angels, who became demons and came to earth to trick
men into worshipping them. "Many of these demons who
were driven out of Heaven preside over the sea, the
rivers, the mountains and the forests...[The devil and
his demons] began to manifest themselves to men under
various shapes and speak with them and to urge men to
offer sacrifices on lofty mountains and in leafy
forests, and to worship them in place of God."[7] Martin
did not deny the reality of the spirits inhabiting the
Gallegan hills, forests and rivers, but he reduced
their status from gods to lesser demons who had been
dismissed from heaven by the one true God. The
official Church's persuasion depended upon the question
of power. Who had more of it, the demons or God?

In Galicia, one of the most persistent forms of

idolatry surrounded mountains and the demons who traditionally had ruled them. Gallegan awe and respect for mountains can be traced in the sources from the earliest periods through the Christian centuries. For example, when the fourth-century virgin, Etheria, travelled to the Holy Land, she saw Constantinople and other great cities; she saw spacious deserts and different peoples, but what she described in greatest detail in her letter to Galicia were the mountains she climbed. Half the pages of the section of her letter describing her travels were devoted to mountains. Etheria's description of Mt. Sinai is typical:

> Now the whole mountain group looks as if it were a single peak, but as you enter the group, [you see that] there are more than one; the whole group however, is called the Mount of God. But that special peak which is crowned by the place where, as it is written, the Glory of God descended, is in the center of them all. And though all the peaks in the group attain such a height as I think I never saw before, yet the central one, on which the Glory of God came down, is so much higher than them all, that when we had ascended it, all those mountains which we had thought to be high, were so much beneath us as if they were quite little hills.[8]

Reading this passage, one senses that Etheria was as
impressed by the physical presence of this magnificent
range as by the fact that God once had graced the
peaks.

Mountain themes also permeated the writing of
Valerius of Bierzo, as he himself noted referring to an
"oft-mentioned" mountain.[9] When Valerius wrote a
commentary on Etheria's letter, he selected to discuss
the mountains she visited and wrote with eloquent awe
of the "fragile woman's" arduous climb up Mt. Sinai
that raised her not only to the clouds, but also closer
to God.[10] Even an anonymous author of a mystic
fourth-century letter spoke of the highest revelation
in a mountain metaphor: "Then to you it shall be
revealed the top of the mountain."[11]

Before Catholicism could penetrate deeply into the
countryside, it had to accept Gallegan reverence for
mountains and provide a suitable replacement for such
"idolatry." Martin's theoretical position that old
mountain gods were demons pointed the way for the
Church to coopt reverence for mountains. On a
practical level, lesser demons would have to be driven
out and replaced with veneration of God as the ruler of
the Gallegan hills. In this spirit, Pope Gregory
advocated a forceful cooptation of pagan holy places.
"The temples of the pagans were to be sprinkled with
holy water; altars and relics were to be placed in
them, and thus the worship paid to demons would be
transferred to the one true God."[12] Without a doubt,
this process was repeated as Christianity spread and
replaced old gods. In Galicia, Valerius vividly
described one such sudden conversion of a pagan
mountain shrine. "Although on the top of a mountain
height people in the stupid and wicked madness of their

blindness were impiously and foolishly venerating unholy shrines of demons according to pagan rites, this outrageous obscenity was finally destroyed by the help of faithful Christians, and with the aid of the almighty Lord a basilica was built in the name of St. Felix the martyr."[13]

While some ancient shrines were consciously converted forcefully to Christianity, traditionally sacred heights were also Christianized in a more subtle and probably more effective way. Would-be holy men who climbed isolated peaks to fight for sanctity had to fight their first battle against the demon to whom the mountain belonged, the "ancient scoundrel," for example, who plagued Emilian during his retreat to Mt. Distercius.[14] As a holy man gained power by displacing the old god, his reputation spread through the neighboring countryside, and even after his death, his remains were believed to protect people from the natural forces of the mountain. As contacts increased between official churchmen and peasants in the course of the Church's missionary attempts to convert the semi-pagan "rustics," bishops heard of miracles at the tomb of an obscure local holy man. Official churchmen recognized the presence of mystery and holiness at places distant from Iberian centers of power and outside the Christian written word. When a parish priest recounted miracles occurring at the shrine of a local holy person, a bishop was less interested in exploring the origins or orthodoxy of the entombed than he was in assembling evidence of miracles to demonstrate holiness. When presented with examples of holiness, official churchmen argued inductively that such evidence of God's grace proved that the proposed saint had lived an orthodox Christian life, and thus was worthy of canonization. Arguing from the miraculous to the orthodox provided one of the principal means for incorporating peasant religiosity into the official religion.

This is not to say that the replacement of old gods with saints caused no basic change in rural religious perspectives. Such substitutions actually changed the traditional locus of religious power. Throughout the pre-Christian centuries, the natural phenomena that occurred at the peaks were attributed to a god residing in the mountain itself. This explanation permitted villagers to attempt to control the relationship between themselves and a mountain by appealing to, or at least not offending, the mountain's god. Christianity explained rockslides, falling trees or seemingly random escape from danger as the will of the one true God who could also be appeased through appeal to His representative, the mountain's saint. Of course, removing God from a mountain to the heavens and leaving the mountain guarded by a mediator increased the complexity of the ritual ordering of the relationship between mountain and peasant. Not only was the saint supposed to transmit local requests to God, but holy men acquired some independent power. People thus had to avoid giving offense to the saint no less than to God. The practical consequence of this increased complexity was that God, the ultimate source of power, became more distant, and reliance was increasingly placed on a secondary power figure, the saint. Faith was less a faith in omnipotent God than in a mediating saint, and since this faith depended upon a relationship (between God and his saint) that was both out of the control and beyond the comprehension of the rural petitioners, it may have been less reassuring than the older form of worship in which gods were more directly accessible. The only way anyone could assess the standing of a local saint with God was to observe the number of miracles performed through a saint's intercession. Cults rose and fell on the basis of miraculous productivity and villagers were always receptive to rumors of more powerful saints who were perhaps closer to God. In the transition from pagan to Christian, the blame for misfortune was inverted spatially. Pagans accused a distant abstract "fate" for misfortune, leaving their local gods intact; Christians accused local mediator/saints leaving the distant all-powerful God untouched by their anger.

In spite of the change in the source of supernatural power, holy people in hermitages and monasteries as well as saints' relics in basilicas did conquer the hills. In effect, the Christianization of Galicia's hills occurred when there were enough monasteries and relics dispersed throughout the countryside to bring most of the villages within the holy space and protection of a holy person. The Church seemingly did not persuade villagers that an abstract God would protect them in the hills, but peasants did look to mountain saints and let the saints intercede for them with a distant God. A saint formed a link between God and his petitioners just as the mountain itself seemed to join the earth with the sky.[15] St. Emilian protected the region of Mt. Distercius; St. Felix guarded the Bierzo; Sts. Justus and Pastor were buried in the hills west of Astorga; St. Fructuosus was buried "...on the little top of a mountain between the city of Braga and the convent of Dumio."[16] These were only the most popular saints, whose lives and reputations have survived. Doubtless, there were many

more local holy men whose names have disappeared in the
mountains that dominated Gallegan peasant geography.[17]

Once the slow process of replacing old gods with
saints had begun, the official Church itself began to
use popular veneration of local saints to combat
idolatry in general. Hagiographic accounts were
modified so that their narrative included official
values,[18] and saints' Lives were also used directly to
combat idolatry. For example, St. Augustine expressed
the Church's conscious use of Saints' cults in his
sermon on Fructuosus the martyr, in which he argued
that it was necessary to use the example of martyrs to
preach against idolatry.[19]

Prudentius' poetry provides one of the best
examples of the Church's use of popular saints to
combat idolatry, as well as giving an excellent
illustration of the way religious impulses moved back
and forth between official churchmen and peasants.
Among Prudentius' writings are a number of hymns to
Spanish martyrs. The poet drew upon oral traditions of
the countryside to create skillful poetry of the
passion of popular martyrs. Transforming popular
religious sentiment into verse made the worship of
local saints a part of the ruling, literate culture.
To complete the circular flow of communication, four of
Prudentius' hymns were included in the Mozarabic
Breviary to be sung on each saint's feast day[20] as a
means of further inspiring peasants who originally had
initiated such worship. The message of martyrdom took
on a more didactic note in the transition from peasant
culture to orthodoxy and back again. Prudentius'
lesson was that the martyrs had died to avoid idol
worship.

>   The proud, impious prefect, fierce and brutal
>   Bade them worship at altars of the demons.[21]

The poet urged peasants to avoid "demon worship" and emulate the saints and martyrs they revered. Prudentius also accused those persisting in idol worship of participating in the guilt of sacrificing God's servants:

> Vascons, once a heathen people, are you
>   not today convinced
> That you stained your hands unwitting
>   in the blood of martyr saints?
> Do you not believe these victims now
>   enjoy bliss with God?[22]

These hymns became powerful weapons in the official Church's fight for uniformity, particularly since they were firmly based in rural religious tradition.

Idolatry expressed the traditional Gallegan explanation for ordering nature. However, rural religion involved more than the belief that nature was ruled by various gods and goddesses. It was also a religion of magic, since natural forces were so immediately crucial to survival. Nature not only had to be explained but also controlled. Therefore, beyond accepting rural perceptions of holiness, the Church also had to provide concrete practices for controlling nature. People had worshipped "idols" for specific practical reasons in order to receive supernatural favors. Elaborate rituals had evolved in the presentation of petitions to old gods as a means of bribing or controlling them. In form, these practices were magical.[23] In the early centuries, the Church had been unable to persuade peasants to accept a doctrine of complete and passive faith, to trust and accept natural disasters as part of God's plan and to look toward a promised afterlife.[24] Instead, the Church had to convince peasants that Christianity offered a more

powerful magic than the old ways. In the seventh
century, Braulio of Saragossa articulated the Church's
practical approach to converting stubborn peasants:
"...with a watchful zeal to restore to the way of
salvation the souls of those who have lost hope, by
setting up a separate science as rival to their own."[25]
Thus, when peasants were converted to Christianity, it
was a Christianity of magic that set up Christian magic
to rival the old magic.[26]

When faced with the many magic rituals that
traditionally had been used to coerce favors from the
gods, the official Church took several different
positions. The Church was remarkably willing to
accommodate a wide range of magical practices as long
as they took the form of petitions addressed to the one
true God. There were some practices, however, whose
intent was less clear, and about these the Church was
ambivalent. Other practices were allied too integrally
with idolatry to be assimilated, and these were
consistently forbidden.

Within the category of practices the Church was
willing to accommodate were traditional fertility
rites. The Church had accepted Gallegan respect for
virgins, who by their presence in the community helped
bring fertility to the land. Nevertheless, there
remained many rituals and formulaic requests for
fertility that usually had prevented famine. The
Church had to provide for comparable magical practices
to help promote fertility.

Fertility offerings traditionally had been
presented to fountains. Fountains not only recalled
the mythological waters guarded by virgins in the
Celtic tradition, but they presented a visual example
of desired fertility, that is, flowing "living" water

springing out of barren rock. Martin of Braga condemned traditional offerings to fountains saying, "For what is burning candles by...the fountains...if not the worship of the devil."[27] In spite of such prohibitions, the Church could not simply bypass fountains in its expansion to the countryside. The Church recognized the supernatural quality that peasants attributed to some fountains and had to drive out the fountain's goddess just as hermits had driven old gods from mountain peaks. At a local fountain shrine in the presence of the community, a priest chanted with appropriate ceremony: "Be exorcised, creature of water, in the name of the Lord God of Hosts, Father almighty, by virtue of His omnipotence, evil and diabolical apparition depart...."[28] While exorcisms may have been dramatic, in fact, they were merely stronger versions of Martin's prohibitions of fountain worship. Since fountains had been objects of veneration for so long, the Church could not simply deny their holiness, but had to provide an acceptable substitute. The Church's exorcism had banished old sanctity from a fountain, but a priest's blessing essentially made the fountain holy again by rededicating it to God.

The blessing began with a recognition that a fountain was an awesome natural wonder: "...pressed by mountains, you [water] were not shut in, when you were beaten with rocks, you were not shattered, when you were diffused in the earth, you did not fail....You press open mountain doors, yet were not consumed...." A priest also acknowledged that the waters contributed to fertility: "...you sustain the arid...."[29] Thus, the blessing articulated Gallegan awe of the miracle of water springing from dry, barren rock.

The sentiments expressed in these passages, however, were too close to nature worship which had been prohibited as idolatry, so the Benedictio fontis moved to the abstract, turning fountains into symbols of God's cosmic mystery. The priest addressed the fountain, saying, "Through your beginning, by your glorious finish...we shall know the end...O Lord, Almighty God, whose goodness is not known, yet...by means of the waters, we shall bring forward a sign of your works."[30] After thus establishing the anagogical value of fountains, the blessing returned again to the concrete, but argued that fountains represented not a miracle of nature, but a Christian miracle of regenerative baptism. The "living" waters that came from the rock were the living waters of baptism, of personal salvation. "Give a healthful draught to those filled with bitterness of fruit [referring to Adam's eating the apple], who having eaten of mortal disease, by your antidote be freed from long lived destruction...by the mystical renewal of the liquid and redeemed they are made new and reborn."[31]

By manipulating the symbolism of "living" waters, the Church converted the practice of fountain worship to official acceptance. At the level of popular belief, however, it is questionable whether veneration of fountains as fertility symbols was completely transferred to veneration for personal salvation through baptism. The blessing was long enough and complex enough to incorporate various levels of belief, and it is reasonable to assume that many who heard the beautiful praise of waters fighting through rock to bring fertility, accepted that image as a true expression and ignored the subsequent theorizing. The fountain blessing represented a skillful attempt by

FOUNTAIN SHRINE AT COVADONGA

official churchmen to convert the meaning of fountain
worship from a rural base to an elite one, but this is
not to say that such a position changed the fundamental
religious views of peasants. At the observable level
of practice, little changed. Villagers continued to
offer candles at local fountain shrines. The Church's
blessing did, however, establish a theoretical
construct that permitted peasant worship to satisfy
official requirements of religious uniformity.

The Mozarabic Liturgy also had many prayers to be
said over the seeds at planting to ask God's blessing
for their abundant germination.[32] These prayers were
to supplant traditional fertility incantations. Even
blessed crops were subject to the hazards of the
unpredictable weather of Galicia. Peasants looked to
holy men to protect crops from storms. Through the
canonization of Vincent, a cult figure, the Church made
magical manipulation of storms part of orthodox ritual.
Nothing is known of the presumed martyrdom of Vincent;
his canonization rested upon popular belief in one
miracle. Vincent's Life relates that the region "a
long time ago" was afflicted by hailstones and falling
stones and was saved by Vincent's relics. From then
on, Vincent was known as the patron saint for
protection against storms.[33] St. Vincent's feast was
incorporated early into the Visigothic liturgy,[34] and a
peasant whose crop was threatened by storms could
appeal through orthodox channels to a holy man who had
demonstrated his power in the Iberian hills. The storm
might or might not be stopped, but appeal to Vincent
satisfied the need for concrete action that was a
fundamental characteristic of religions of magic.

After the crops had been harvested, peasants had
to face the problem of rodents. Appealing to the

practical side of villagers, Martin of Braga scorned traditional methods of rodent control: "If the bread or cloth is not taken away from them [moths and mice] and protected in a little box or basket, they will never spare what they find simply for your dedicating a holiday to them...These idle sacrifices do not defend you from the many...tribulations which an angry God sends you."[35] Martin offered the most convincing argument of all for not continuing these practices: they did not work. He offered the community more powerful magic and a concrete talisman to grant protection: "Why does no augury harm me or any other upright Christian? Because when the Sign of the Cross goes before, the sign of the devil is naught."[36] By the seventh century, references to feast days for mice and moths disappear from the sources, so the practice may have slowly died out. The impact of Martin's sermon, however, perhaps may best be seen in the architecture of the horreos in the western portion of the province (Martin's diocese) that are crowned with wooden crosses to protect the stored grain (see figure 1, page 20).

In addition to positive Christian rituals designed to procure an adequate food supply, the church also used threats to win peasants from traditional fertility practices. If Christian symbols and rituals helped the harvest, the opposite was also true. Paganism and idolatry would bring disaster. Such threats emerge not only directly, for example in Martin's warning of the "tribulations which an angry God sends you," but also in the interpretations of events promulgated by members of the official Church. In the seventh century, Leander of Seville expressed the consequence of heterodoxy, lamenting that when Arians conquered

Galicia, "...the soil itself...lost its former fertility."[37] In a more general expression of the same thought, King Egica, addressing the Sixteenth Council of Toledo in 693, argued that misfortunes were punishments by God for people's sins, and the King attacked idolatry and other "diabolical superstitions" that had to be eradicated, presumably for the well-being of the Christian kingdom.[38]

Fertility was not the only concern of traditional village life that was highly ritualized. Celtic Gallegans also ritualized the gathering of medicinal herbs[39] and in the early fourth century, Gallegan villagers demonstrated their skill with medicinal herbs by offering Fructuosus a "specially prepared drink" to ease the pain of his imminent martyrdom.[40] Priscillian and his followers also inspired awe through their knowledge of abortive herbs that were collected with appropriate ceremony.

Obviously, the Church could not, and did not, object to the collection of medicinal herbs. Churchmen were concerned, however, with rites surrounding the collection. The faithful were not to forget that the benefit of herbs ultimately came from God. Traditional ceremonies surrounding herb gathering were forbidden, for "What is muttering incantations over noxious herbs and invoking the names of demons, if not the worship of the devil?"[41] Instead, Christians should collect medicinal herbs using divine Christian symbols and chanting the Lord's prayer.[42]

In all these examples of Christian magic, the goal of the magical petition was clear. It was to make fields fertile, to protect crops, and to strengthen the healing power of herbs. Some traditional rituals, however, had less specific goals and were thus more difficult to replace with a comparable Christian ritual. Walking barefoot was one such practice that was probably impossible to eradicate because of its nonspecific nature. Simple blanket prohibitions would have been ludicrous, for obviously every time a peasant went shoeless he was not necessarily indulging in a pagan ritual. Priscillianists had been condemned for believing that there was a connection between barefootedness and the effectiveness of prayer, but was it wrong to say orthodox Christian prayers while barefoot? What of people who went unshod for a time in order to invoke good luck or as an expression of orthodox asceticism? Martin warned peasants against"...pedem observare..."[43] probably intending to prohibit ritualization of walking barefoot. The vagueness of Martin's prohibition was in striking contrast with his usually detailed descriptions, and his imprecision foreshadows the Church's problems in identifying and eradicating the practice. As Augustine noted, it was "...easier to persuade a confirmed drinker to forsake his bottle than to dissuade a man from walking barefoot for eight days, so great is the force of cultic custom."[44]

The Church's approach to this custom reveals both the complexity of the traditional reasons for the ritual and the impossibility of eradicating it. Most often, churchmen probably chose to ignore that which they could not change, defining the practice of going barefoot as an innocuous secular act rather than a threatening pagan superstition. At other times, walking with bare feet was viewed as a symbol of Christian asceticism. St. Fructuosus "...entered barefoot into a forest overgrown with vines..."[45] and holy men regularly demonstrated sanctity by choosing to walk instead of riding.[46]

As an effort to reduce the ritual importance of bare feet, the Church seems to have occasionally treated shoes as ritual objects. For example, a type of shoe which was "held securely on the foot of mountain people"[47] was a relic of the shepherd saints, Justus and Pastor. There is nothing in the account of their martyrdom that associates the saints with a shoe, and it is possible that chance alone determined the shoe's association with the saints. The official description, however, accentuating the shoe's firm adherence to the foot, suggests elements of official efforts to transfer symbolic importance from bare feet to shod ones.

That the transfer was never fully made even at the level of official hagiography can be seen in the account of the passion of the martyr Fructuosus of Tarragona. In a short account of the arrest, interrogation and martyrdom of Bishop Fructuosus and two deacons, a disproportionate amount of attention was given to Fructuosus' feet. When the soldiers came to his house, Fructuosus asked to be permitted to put on his shoes. So dressed, he endured six days in jail and withstood Judge Emilianus' efforts to force him into idolatry. He was then marched to an amphitheater where he would receive his martyr's crown. At the amphitheater, a lector tearfully begged Fructuosus for the privilege of removing the Bishop's shoes. Fructuosus refused and "...strong and rejoicing and certain of God's promise, Fructuosus removed his own shoes."[48] Consistent with traditional Gallegan values, Fructuosus was barefoot for his most sacred moment, his martyrdom.

The story of Fructuosus may suggest a certain victory of "barefootedness" in this instance, but that was not necessarily the case in all circumstances. Instead, the manner with which the Church dealt with the issue of ritually bare feet suggests that the official Church was ambivalent about rituals considered generally holy rather than rituals clearly identified as specific magical acts. Another example of a generally holy act was the lighting of candles. To light a candle could be a purely secular act, a forbidden pagan ritual when done at a crossroad or in front of a tree, or an orthodox Christian act performed at an altar or shrine. Just as in walking barefoot, it was the circumstances surrounding the practice that determined orthodoxy, not the act of lighting itself.

There were, however, some traditional practices that were too closely allied to idolatry for the Church to accommodate in any form. The two broad categories of practices that the Church consistently forbade were divination, the attempt to foretell the future by means of signs, and black magic, the attempt to inflict harm on others by supernatural means. Divination had always been an integral part of pagan worship (whether Celtic or Roman paganism). Divination was usually recognizable because of its association with particular objects used to foretell the future, whether sacrificial entrails, birds or any of a number of items that were endowed with the supernatural capacity to predict the future. Official churchmen looked upon this elevation of everyday items as idolatry. As Martin of Braga warned, "What is divination and augury...if not worshipping the devil?"[49] Similarly, anyone who associated with soothsayers (<u>divinos et sortilegos</u>) was associating with evil.[50]

Of course, it was always possible that some visions of the future were sent by God. For example,

Saint   Emilian   foretold Leovigild's   invasion   of
Cantabria.[51] The Church distinguished between orthodox
and heretical visions primarily by determining their
origin.   If a vision were unsolicited, then it probably
came from God, for God had chosen what to reveal and to
whom.   An individual then became a passive vessel for
God's revelation. By divination, on the other hand, an
individual   took   the initiative and attempted to use
traditional rituals to force a knowledge of the future.
Since God is too powerful to succumb to ritual bribery,
forced foreknowledge must have come from the devil,
making divination almost synonymous with idolatry.

        Black   magic was also consistently and repeatedly
forbidden.   Black magic emerged from the same view of
the world that made villagers ritually petition God for
blessings.   While the Church was willing to permit
Christianity to be a religion of white magic (at least
during the centuries under discussion),[52] churchmen
insisted that people not try to invoke supernatural
help to punish evil, for punishment belonged to God.
Consider, for example, traditional Gallegan concern for
storms.   It was lawful to offer prayers and candles to
St. Vincent asking him to intercede with God to stop a
damaging storm. On the other hand, it was forbidden
for "enchanters and invokers of tempests, who, by their
incantations,   bring hailstorms upon vineyards and
fields of grain."[53] The official Church did not deny
that it was possible to invoke demons to hurt others,
but it forbade the malevolent practice.   A law was
passed to try to protect people and their property from
the anger of those who could invoke the supernatural:
"[If anyone]...should attempt to employ, or should
employ, witchcraft, charms, or incantations of any kind
with intent to strike dumb, maim, or kill either men or

animals; or injure anything movable; or should practice said arts to the detriment of crops, vineyards, or trees; he shall suffer in person and property the same damage he endeavored to inflict upon others."[54]

The forms of black magic most feared were rites designed to bring death to an enemy. The Council of Elvira pronounced perpetual excommunication upon anyone who had killed by magic.[55] Efforts to cause someone's death by magic survived well into the Christian era and, indeed, Christian rituals themselves at times were used for this form of black magic. In order to harm someone, a cleric would at times put on garments of mourning, close the doors of the church and strip the altars bare.[56] Although the Church forbade this practice, even one of Galicia's most famous saints succumbed to it when he was filled with righteous anger: When Fructuosus of Braga was enraged at his brother for removing his inheritance from a monastery, the saint "...at once removed the veils of the church, stripped the sacred altars and covered them with sackcloth; he also wrote and sent to...[his brother] a letter of shame and reproach and divine warning."[57] Even more extreme was the practice of saying requiem mass for the living in order to bring about their death.[58] The late proscriptions of such practices strongly suggest that the Church was never able to eradicate completely the attempt to kill by black magic.

The Christian villagers of the seventh century remained preoccupied with the ancient and crucial problems of ordering the world of nature and ritually coercing the land to produce enough to ensure survival. The Church's success in winning peasants to Christianity was not due to changing rural religious views. Instead, the Church largely accepted peasants' perceptions of the holy and expanded the boundaries of orthodoxy to include traditionally holy mountains, fertility rites and other religious forms that had persisted in the hills. Even though the Church fought against those practices that were blatantly idolatrous or harmful, the Christianity that converted peasants was as surely a religion of magic as the paganism that preceded it.

Notes

1. "Concilium Eliberitanum," PL 84:301-02.

2. III Tolet, PL 84:341.

3. Stephanie R. Jernigan, "Origins of the Early Christian Architecture of the Iberian Peninsula," (Ph.D. diss., University of Missouri, Columbia, 1974), p. 7.

4. III Tolet, XVI, PL 84:354; reaffirmed in XII Tolet, XI, PL 84:478.

5. II Bracara, I, PL 84:571. "...convocata plebe ipsius ecclesiae doceant illos ut terrores fugiant idolorum."

6. C.W. Barlow, ed., Martini Bracara Opera (New Haven, 1950), contains the complete works of Martin of Braga, including "De Correctione Rusticorum" and is the first to supersede the classic work by C.P. Caspari, Martin von Bracara's Scrift De Correctione Rusticorum (Christiana, 1883). The manuscripts used by Barlow were analyzed by A. Kurfess, and he concluded that "Barlow's erste Gesamtausgabe der Opera Sancti Martini Episcopi Bracarensis verdient hohes Lob." (A. Kurfess, "Textkritisches zu Martini episcopi Bracarensi opera." Athenaeum 32 [1954] p. 409.) I accepted Kurfess' well supported judgment and used Barlow's edition as a check against the other published versions of Caspari and Palmer.

7. Palmer, pp. 26-28.

8. Etheria, The Pilgrimage of Etheria, trans. M.L. McClure and C.L. Feltoe (New York, 1919), pp. 2-3.

9. Valerius of Bierzo, Valerio of Bierzo - An Ascetic of the Late Visigothic Period. The Catholic University of America Studies in Medieval History, New Series, vol. XI, trans. Consuelo Maria Aherne

(Washington, 1949), pp. 124-25, "...saepe dicto
monte..."

10.   Valerius of Bierzo, "Epistola de B. Echeria,"
PL 84:423.   "...ad montem sanctum Sinai unde eum
speramus in nubidus coeli suo tempore advenire, femina
fragilitate oblita, hujus montis ardua proceritate
cujus cacumen usque ad nubium altitudinem contiguum
eminet, infatigabili gressu dextra divina sublevata..."

11.   "Deux lettres mystiques d'une ascète
espagnole," G. Morin, ed., Revue Benedictine 40 (1928),
p. 298.

12.   McKenna, p. 133.

13.   Aherne, trans. Valerio of Bierzo, p. 114.

14.   Braulio of Saragossa, "Vita Sancti Emilian"
The Fathers of the Church - Iberian Fathers, C.W.
Barlow, ed. (Washington, 1969), 2:122.   Peter Brown
explored the relationship between holy men and
mountains: "The hermit placed himself on the mountain
tops, as a usurper of the power of ba-alim."   (Peter
Brown, "The Rise and Function of the Holy Man in Late
Antiquity," Journal of Roman Studies 61 [1971], p. 83.)

15.   Traian Stoianovich, A Study in Balkan
Civilization (New York, 1967), pp. 43-44.

16.   Frances Clare Nock, trans., The Vita Sancti
Fructuosi, The Catholic University of America Studies
in Medieval History, New Series, Volume VII
(Washington, 1946), p. 124.

17.   While the sources are not as full of
information regarding the great rivers that had been
traditionally ruled by pagan gods, it appears that
saints also replaced old gods as patrons of rivers.
For example, St. Vincent of Braga was martyred during
the late empire, and his Vita makes a point to say that
a sepulcher was erected to him next to the river

Aleste. (Henrique Flórez, España Sagrada [Madrid, 1759] 15:265.)

18. See above, Chapter V.

19. Augustine, "Sermon No. 273," Actas de Los Martires, Daniel Ruiz Bueno, ed., (Madrid, 1962), p. 796.

20. [Prudentius] The Poems of Prudentius, trans. M. Clement Eagan (Washington, 1962), p. xxi.

21. Ibid., p. 170.

22. Ibid., p. 103.

23. C. Grant Loomis, White Magic (Cambridge, 1948), p. 3: "Magic is a practice which seeks to turn events or to control nature in an unnatural and unexpected fashion."

24. Malinowski's distinction between religion and magic corresponds to my distinction between official and peasant religiosity: "Religion refers to the fundamental issues of human existence while magic always turns round specific concrete and detailed problems." (B. Malinowski, A Scientific Theory of Culture and Other Essays [Chapel Hill, 1944], p. 200.)

25. Braulio, "Letter No. 21 to Pope Honorius I," Fathers of the Church, p. 52.

26. Keith Thomas, Religion and the Decline of Magic (New York, 1971), p. 25: "[Missionaries] have frequently been assisted by the belief of converts that they are acquiring not just a means of other-worldly salvation, but a new and more powerful magic." Raoul Manselli noted that Christianity only began to change from a religion of magic in about the eleventh century. (Raoul Manselli, La Réligion populaire au moyen âge - Problèmes de méthode et d'histoire [Paris, 1975], p. 48.) My analysis of magic differs sharply from that of A.A. Barb, who viewed incantations as "...the product

of highly educated people, becoming more and more
childish by a long process of dilapidation. They are
not products of some nebulous primitive folk-lore
dating from an age before religion was invented...Magic
derives from religion, decayed and decomposing." (A.A.
Barb, "The Survival of Magic Arts," Paganism and
Christianity in the Fourth Century, A. Momigliano, ed.
[Oxford, 1963], p. 124.) On the contrary, I find that
magical practices derive from a different kind of
religion, one of active persuasion, not of passive
acceptance.

27. Palmer, p. 20.

28. Le Liber Ordinum en usage dans l'eglise
wisigothique et mozarabe d'Espagne du cinquieme au
onzieme siecle, D. Marius Ferotin, ed. (Paris, 1904),
p. 18.

29. Ibid., p. 29. "...que montibus pressa non
clauderis, que scopulis inlisa non frangeris que terris
diffusa non delicis...portas monium pondera, nec
demergis...Tu sustines aridam."

30. Ibid., p. 30. "per te initium, per te finis
exultat, vel potius ex Deo tuum est ut terminum
nesciamus...Domine, omnipotens Deus, cuius virtutem non
nescii, dum aquarum merita promimus, operis insigna
predicamus."

31. Ibid., p. 30. "Da salutarem potum, male
saturatis acerbitate pomorum: ut indigesta mortalium
lues, et annosa permicies divino soluantur
antidoto...ut misticis innouati liquoribus, et redemtos
se nouerint, et renatos."

32. Liber Ordinum, pp. 166-67.

33. "De S. Vincentio," Acta Sanctorum Septembris
Toma I, p. 206. "...quod sib patronus contra
tempestatem..."

34.   Liber Ordinum, p. 477.

35.   Palmer, pp. 15-16.

36.   Ibid., pp. 20-21.

37.   Leander of Seville, "Homilia in Laudem Ecclesiae ab conversionem gentis, post concilium et confirmationem canonum edita," PL 72:894.

38.   XVI Tolet, Tomus, PL 84:535.

39.   Strabo, The Geography of Strabo, trans. Horace Leonard Jones (New York, 1917), 2:III, 4, 18.

40.   "Vita Sancti Fructuosi," Ruiz Bueno, p. 791. "Cumque multi ex fraterna caritate eis offerrint, uti conditi permixti proculum sumerent." This event recalls Christ's procession to be crucified, when he was offered wine mixed with myrrh. (Mark, 15:23.)

41.   Palmer, p. 35.

42.   "Canones Martini LXXIV," PL 84:584: "Non liceat in collectione herbarum quae medicinales sunt aliquas observationes aut incantationes attendere, nisi tantum cum symbolo divino aut oratione dominica, ut tantum Deus creator omnium et dominus honoretur."

43.   Palmer, p. 20.

44.   Henry Chadwick, Priscillian of Avila (Oxford, 1976), p. 19.

45.   Nock, p. 94.

46.   Ibid., p. 110. "...pede proprio, ut ei semper mos erat." Braulio, "Vita Sancti Emilian," PL 80:708. "...pedibus suis non vehiculo est profectus." "Vita Patrum Emeritense," Florez, 13:380. "...absque vehiculi invamine." See also, Nock's discussion of the ascetic value of walking over riding, p. 142.

47.   "De SS Justus and Pastor," Acta Sanctorum Aug. Tom I., p. 150. "...ex calceo quoque unum ultriumque locum prodit, ad calceum more gentis montanae, pedi adstringendium."

48. Ruiz Bueno, pp. 788-91. "Eamus; aut si vultis calceo me...lector eiusdem, cum fletibus deprecans, ut eum excalcearet. Cui beatus martyr respondit: Missum fac, fili, ego me excalceo, fortis et gaudens et certus dominicae promissionis."

49. Palmer, p. 34.

50. II Bracara, "Canones Martini, LXXI," PL 84:584.

51. Braulio, "Vita Sancti Emilian," Fathers of the Church, pp. 135-36.

52. Keith Thomas' observation of the Christianity of Medieval England also applies to Medieval Galicia: "The line between magic and religion is one which it is impossible to draw in many primitive societies; it is equally difficult to recognize in Medieval England." (Thomas, p. 5.) For a discussion of magic in the Medieval Church, see Thomas, pp. 25-51.

53. The Visigothic Code, trans. S.P. Scott (Boston, 1910), Book VI, title II, ch. III, p. 204.

54. Ibid., ch. IV, p. 205.

55. "Concilium Eliberitanum VI," PL 84:302-03: "Si quis vero maleficio interficiat alterum, eo quod sine idolatria perficere scelus non potuit, nec in finem impertiendam esse illi communionem."

56. XIII Tolet, VII, PL 84:494.

57. Nock, p. 92.

58. XVII Tolet, V, PL 84:557. "De his qui missam defunctorum pro vives audent malevole."

CHRISTIAN VILLAGE: SOCIAL ORDER

The survival of Gallegan peasants depended not only upon an harmonious relationship with nature. Quite as important were the interactions that bound villagers together. Thus the Church also had to acknowledge and ritualize the social order of Christian villages. In Galicia's Celtic villages, feasting was at times a ritual occasion. Extended families and friends met together in stone huts for a meal. Everyone sat on a circular bench affixed to the inner wall of the round huts, and passed the food in order of "age and dignity."[1] The meal was a time to reaffirm village ties and to acknowledge each person's standing within the village structure. The shared food represented the success of the hard work required to persuade a reluctant land to provide a sufficiency, and the feast celebrated the village's collective survival.[2] Bakhtin captured the ritual significance of food:

> The encounter of man with the world, which takes place inside the open, biting, rending, chewing mouth, is one of the most ancient, and most important objects of human thought and imagery. Here man tasts the world, introduces it into his body, makes it part of himself.[3]

The Christian tradition, too, incorporated the pervasive symbol of food. In the "Lives of Merida," a

sick boy, Augustus, had a vision of heaven, which to
him was a banquet. "The dishes were not of any kind of
meat but only of fowl...and there were tables and
flowers." Heaven's saints came and ate and then
discovered the boy's presence. But Jesus, Himself,
intervened, saying, "Fear not, my son, I shall always
feed you...."[4] As with all traditions that moved from
the village to elite culture, the concept of ritual
eating was modified. Official religiosity tended to
abstract the concrete cohesive quality of sharing a
meal, making it symbolic. The Church provided the Mass
as a symbolic feast during which spiritual food was
passed to villagers to be shared in appropriate social
order. Churchmen interpreted Jesus' promise to feed a
hungry boy as an offer of spiritual food through His
body and blood, not as a promise of a plate of fowl.
The "Mass of the Lord's Dinner" in the Visigothic
sacramentary explained the spiritual quality of the
Eucharistic feast: "...it is not only food for the
flesh, but an instrument of virtue; not so much
nutrition for the temporal life, but for life
eternal."[5]

Spiritual food, however, also contributed to
community fellowship. In pre-Christian villages,
peasants forged communal ties at a meal; Christian
villagers formed the same ties at the sacramental meal.
In his analysis of Church fellowship, Werner Elert
noted, "...one cannot conceive of a Christian
congregation which does not meet to celebrate the Holy
Supper and for common prayer. These are exactly what
make a congregation out of a cluster of believers."[6]
Elert, however, explored the difference between
Christian fellowship and secular communities and, in
doing so, he revealed both the tension between elite

and traditional views of communal eating as well as the balance struck between the two. He felt Christian villagers were bound together because they were joined with Christ through the Mass: "We eat one bread and by that, by that eating, we become one body.... The Sacrament is not constituted horizontally by men being gathered together, but much rather by a higher authority independent of them, that is, vertically."[7] Leaving aside the question of whether such vertical bonding gave village fellowship a more "profound depth" as Elert argued,[8] it is plain that the Mass as a ritual meal became part of the traditional expression of peasants to consolidate their communal ties by eating together.

To increase the importance of spiritual communion, spiritual and secular eating were increasingly separated. For example, the Third Council of Braga ordered excommunication for anyone who used the sacred plates and goblets of the Mass for secular meals.[9] Furthermore, as the distinction between spiritual and secular food increasingly was accented, more significance was given to not eating. As eating came to be seen as less a concrete celebration of abundance than a symbolic spiritual act, there came to be times when a Christian should avoid eating for ritual reasons. The story of the passion of Saints Facundus and Primitivus illustrates this idea. Atticus, the consul of the province of Leon, arrested Facundus and Primitivus for refusing to worship idols. They were tortured then jailed. While Facundus and Primitivus were in jail, Atticus sent them fine food to weaken their resolve. The martyrs refused to eat. In a rage, Atticus ordered them placed in an oven for three days, an ordeal which they endured with a firm faith. Once

the   saints   had   withstood   both   the   temptation   of
abundant   food   and   the   ordeal   of   the   oven,   they   ate
heartily,   saying   that   this   food   was   for   the   glory   of
God.[10]   Plainly,   these   martyrs   grew   in   spiritual
excellence   by   avoiding   food   at   an   inappropriate   time
and   eating   only   once   their   faith   had   been   tested.

Fasting,   or   the   avoidance of   secular   food   at
certain   times,   increased   the   efficacy   of   the   spiritual
food   of   the   Mass   by   reinforcing   the   separation   of   the
two.   It   was   expected   that   all   the   faithful   would   fast
immediately   before   taking   communion.   The   Lenten   fast
was   a   long   preparation   and   purging   to   prepare   for   the
Church's   holiest   feast   of   Easter.   To   further   accent
the   separation   of   secular   and   spiritual   food
particularly   in   the   Easter   season,   the   Council   of
Elvira   decreed   that   everyone   should   fast   all   day   on   the
Saturday   before   Easter.[11]   (Fasting   in   Lent   also   had   a
quality   of   making   a   virtue   of   necessity,   since   it   came
in   early   Spring,   a   time   when   food   was   growing   scarce
after   winter   stores   had   been   depleted.)

Thus,   peasants   in   Galicia's   Christian   villages
regularly   shared   the   spiritual   food   of   the   Mass,   which
contributed   both   to   their   salvation   and   to
reaffirmation   of   community   solidarity.   Spiritual
eating   was   interspersed with   religious   fasting   and
villagers   demonstrated   their   orthodoxy   not   only   by
taking   communion   at   appropriate   times,   but   also   by
observing   orthodox   fasts   and   avoiding   unorthodox
ones.[12]   While   symbolic   feasting   at   the   Mass   satisfied
some   elements   of   traditional   village   feasts   by   offering
shared   spiritual   in   place   of   secular   food,   popular
festivals   involved   more   than   simply   sharing   food.   They
were   joyful   celebrations   with   singing   and   dancing   along
with   a   ritual   meal.   The   Church   also   provided   for

specific feast days incorporating festival songs and dances to supplement the symbolic feast of the Mass.

After Celtiberians had feasted in the tribal huts, they joined together to dance to tunes played on flutes and trumpets.[13] There were many kinds of dances,[14] depending on the season or the occasion. Probably the most common were variations on traditional circle dances. In Celtic Iberia, women joined the dance circle,[15] held hands with men and participated in the solidarity and magic evoked by a particular dance. Regardless of the theme, a dance in itself expressed the nature of village culture and religiosity.[16] Each dance had traditional patterns and forms that were familiar to the participants. Within the established structure of the dance, however, there was room for a diversity of expression by each dancer, a slight variation of the steps, hand motions and body movement. Rather than detracting from the dance, these individual differences contributed to the fluidity and expression of emotion, making each execution both as old as the village culture and as new as the moment that called forth the celebration.[17]

The early Church incorporated a form of these traditional dances. Although the sources from Visigothic Spain are sparse regarding early Christian dances, E. Louis Backman, in Religious Dances, notes that "...Spain is the country in which the religious dance flourished...abudantly and...most vigorously."[18] We may then assume that in the early Middle Ages the Spanish Church followed the custom of religious dances that characterized the Church elsewhere in Europe.

Many Church fathers defended the practice of dancing in the Church. Basileios of Caesare, for example, wrote: "Could there be anything more blessed

GALLEGAN MUSICIANS IN TRADITIONAL COSTUMES

than to imitate on earth the ring-dance of the
angels...."[19] The spirit of Christian dancing is best
expressed by Backman's summary of Philo's words:

> God leads the ring-dance of
> the heavenly bodies. God
> leads inside the ring, he
> dances with the praying soul
> and holds it by the hand as it
> hops, dancing. For prayer is
> nothing else but a dance hop
> in so far as it releases us
> from earth and strives towards
> heaven.[20]

Throughout Europe, there were dances associated with
baptism, weddings, death rituals and martyrs' feast
days,[21] and it is reasonable to assume that this was
also the case in Visigothic Spain.

Strabo also observed Celtiberians singing old
songs and epic poetry on their festival occasions,[22]
and it is easier to trace Visigothic Christian
traditions of singing than dance, since the hymns were
written down and preserved. Christian singing took
place frequently. There were hymns to invoke divine
aid against illness and hymns to celebrate important
occasions such as the consecration of a king or a
bishop or the dedication of a church.[23] Most of the
hymns, however, were to commemorate saints' feast days,
which, by the fourth century, were the most frequent
occasions for Christian festivals.[24] An examination of
Christian hymns is particularly revealing of the
Church's attitude toward popular festivals. An example
of one such Christian hymn is Prudentius' song
celebrating the healing miracles of Saints Emeterius
and Chelidonius:

> Join, O mothers, in the vigil, raise
>   glad voices in the hymns,
> Giving thanks for cure of husbands and
>   your children raised to life;
> Let us with a holy joy celebrate
>   this festal day.[25]

Such a holiday incorporated the popular elements of
singing and feasting, but was tempered with the
Church's warning that it was to be celebrated with a
holy joy. Deeds of saints could be sung in the same
way that old heroes were euologized in song, but the
Church always was concerned that these festivities
should have a tone appropriate to the religious nature
of the feast. A sense of appropriateness was more
explicitly stated at the Fourth Council of Toledo, when
bishops forbade the singing of the Allelulia hymn
during Lent, since Lent was to be an observance of
sadness, and the Allelulia was a hymn of joy. Only
after Easter could it be sung again.[26]

Providing festivals that were Christian both in
purpose and spirit fulfilled part of the desire of
peasants to recognize their village ties by celebrating
together. However, official feasts which stressed a
seriousness appropriate to a Christian occasion could
not replace another kind of popular festival, the
carnival feast, which by definition violated the
Church's requirement of a decorous celebration.
Bakhtin's description captures the quality of a
traditional carnival celebration:

> Actually the official feast
> looked back at the past and
> used the past to consecrate
> the present. Unlike the
> earlier and purer feast, the

> official feast asserted all that was stable, unchanging, perennial...This is why the tone of the official feast was monolithically serious and why the element of laughter was alien to it... As opposed to the official feast, one might say that carnival celebrated temporary liberation from the prevailing truth and from the established order; it marked the suspension of all hierarchical rank, privileges, norms, and prohibitions.[27]

The joyous quality of popular feasts temporarily inverted the social order of the village and the society. Food, which was usually scarce, was consumed in abundance. Serious matters were made the subject of humor. Clowns were momentarily treated as kings, and rulers were mocked. This temporary inversion of the social order was consistent with the world view that caused peasants to feed mice to persuade them not to eat and leave one mountain unplowed so that others would be fertile. Similarly, in the village social order was at times suspended precisely in order to preserve it. However these irreverent celebrations were inconsistent with official feasts that were to be conducted with appropriate "holy joy." Truly traditional festivals had to "...be turned over to the popular sphere of the marketplace."[28] Isidore of Seville wrote a marvelous description of a popular festival that temporarily reversed reality:

> These miserable creatures,

and, what is worse, some of
the faithful, assumed
monstrous forms and
transformed themselves into
wild shapes; others womanized
their masculine faces and made
female gestures--all romping
and stamping in their dances
and clapping their hands, and,
what is still more shameful,
both sexes danced together in
the ring-dance, a host with
dulled senses and intoxicated
with wine.[29]

The Church repeatedly condemned such popular
festivals. Bishops at the Third Council of Toledo
discussed with horror the "rabble" who by "irreligious
custom" danced and sang "shameful" songs so loudly as
to disturb religious services. Conciliar legislation
called for priests and judges alike to work to banish
this custom and accustom people to "holy festivals."[30]

While the Visigothic sources briefly refer to the
popular feasts that continued to express village
religiosity, the sources do not permit an analysis of
precisely when such celebrations took place. Probably
some feasts celebrated joyous events in the village: a
wedding, a birth or a particularly abundant harvest.
Undoubtedly, some celebrations continued the festive
spirit that was evoked with a holy joy on spiritual
occasions: saints' days or other Church holy days. In
spite of the continuation of "irreligious" feasting,
the Christian villagers nevertheless structured their
year of feasts and fasts around the official Church's
calendar.

In his study of Italian peasants, Rudolph Bell observed that "Agrarian cultures tend to perceive time as a cyclical alternation of paired opposites in accordance with the regular passing and return of the seasons, of occasions for commemoration, of life and death."[31] In the seventh century villages of Christian Galicia, these seasonal cycles were given orthodox legitimacy by being incorporated into the Church's calendar. Christian festivals were tied to cycles of scarcity and abundance, planting and harvesting, work and leisure. Christian feast days thus were deeply affected by traditional festivities.[32]

Spring, the season of joyous rebirth, appropriately began with the celebration of the Conception of the Virgin Mary on March 20. The symbol of the fertile virgin introduced the season of preparing the soil and planting. After this fixed feast, spring was dominated by the movable feasts of Easter, the Ascension of Jesus (forty days after Easter) and Pentecost (fifty days after Easter). On Easter Sunday, villagers ate spring lamb, celebrating both Christ's resurrection and their survival through the winter. In this time of planting, however, food was not yet abundant enough for many feasts, and peasants were too busy preparing their fields to have time for festivities. Easter was merely a promise of rebirth both of the soul and of the soil, and there appear to have been no more feast days in the spring.

May, June and July were also months of hard work and a relative scarcity of food during which no festivals were commemorated. Only beginning in late July did the promise of Easter begin to be fulfilled with the onset of the harvest and the festivals that accompanied it. Many local festivals were observed at

varying   times   during   the   harvest   season.   The
Visigothic   laws even set aside the month between   July
16 and August 16 as a time of harvest festivals   during
which   no legal business would be transacted.   During
this month of harvest, "no one shall presume to subject
another   to annoyances either for the trial of a   case,
or   for   the payment of a debt."[33]   Harvest   time   had
always   been   a time for celebrations.   The   Celts   had
observed   the feast of Lugus or Lug on August 1,[34]   and
the   Hispano-Romans had celebrated   Vulcanalia   (August
23)   as   a   harvest   festival.[35]   In   the   Christian
villages, several popular saints' days were   celebrated
during harvest time.   The martyrdom of Felix of   Gerona
was commemorated on August 1, Lug's day, and on   August
6, the Church recognized the feast of Saints Justus and
Pastor.

Harvest   began   the season of   increased   feasting
that celebrated the village's victory over the   hazards
of   planting.   The festival season began   in   earnest,
however, after the vintage celebrations from   September
15,   to   October   15.[36]   Villagers   celebrated   the
preparation of wine, which completed their annual cycle
of   work.   October 15, the end of the   vintage   season,
introduced a period when the Church calendars   provided
for   numerous   feast   days throughout   the   fall,   when
villagers had both food and leisure.   In late   October,
people   celebrated the feasts of Marcelo the   Centurion
(October   29)   and   Claudio, Lupercio   and   Victorico
(October   30).   November brought the feast days of   St.
Emilian   (November   12)   and   Facundo   and   Primitivo
(November 27).   There were three saints' days   observed
in early December (Eulalia on December 10, Leocadia   on
December   9   and   Fausis, Januarius   and   Martialus   on
December   13).   Roughly coinciding with the   old   Roman

Saturnalia (beginning on December 17), the fall feasts culminated with the feast of "expectation of birth" beginning on December 18 and continuing for the eight days until Christmas.[37] Roughly coinciding with the winter solstice, Christmas marked the end of celebrations of a victorious harvest and introduced a time of looking forward. While Christmas was not as important as Easter during the early Christian centuries, the feast of the infant Jesus nevertheless was a promise of the salvation that would come in the spring with His resurrection.

The dark, rainy days of January during which outdoor work virtually ceased were from time to time relieved by feast days. Gallegans had adopted the Roman custom of celebrating the Kalends of January to mark the New Year, but Martin of Braga condemned this practice, saying that January 1 was not the beginning of the year. Martin and other local churchmen began the year at the vernal equinox (approximately the Feast of the conception) and forbade celebrating the Kalends as a remnant of paganism.[38] The Church did permit a small celebration on January 1 for the circumcision of Christ, but decreed that January 2 should be a day of fasting to prevent the several days of winter festivities that had traditionally accompanied the Kalends. The Christmas season culminated on January 6 with the celebration of the Epiphany, Christ's recognition by the Magi. The winter feasts ended late in January with the days of the martyrs, Saints Fructuosus and Vincent (January 21 and 22).

Then began the winter days of waiting for spring. Food, becoming scarcer, was something to use cautiously, not with festival abandon. There were no saints' days in February and through most of March.

(Some calendars show two saints' days in early March,
Emeritus and Chelidonius on March 3 and Perpetua and
Felicia on March 7, but their cults were never widely
observed, and it is questionable whether the days were
observed with many festivities.) Bishops in Toledo
recognized this relationship between feast days and the
larger seasonal cycles, for they noted that it was
impossible to celebrate the incarnation of the Virgin
Mary since it would usually fall during Lent.[39] Lent,
which began in February or early March, made the winter
days a time of somber penance in preparation for the
new beginning and new hope which came with the vernal
equinox and the Lord's resurrection. The Church's
calendar thus marked the cyclical turnings of the
seasons that shaped the life of the village.

It is significant that the major Church holy days,
Christmas and Easter, were feasts that coincided with
cosmic happenings, not with local events. The date of
Easter depended upon the vernal equinox, the moment
when God divided time into equal portions of day and
night; Christmas coincided with the winter solstice,
the moment when the sun began to return to lengthen the
days. Neither event provided the immediate result of
food or wine on the table. Instead, both affirmed that
the yearly cycles continued as part of God's plan. The
local celebrations of harvest victories were dedicated
to saints, God's local intermediaries. Thus, the
cycles of village festivals were consistent with the
natural order of the rural Christian world, in which
God ruled universals and saints ruled mountaintops.

The Christian festivals throughout the year
centered at the parish church. However, the church
building was not only a place where villagers met
periodically to worship; it was a symbol of the unity

of the village. Pascual Perez in La imagen de la
Iglesia en la Liturgia Espanola, observed that the
image of the Church existed on two levels. First was
the theoretical view of "Church," which represented an
abstract concept of the universal church. Second was
the manifestation of the church in liturgical
celebration, or the church in space and time.[40] For
peasants, the latter image predominated. The Church
meant the building in the village and the hallowed
ground upon which it stood,[41] but more than that, the
Church stood for the people who frequented it. Pascual
Perez noted that in the Visigothic liturgy the most
frequent synonym for Ecclesia was populus Dei.[42] The
small, dark village churches were the loci for
celebration in time of joy, for consolation in time of
trouble, and for refuge in time of need.

   The church's refuge extended to criminals seeking
sanctuary in the building.[43] The laws provided a
penalty for anyone violating the sanctuary of the
Church: "...the offender shall be compelled to pay a
hundred solidi to the church which sustained the
injury."[44]   The language of this passage is
significant, because the penalty assessed was not one
of penance to appease an offended God, but a wergeld to
repay offense to a person. Indeed, a violation of the
village church was a crime against God's people for
whom the church was the center of the village's social
as well as spiritual world.

   Since feasting together asserted and reinforced
peasants' social ties, those who by their actions had
placed themselves outside village morality were
excluded from the village feast. This was true during
the tribal period[45] and it remained true in the
Christian villages. The early conciliar legislation

explicitly associated sinning with exclusion from communal eating. The First Council of Braga decreed that the faithful of a community were forbidden to eat with a sinner until he or she had completed an appropriate penance,[46] and the First Council of Toledo decreed that if the wife of a clergyman sinned, he was not to eat with her.[47] The Second Council of Braga similarly decreed that "If a bishop, presbyter or deacon marries a widow, no religious person shall feast with them."[48] By the seventh century, exclusion from the symbolic, spiritual communion of the Mass had replaced ostracism in the conciliar legislation. Sinners were excommunicated, excluded from the Mass, which symbolically excluded them from the fellowship of the Christian community. The principle remained the same, however. In the sixth century, secular food was not shared with sinners, and by the seventh century, spiritual food was not shared. To complete a sinner's exclusion from the community, he or she was banned from the church building. A priest who discovered sinners was to excommunicate them and throw them out the church door,[49] thus vividly removing them from the community.

Such legislation suggests that, at the village level, sin was a social matter involving temporary expulsion from the close-knit community. Therefore, penance, the path to reacceptance, also had to take a public form.[50] Martin of Braga's legislation provides a striking picture of public penance: a murderer or perhaps someone who "sinned with an animal" must humbly lie at the church door, pleading for readmittance to both church and community.[51] After the prescribed period of penance had passed, the penitents were readmitted into the Church during a solemn public ceremony before the Mass, which usually took place on

Holy Thursday.[52] Active community involvement in both
penance and reconciliation contrasts sharply with
internal penance practiced by members of the official
Church, whose prayers and concern with guilt and
recrimination were described by Isidore of Seville as
"torturing the soul."[53] For the elite, penance
provided a way for an individual to earn forgiveness in
God's eyes. In the village, however, excommunication
and penance not only were matters between a person and
his or her priest, but also a means for regulating
ritually the membership of the village as a social
unit.

While the Church ordered the social unity of the
village as a whole, it also provided rituals to
establish the social relations of the people within the
village. The first step in ordering village
relationships was the initiation of adults and later
infants into the Christian society. Baptism was the
ritual means of acceptance into the community. Like
most church rituals, baptism was significant on several
levels. At the individual level (which was stressed by
church doctrine), baptism was the path to individual
salvation. A sinner was cleansed and "...made new and
reborn."[54] Along with this private purpose, however,
baptism represented an individual's initiation into the
community of the Christian village.[55] At least as
early as the third century infants were baptized along
with adult catechumens.[56] By the seventh century,
however, most of the baptisms would probably have been
of infants, and just as surely as the child was
presented to and accepted by God, he or she was
presented to and accepted by the villagers.

Unless serious illness imposed urgency upon
baptism, most people were received into the Church on

Easter, the feast of renewal. The doors of the
baptistries were locked during Lent,[57] while the
faithful fasted and prepared for Easter. On Palm
Sunday, the heads of children were washed to prepare
them for the Easter presentation.[58] On Easter Sunday,
children were brought to the altar, where first the
priest breathed upon them to exorcise "unclean spirits"
that inhabited the unbaptized.[59] Then a child was
anointed with oil and baptized with holy water. Unlike
the rest of Spain, Galicia appears to have adhered to
the practice of triple immersion, looking backward to
the precedent legitimized by Pope Vigilius in the fifth
century.[60] Immediately after baptism, the candidate
was confirmed by the priest's laying on of hands.[61]
Since baptism, the washing of sins, and confirmation,
the full acceptance into the Christian community,
occurred virtually simultaneously, when a child was
taken from the church on Easter Sunday, he or she was
fully a member of the Church and could participate in
the feasts and communion of the Christian yearly cycle
that began with Easter.

That baptism was both an individual and a social
matter can be seen in the legislation surrounding the
ritual. As an individual rite of passage, baptism
washed away sins and the sign of the cross on the
forehead gave the child the possibility of eternal
life.[62] This rite was one in which individuals had to
participate for themselves. For example, if a pregnant
woman were baptized, the unborn child was not
considered to have received the sacrament.[63] The
Church made it clear, however, that individual rebirth
through baptism did not supersede other social ties.
For example, if an adult received baptism after
marriage, this rebirth did not permit the previous

spouse to be set aside.[64] On the contrary, baptism reinforced and increased village ties, not only by legitimizing a child's membership in the village, but by formalizing fictive kinship ties of godparents, which joined villagers together in more complex patterns than had existed with strictly blood and marriage ties. So important was baptism as a social rite of passage into the community, that by the seventh century, any child who died before being baptized could not inherit.[65]

Marriage, too, was a social matter that aligned families and consolidated and rearranged property. This was, of course, most clearly visible among the nobility, but since villagers too might own land, particularly in the early Middle Ages, it was also important that village family ties be governed and controlled in an orderly way through marriage ties. Choice of a marriage partner was a matter for families to decide, and it was not left to the passions of young lovers. The Visigothic Code forbade "bride snatching," with or without the bride's consent, since this was a way for couples to choose to marry without the consent of their families.[66] The laws governing marriage also provided for a way to maintain the social barriers between peasant and elite by forbidding marriage outside one's social class: "...as an inferior rank is ennobled by the gift of freedom, so, in like manner, an illustrious race is disgraced by marriage with an inferior caste."[67]

After choosing a suitable mate for their child, parents conducted a betrothal ceremony in the presence of both families and witnesses. At this ceremony, a ring was given as a pledge of the couple's intention to marry, and dowries were exchanged between the families.

The   laws decreed that each noble family would give   to
the other one-tenth of its property, but when the   laws
referred to non-noble families, they only mentioned a
gift to be given by the groom's family to the bride:

> In   regard   to   others
> [non-noble] who desire to make
> marriage contracts, we deem it
> proper, and so decree; that
> whoever is known to possess
> ten   thousand solidi, shall
> give to his bride as a dowry,
> as much as a thousand solidi
> out of all his possessions.
> And he who has only a thousand
> solidi shall, in   the   same
> proportion, give a hundred as
> a dowry.[68]

The father of the bride kept the   dowry until the
wedding, at which time it would be turned over to   his
daughter.[69]   With the exchange of the dowry at   the
betrothal ceremony,   the   contract was   considered
binding, whether or not any written contract had been
executed.   In the village, it was unlikely that a
written contract would have been prepared, but families
remained bound to the promise pledged at the betrothal
feast.

The sources stress the moment of betrothal and
dowry exchange as the important event in marriage
alliances. The wedding itself, which was to take place
no later than two years after the betrothal (unless the
couple had been pledged as young children), was less
recognized since it was merely the last step of family
alignments that had been created at the betrothal.   As
the laws stated, "conjugal dignity" depended less on

the wedding than on adhering to propriety in the
betrothal:

> Marriage is recognized to have
> greater dignity and honor,
> where the dowry is given
> before the nuptial contract
> has been entered into in
> writing. For where the dowry
> has been neither given, nor
> stated in writing, what
> expectation can there be of
> future conjugal dignity, when
> propriety does not confirm the
> celebration of the marriage,
> nor the honorable obligation
> of the written contract
> accompanying it?[70]

The wedding itself was celebrated with a feast,
and the all-important dowry was then turned over to the
couple. Perhaps as an echo from their Celtic
matrilinear tradition,[71] women in the north of Spain
enjoyed an unusual position before the law.[72] The
bridegroom's endowment "...became in full the property
of the wife, who, at her death, could dispose of it as
she pleased if the marriage had produced no
children...." Even the law recognized a woman as a
person sui juris, exercising guardianship of her
children, freely contracting agreements, testifying in
legal cases, acting as guarantor in civil or judicial
actions, and acting as executor of wills.[73]

Customs and law surrounding marriage combined to
regulate the social order of villages as well as the
kingdom as a whole. Other conciliar and legal decrees
were promulgated to perform the twin tasks of keeping

the faithful from carnal sin and preserving the
marriage ties. The Church wanted the marriage bond to
be stable and forbade concubinage and divorce (except
for adultery).[74]

Adultery was a sufficient threat to the social
order to bring strict penalties. By not adhering to
the sexual mores of the community, both parties not
only suffered excommunication[75] but forfeited the
rights previously granted them by their position in the
community. For example, when a man found his wife
guilty of adultery, both she and her lover were to be
"given up to the husband, to be disposed of in any way
he may select."[76] If a wife discovered her husband in
an adulterous relationship with an unmarried woman, the
woman was surrendered to the wife "that the revenge of
the woman injured may be fully satisfied."[77]   The
penalty was left to the discretion of the wronged
party.   The guilty could be killed[78] or become the
slave of the wronged spouse.[79]

Not only did adulterers lose the right of personal
freedom, but they also forfeited their property and
inheritance rights:

> If   neither adulteress   nor
> adulterer   should   have
> legitimate children by a
> former marriage, the entire
> inheritance of both of them,
> along   with   their   persons,
> shall be delivered up into the
> power of the husband of the
> woman.   But if the adulterer
> should   have   legitimate
> children by a former marriage,
> his   property   shall   belong

> entirely to them, and only his
> person shall be surrendered to
> the   husband   of   the
> adulteress.[80]

The laws make no specific mention of the obvious fact that adultery might bring into question the legitimacy of any children born of a woman who was suspected of adultery.[81] There is one reference, however, that seems to address the desire for inheritance to be unambiguously legitimate. The law states that "after the adulterous wife has been brought back into the power of her husband it shall not be lawful for any marital relations to exist between them."[82] Adherence to this provision would ensure that any children born of an adulterous woman would clearly be illegitimate and thus not entitled to inherit. Furthermore, if a wronged husband violated this provision, he lost his right to his wife's forfeited property, which would then pass to her legitimate children.[83]

Lawmakers were so anxious to curtail adultery that they permitted the usual legal procedures to be suspended, permitting relatives of a wronged husband to bring a case to court in the event that a husband was rendered incapable of testifying by "...certain wives who hate their husbands [and] abandon themselves to adultery, and so affect the minds of their husbands, either by the administration of drugs, or by the devices of witchcraft...."[84] It is curious that this law mentions only women adulteresses as witches. This suggests that adultery by a man was considered less serious, or that men were not assumed to possess a knowledge of herbs or magic to delude their spouses. It may simply be that the phrasing of the law reveals that male lawmakers feared being cuckolded. In any case,

the abundance of legislation in general concerning the
punishments for adultery testifies to the importance of
marriage ties to the kingdom's social organization.

Adultery, however, was not the only threat to
family ties. Incest to the sixth degree of
relationship was also prohibited.[85] In order to
preserve harmony within the family, incest prohibitions
also extended to concubines of family members so that
"...the bed of the father or brother be not
polluted...."[86] This law contradicts the law against
concubinage by recognizing its existence. This may
suggest that preserving harmony in the family by
extending incest prohibitions to concubines was even
more important than concern for the individual soul of
the adulterer.

Marriage legislation was designed not only to
regulate the relationships between men and women in
ways designed to maintain a harmonious social
structure, but to ensure the continuation of a family
by providing heirs. "The law of nature is framed in
the direct hope of progeny when the nuptial contract is
entered into with all due solemnity."[87] This law was
framed to prevent families from uniting only for
considerations of property. "We sometimes see persons
who, not observing the laws of nature, but induced by
avarice, dispose of their children in marriage so
improperly, that neither the age, rank, or morals of
the parties concerned are considered by them." To
correct this, the law ordered that "...hereafter, women
shall always marry men who are older than themselves,
and a marriage under other circumstances shall not be
valid...."[88] While one could certainly question
whether this law was strictly enforced or even whether
simply enforcing such an age difference between

marriage partners would guarantee children, the spirit of the law is clear. The purpose of marriage was to produce heirs and guarantee the family's survival.

Just as festivals, baptism, and marriage rituals combined to maintain and order the social organization of the village, so death repeatedly disrupted it. In the village, death was accepted as a natural part of village life. As Philippe Aries noted in his analysis of death in the early Middle Ages, "It was a public ceremony...It was essential that parents, friends and neighbors be present."[89] As family and neighbors frequently feasted together to celebrate the cohesiveness of village life, they were present to recognize a neighbor's death. After death, mourners beat their breasts in grief[90] and joined together to carry the body to the cemetery in a procession which involved songs and ritual dance steps.[91] Just as the Church tried to regulate feasts to that they would be celebrated with "holy joy," so it tried to mold the traditional funeral procession so that grief would be expressed by "holy" sadness. The Third Council of Toledo forbade traditional funeral songs and immoderate breast slashing, for such activities impeded "faith in the hope of resurrection." Instead, appropriate psalms should be sung during the procession to the cemetery.[92] The body was buried in the parish churchyard and the grave was simply marked. As Aries noted, during the early Middle Ages individually marked and preserved graves were not particularly important. "The body was entrusted to the Church. It made little difference what the Church saw fit to do with these bodies...."[93] In effect, churchyard burials were communal in that graves could be opened and bones moved without regard for an individual's resting place.

The bodies were buried simply, for by the early seventh century, when the kingdom had largely accepted Catholicism, the old Gothic custom of burying goods along with the dead had been abandoned.[94] An unusual burial practice did persist into the Visigothic period in the northern mountains of Iberia. Hugo Obermaier has detailed excavations revealing a practice of staking corpses with iron pegs of various lengths. The stakes were driven through many parts of their bodies; along the leg and arm bones, and through the skull and abdomen. Some of the excavated gravesites were Celtic, while others were dated Visigothic in the Christian era.[95] It was not an occasional corpse that was staked; for example, in one cemetery, 38 out of 57 corpses were staked, and this included some children's bodies.[96] While it is very difficult to find more information on this practice, it is at least possible that the dead were affixed to their graves to protect the corpses from either demons or graverobbers, who used corpses for magical purposes. In either case, the practice reflected a concern that the dead rest undisturbed. A village priest addressed this concern when, at the burial, he asked "...God to free this last resting place from the attacks of the devil."[97]

Once the deceased had been buried and entrusted to the care of the Church, the involvement of the living with the dead did not end. Customarily, women kept a vigil in the cemetery at night, lighting candles for the dead.[98] Peasants also came to the cemetery to bring offerings to the dead and feast at the gravesides.[99] Feasting at the cemetery confirmed that kinship and community ties existed not only in the space of the village but through time. While the Church was advocating a concern for personal

immortality, through traditional rituals peasants were
achieving a collective immortality: the continuation
of the village as a unit.[100] Catholic leaders preached
against these traditional practices, seeing them as
remnants of paganism and as a distraction and threat to
the pursuit of individual salvation. The Church
forbade individuals to make private offerings to the
dead and placed itself between the living and the dead
to be the exclusive mediator between the secular and
spiritual worlds. The Council of Elvira prohibited
offering candles at cemeteries, for "the spirits of
saints are not to be disturbed."[101] The First Council
of Braga further decreed that any offerings to the dead
should be collected by priests to become the property
of the Church.[102]

Along with offerings, peasants traditionally
brought meals to the cemetery to eat in the presence of
the dead. Martin of Braga wrote that it was improper
for Christians to bring food to the cemetery.[103] The
Church offered the communion meal as a substitute for
pagan feasting with the dead, but parish priests, who
shared many of their parishioners' sensibilities,
combined Christian and pagan rituals. The bread and
wine of the Mass were taken to cemeteries where the
living had traditionally shared a meal in the company
of the dead. The Catholic hierarchy strongly
disapproved of this practice: "It is not appropriate
for clergy to go into the country and hold mass in the
cemetery but only in basilicas where martyrs' relics
are deposited."[104] The living could continue to be in
communion with the dead, but only symbolically. Relics
of a venerated saint were to represent generations of
peasants tied to the village social structure through
time and space by timeless rituals.

Galicia's villages contained a complex social order that was carefully ritualized to preserve the social patterns that had guaranteed the village's continuance. By the seventh century, the center of the Christian villages had become the parish church, where priests legitimized and made holy the patterns of relationships within the village. The priest accepted individuals into the Christian community through marriage, provided feasts at which peasants could reaffirm community ties while celebrating the cycles of life, and commemorated both an individual's death and his or her immortality. The Church did not create the means for ordering village social life, but by coopting, subtly modifying and recording traditional rituals, it guaranteed that much of the pre-Christian religiosity survived in a larger, more complex and literate society.

Notes

1. Strabo, The Geography of Strabo, trans. H.L. Jones (New York, 1917), III:3, 7.

2. Mikhail Bakhtin, Rabelais and his World (Cambridge, 1965), p. 281. "It must be stressed that both labor and food were collective; the whole of society took part in them."

3. Ibid., p. 281.

4. J.N. Garvin, trans., Vitae Sanctorum Patrum Emeretensium (Washington, 1946), I:7-19, pp. 141-42.

5. D. Marius Ferontin, ed., Le Liber Mozarbicus Sacramentorum et les manuscrits Mozarabes (Paris, 1912), p. 235.

6. Werner Elert, Eucharist and Church Fellowship in the First Four Centuries, trans. N.E. Nagel (St. Louis, 1966), p. 65.

7. Ibid., pp. 33 and 37.

8. Ibid., p. 37.

9. III Bracara II, PL 84:588.

10. Henrique Flórez, España Sagrada (Madrid, 1759), 34:325.

11. Eliberitanum XXVI, PL 84:305.

12. I Caesaraugustanum II, PL 84:315 forbade fasting from December 17 through January 6, since that was reminiscent of a Priscillianist fast.

13. Strabo, III:3, 7.

14. Julio Caro Baroja, Los Pueblos del Norte de la Península Ibérica (San Sebastian, 1973), p. 237. The author observed various types of dances among the northern Iberians: "Danzas agrícolas, danzas de aire guerreo, que en casos, pueden tener significación agraria; danzas sociales; danzas animales de significado problemático...."

15. Strabo, III:3, 7.

16. E.O. James, Christian Myth and Ritual (London, 1933), p. vii: "Always and everywhere man has tended to 'dance out his religion,' a vital faith finding its natural expression in action both symbolic and practical."

17. This analysis of village dances emerged from numerous conversations in Iceland on the subject with Rubek Rubekson, an expert on Faroese Island folk dances.

18.   E. Louis Backman, Religious Dances in the Christian Church and in Popular Medicine, trans. E. Classen (London, 1952), p. 95.

19. Ibid., p. 25.

20. Ibid., p. 37.

21. Ibid., p. 38. Backman summarizes the types of dances performed at various Church festivals.

22. Strabo, III:4, 18.

23.   Ruth E. Messenger, "Mozarabic Hymns in Relation to Contemporary Culture in Spain," Traditio 4 (1946), p. 165.

24. Camen García Rodríguez, El Culto de los Santos en la España Romana y Visigoda (Madrid, 1966), pp. 78 and 377. The author has an excellent analysis of the development of saints' feast days.

25.   Prudentius, "SS Emeterius and Chelindonius," The Poems of Prudentius, trans. Sister M. Clement Eagan (Washington, 1962), p. 105.

26. IV Tolet, XI, PL 84:370.

27. Bakhtin, pp. 9-10.

28. Ibid., p. 9.

29. Backman, p. 35.

30. III Tolet, XXIII, PL 84:356. "Exterminanda omnino est irreligiosa consuetudo quam vulgus per

sanctorum solemnitates agere consuevit, ut populi qui debent officia divina attendere saltationibus et turpibus invigilent canticis, no solum sibi nocentes sed et religiosorum officiis perstuepentes: hoc enim ut ab omni Hispania depellatur, sacerdotum et judicium a concilio sancte curae committitur."

31. Rudolph M. Bell, Fate and Honor, Family and Village (Chicago, 1979), p. 34.

32. To determine the cycles of feast days in seventh-century Galicia, I used the calendars that were analyzed by D. Marius Férontin, Le Liber Ordinum en Usage dans L'Eglise Wisigothique et mozarabe d'Espagne du cinquième au onzième siècle (Paris, 1904) and Jose Vives and Angel Fábrega, "Calendarios Hispánicos Anteriores al siglo XIII," Hispania Sacra (1949) I:119-146, II:339-380. When using these calendars (which date from the eleventh century), I used only those saints' days whose cults I can demonstrate existed in the seventh century. Along with the calendars, I used references to particular feast days in the Visigothic laws, conciliar legislation and other early sources.

33. Visigothic Code, trans. S.P. Scott (Boston, 1910), Book II, title I, ch. X, p. 21.

34. John T. McNeill, The Celtic Churches: A History A.D. 200 to 1200 (Chicago, 1974), p. 7. It is also worth noting that the important Gallegan city of Lugo was named after this harvest god.

35. Harold F. Palmer, "Martin of Bracara, De Correctione Rusticorum," (M.A. Thesis, Catholic University of America, 1932), pp. 34-35. "What is keeping the Vulcanalia...if not worshipping the devil."

36. Visigothic Code, Book II, title I, ch. X, p. 21. "...the vintage from the fifteenth Kalends of October to the fifteenth Kalends of November."

37. X Tolet, I, PL 84:441. This canon established the feast of expectation of birth.

38. Palmer, p. 29.

39. X Tolet, I, PL 84:441.

40. Arturo Pascual Pérez, La imágen de la Iglesia en la Liturgia Española (Madrid, 1971), p. 34.

41. The Twelfth Council of Toledo indicated that the hallowed ground was thirty paces around the Church. XII Tolet, X, PL 84:478.

42. Pascual Pérez, p. 71.

43. Visigothic Code, Book IX, title III, ch. 1, p. 331.

44. Ibid., Book IX, title III, ch. 3, p. 331.

45. E.A. Thompson, "The Passio S. Sabae and Early Visigothic Society," Historia 4 (1955), p. 333. Thompson described how Sabas received no help from the villagers after he removed himself from the village protection by refusing to participate in a sacrificial feast.

46. I Bracara, PL 84:568.

47. I Tolet, VII, PL 84:330.

48. "Canones Martini, XXIX," PL 84:579.

49. I Bracara, PL 84:568.

50. I Tolet, II, PL 84:329.

51. "Canones Martini, LXXVIII," PL 84:585: "...ad janum ecclesiae catholicae semper subjaceat..." See also canon LXXXI, "...quindecim annis in humilitate subjaceat ad ecclesiae januam..."

52. IV Tolet, VII, PL 84:368. At this council the penitential ceremony was officially introduced in the church liturgy, and the special prayers are preserved in Férotin, Le Liber Ordinum, p. 99.

53. Isidore of Seville, "De Ecclesiasticis Officiis" II, 17, 6, PL 83:786: "...poenitentia nomen

sumsit a poena, qua anima cruciatur..." Justo
Fernandez Alonso, "La disciplina penitencial en la
Espana Romanovisigoda desde el punto de vista
pastoral," Hispania Sacra (1951), p. 251, described
Isidore's view as reflecting a "juridical mentality"
which certainly is characteristic of the official
culture.

54. See above, Chapter VII.

55. Keith Thomas, Religion and the Decline of
Magic (New York, 1971), p. 37: "The social
significance of the baptismal ceremony as the formal
reception of the child into the community is obvious
enough, and it is not surprising that greater meaning
should have been attached to the ceremony than the
Church allowed."

56. See T.C. Akeley, Christian Initiation in Spain
c. 300-1100 (London, 1967), for the development of
infant baptism. See also Stephanie R. Jernigan
"Origins of the Early Christian Architecture of the
Iberian Peninsula," (Ph.D. Diss. University of
Missouri-Columbia, 1974), p. 66, for archeological
evidence of infant baptism.

57. XVII Tolet, I, PL 84:555-56.

58. Jernigan, p. 66.

59. H. Jenner, Catholic Encyclopedia, X:622:
"Exorcizo te immunde spiritus hostis humani generis."
This ritual is reminiscent of the practice of
exorcizing spirits of water before consecration.

60. "Epistola Vigilii Papae ad Profuturum
Episcopum," VI, PL 84:832.

61. Zacarias García Villada, Historia
Ecclesiastica de España (Madrid, 1932), I:233.

62. Jenner, p. 622: "Signum vitae aeternae quod
dedit Deus Pater Omnipotens per Jesum Christum Filium
suum credentibus in salutem."

63. "Canones Martini, LIV," PL 84:582.

64. Innocent I, "Epistola III," PL 20:493.

65. Visigothic Code, Book IV, title II, ch. 12, p. 128. While this law may raise the question of how a dead child could have an inheritance, the issue became important when, for example, a child was due to receive an inheritance from his or her grandparents. If the child had been baptized before dying, the child's parents could keep the inheritance. If the child had not been baptized, the inheritance would go to the next person in line from the grandparents, which could bypass the child's parents.

66. Ibid., Book III, title III, chs. 1, 2 and 3, pp. 83-93. The practice of bride snatching may have been forbidden, but it seems to have been sufficiently established in Spanish tradition to have continued well beyond the Visigothic era. (Heath Dillard, "Rape, Seduction and Elopement in Reconquest Castile," [Paper delivered at the Fourth Berkshire Conference on the History of Women, Mount Holyoke College, Massachusetts, August 25, 1978].)

67. Ibid., Book V, title VII, ch. 12, p. 189.

68. Ibid., Book III, title I, ch. VI, p. 80.

69. Ibid., Book III, title I, ch. VII, p. 80.

70. Ibid., Book III, title I, ch. I, pp. 75-76.

71. Jaime Vincens Vives, An Economic History of Spain (Princeton, 1969), p. 53.

72. John Frank Stephens, "Church Reform, Reconquest and Christian Society in Castile-Leon at the Time of the Gregorian Reform," (Ph.D. Diss., State University of New York at Binghamton, 1977), pp. 2-3. Stephens argues that Rome had very limited impact on the old matriarchal tradition in the North, and in fact two systems were created in Iberia: an

urban/patriarchal in the South and a matriarchal/agropastoralist in the North. While this position cannot be maintained too rigorously, it is useful in understanding the broad cultural developments of the peninsula. It is also interesting to note current Spanish generalizations in which southern men consider northern women to be too independent and headstrong.

73. Claudio Sanchez Albornoz, "La Mujer Musulmana y la Mujer Cristiana hace mil años," Del Ayer de España (Madrid, 1973), pp. 105-06. "El marido dotaba a su esposa según su fortuna y condición. Los novios ricos haciandotes muy cuantiosas...La dote pasaba a ser plena propriedad de la mujer, que disponía de ella a su muerte por entero, si no le nacían hijos del marido.... La mujer era persona sui juris, ejercia la tutela de sus hijos, podía contraer obligaciones libremente, deponer y ser parte en juicio, ser fiadora en acciones civiles o en actos judiciales y hasta acuar como ejecutora...de expresion de ultimas voluntades." See also Visigothic Code, Book II, title III, ch. VI, p. 50 and Book IV, title II, chs. 1 and 9, p. 121 and 123.

74. I Tolet, XVII, PL 84:331, XII Tolet, VIII, PL 84:476.

75. "Canones Martini, XXVIII," PL 84:579.

76. Visigothic Code, Book III, title IV, ch. III, p. 96.

77. Ibid., ch. IX, p. 98.

78. Ibid., ch. IV, p. 96.

79. Ibid., ch. II, p. 95.

80. Ibid., ch. XII, p. 99.

81. Keith Thomas, "The Double Standard," Journal of the History of Ideas, 20 (1959), pp. 195-216.

82. Visigothic Code, Book III, title IV, ch. XII, p. 99.

83.   Loc. cit.   "If...such relations should
thereafter exist, he [husband] himself shall have none
of her property, and all of it shall be given to her
legitimate children; or, if there are no children, to
her other heirs."

84. Visigothic Code, Book III, title IV, ch. XII,
p. 100.

85. Ibid., Book III, title V, ch. I, p. 106.

86. Ibid., Book III, title V, ch. VII, p. 111.

87. Ibid., Book III, title I, ch. V, p. 77.

88. Ibid., Book III, title I, ch. V, p. 78.

89.   Philippe Ariès, Western Attitudes toward
Death: From the Middle Ages to the Present (Baltimore,
1974), pp. 11-13.

90. Gregory of Tours, "De Virtutibus S. Martini,"
in Claude W. Barlow, ed., Martini Episcopi Bracarensis
Opera Omnia (New Haven, 1950), p. 300.   "...at that
time, blessed Martin...died, and his people greatly
beat their breasts as a sign of grief."

91. I Bracara XVI, PL 84:567.   "...cum psalmis ad
sepulturam eorum cadavera deducantur...." See also,
Backman, p. 2, regarding Germanic dance rituals
associated with the dead.

92. III Tolet, XXII, PL 84:356.

93. Ariès, p. 22.

94.   E.A. Thompson, The Goths in Spain (Oxford,
1969), p. 108.

95. H. Obermaier, "Leichennagelung im spanischen
Mittelalter," Forschungen und Fortschritte (Berlin,
1933), p. 169.

96. Ibid., p. 171.

97. Stephen McKenna, Paganism and Pagan Survivals
in Spain up to the Fall of the Visigothic Kingdom: The
Catholic University of America Studies in Medieval
History, New Series, Vol. 1 (Washington, 1983), p. 144.

98. Eliberitanum XXXIV and XXXV, PL 84:305. Also, Joan Morris, The Lady Was a Bishop (New York, 1973), p. 7: "Women in pre-Christian times and in the Christian era have always been to the fore in funeral celebrations. It was considered their special duty."

99. Aries, pp. 23-25, describes singing and dancing at cemeteries as part of the early medieval tradition of maintaining a proximity of the living with the dead.

100. Ariès, p. 104: "But from the Middle Ages on, among the literate, in the upper classes, it [an indifference to the individual form of the personality] was subtly modified [toward more individualistic perception of death and immortality]."

101. Eliberitanum XXXIV, PL 84:305.

102. I Bracara XXI, PL 84:568.

103. "Canones Martini, LXIX," PL 84:584.

104. Ibid., LXVIII, PL 84:583.

CONCLUSION

During their long settlement in northern Iberia, the Celts had established patterns of life, thought and ritual that were well suited to the gallegan hills. Many of these patterns persisted through the Roman, Suevic and Visigothic conquests of the region and formed a base which subtly shaped the future development of the region.

Even after cultural assimilation had gone on for centuries among these various groups, the seventh century Visigothic state was not a homogeneous kingdom under one king and one God, but rather it contained two interacting cultures, peasant and elite. Furthermore, each culture possessed its own perception of the world and thus its own view of religion. The peasant culture existed in the villages of the Gallegan hills and along the stormy coasts of the northwest. The culture of the elite ruling groups belonged to the towns, manorhouses and the centers of Visigothic power, Toledo and Braga.

The villages provided the economic base upon which the Visigothic rulers built their kingdom. The peasants had to produce enough food not only to sustain themselves, but also the lay and ecclesiastical nobility. The rulers, in turn, provided a measure of protection, a body of laws to structure the kingdom and an ecclesiastical hierarchy to guide the spiritual life of the faithful. In these ways, both peasants and rulers contributed to the functioning of the larger society. While peasants and rulers were independent of each other in pursuing their own lives and interests, there existed a symbiotic relationship between the two groups that required a measure of interaction on several levels. The exchange of goods between villages

and towns took place through a network of tax
collectors and merchants that connected the economies
of the villages with the kingdom as a whole.
Similarly, the political unification of the kingdom was
effected by local officials and judges enforcing on the
local level laws promulgated in the Visigothic centers
of power. The interactive nature of Visigothic society
was central to the economy of peasant and elite, the
power structure of ruled and ruler, and the
confrontation of differing religious points of view.
Moreover, peasant and elite were interdependent, tying
the kingdom together in a series of complex
relationships. Religious interaction not only
illuminates the development of the early Church, but
also reflects the complexities that permeated all the
other interactions between the two groups.

The sources pose a problem for studying the
religiosity of mountain villagers. Written by elite
churchmen, the texts reflect the bias of official
religion and make it difficult to delineate the special
features of popular religion. Yet, even official
sources are rich enough to permit an outline of the
broader elements of rural popular religion. In their
religion peasants primarily wanted to understand and
control their interactions with nature and with village
society. The details of persistent rural practices
provided by the sources contribute to a fuller
understanding of these basic motivations. The
religiosity of the elite, on the other hand, was
primarily concerned with power, uniformity of practice,
administration and formal religious doctrine
surrounding ethics and theology. Religious
perspectives separated and defined village space from
elite space as clearly as the walls of Lugo and Astorga
separated countryside from town.

While the economic, political and social spheres of peasant and ruling cultures could continue to operate fairly independently, joined only at the points of contact required for the functioning of the kingdom, the religious differences could not remain so sharply differentiated. The Catholic Church claimed to be neither solely of rulers nor of subjects; it was universal.

To bring the remote corners of the kingdom into the universal Church, the rulers erected an ecclesiastical hierarchy to facilitate the transmission of official religiosity from towns to isolated villages. The metropolitan bishop of Toledo conveyed decisions concerning religious practice and policy to bishops of all the provinces. These bishops in turn instructed their parish priests who were to return to their villages and bring their parishioners into conformity with the religious laws of the land. While bringing official religious views to the countryside and caring for the souls of their parishioners, parish priests fulfilled the traditionally important tasks of ritualizing village social relationships. The priest baptized village children, marking their entrance to both the kingdom of God and the community of the village. The priest also presided over weddings that united village families and shared the community's mourning at the death of a neighbor. As he served as the center of village life, a priest was also the officially designated mediator of orthodox religiosity. At the same time, however, parish priests made bishops aware of religious impulses arising out of the village culture in which they participated. For example, bishops in Braga learned of sacred fountains that had traditionally brought fertility to the land. Bishops also learned of men and women whose sanctity derived not from the promotion of the official Church, but from the veneration of country people.

Villagers venerated hermits (and their predecessors, martyrs) for their ability to control nature, at least to a certain extent. Aspiring holy men removed themselves from the community to fight solitary ascetic battles in the hills. Once a man had proven himself victorious over hunger, thirst, fear and exposure to cold, storms and wild beasts, people recognized his supernatural power and looked to him to perform similar miracles on their behalf. Holy men stopped storms, halted rising waters and cured illness by means of God's grace that had come to them during their withdrawal to solitude. These soldiers of Christ fought not only for their own souls, but through miracles worked for the good of the community from which they had withdrawn.

Women were venerated as holy not because they actively fought to gain supernatural power by ascetic battles, but because they preserved power they inherently possessed as virgins. When a woman chose to forego being fertile by bearing children, peasants perceived that she bestowed fertility and prosperity to the public sector. Virgins, too, removed themselves from the community life of marriage and thus contributed to the community's well-being.

The presence of holy men and women in the community satisfied some of the fundamental requirements of rural religion that had persisted from Celtic times by providing the means for possibly controlling nature. Through the intercession of holy people living close to God, peasants in an infertile land might be able to grow food and avoid some of the hazards of living in stormy, inhospitable mountains.

These holy people did not remain isolated. They traveled and spoke to both peasants and official churchmen, thus serving along with parish priests as mediators of religious information. Unlike parish priests, however, their role of mediator was not delegated by the official Church but derived from the people who initiated the veneration. The religious knowledge of hermits and virgins came from God, not from an ecclesiastical superior; therefore members of the official Church were never certain that the information transmitted by charismatic holy people was strictly orthodox. Throughout the seventh century this suspicion was reflected in the persistent efforts by the Church to bring holy men and dedicated virgins within the control of the Church hierarchy. The Church accepted and promoted cults of saints whose veneration rested upon the oral traditions of the countryside. The supernatural power that remained in a saint's relics brought the prosperity and performed the miracles previously done by the holy man or woman. Bishops recorded or rewrote the lives of these saints so that the example set by the saint was orthodox.

The Church also worked to bring living holy men and women into its control. Wandering holy men and informally dedicated virgins were repeatedly ordered to enter communities and bind themselves to vows of obedience to abbots, abbesses and bishops. While the charismatic power of each individual monk and nun was considerably less than that possessed by holy men and women in earlier centuries, the collective power of a community of men and women living close to God helped bring villages in their vicinity under God's protection. In the seventh century monastic houses were dispersed throughout the hills of Galicia and became stopping places for travelers. Their location near travel routes and their proximity to villages made monasteries points at which peasant and rulers exchanged religious views.

The accommodation of official religion to rural religion was made possible largely because of the religious information that was transmitted through the mediation of parish priests and monks and nuns. It is important to recognize that these people would not have been successful in Christianizing the countryside if they had not also fulfilled the religious tasks of ritualizing village social relationships and controlling nature. Both functions had always been central concerns of Gallegan villages. It would have been impossible for the official Church to impose religious leaders or religious ideas unless they had been in some way consistent with peasants' religious perspectives. Somewhat paradoxically, it was their consistency with peasant religiosity that permitted priests, monks and nuns to be effective mediators of official religiosity.

When the Christian Visigothic kings began their attempt to bring their recently unified kingdom into conformity with Catholic orthodoxy they were challenged by the heresy of Priscillianism, which was popular in the Gallegan province. Priscillianism was difficult to eradicate because it had achieved precisely the synthesis between peasant and elite religiosity that the Church would have to attain. By the mid-sixth century, the Church had managed to eradicate the obvious remnants of Priscillianist practices. The Church then slowly expanded the bounds of orthodoxy to encompass the rural space of the Gallegan hills.

Throughout the seventh century, the process of

elite accommodation to popular religion progressed
slowly. The Church not only canonized holy people who
had traditionally been venerated,but also incorporated
specific prayers and rituals designed to satisfy the
needs of peasants living in the villages of the hills.
The Church recognized the need for fertility rites and
incorporated them into accepted practice as prayers to
bless crops and to acknowledge the importance of
traditionally sacred objects, such as fountains. The
Church also provided for festivals, songs and dances
that had always served to recognize and reinforce
village social ties. Peasants living in the Christian
villages of Galicia structured their year around the
festivals of the official Church calendar. These
festivals, however, were organized to conform to
peasants' traditional cycles of scarcity and abundance,
work and leisure. Thus the lines of religious
difference between peasant and elite were slowly
blurred and the Church achieved the appearance of
universality that it sought. Peasants largely accepted
the abstract, ethical theology that was brought into
the hills, along with the hierarchy and administration
that accompanied it. Rulers and townspeople, in turn,
venerated saints who had first proven their sanctity in
the hills, and cities structured their Church year
around cycles established in the villages. It was only
later in the Middle Ages that churchmen would question
the orthodoxy of the lingering "pagan" survivals that
made up the syncretic accommodation that had been
established in the early centuries of Christianity.
The triumph of the universal Church in the seventh
century lay not in its ability to convert villagers to
official religiosity, but ultimately in its willingness
to call peasants orthodox even though they persisted in

their traditional beliefs that had proven successful from the earliest Celtic settlements.

BIBLIOGRAPHY

Manuscripts
Biblioteca Nacional:
        MS.   51
        MS.   494
        MS.   822
        MS.   10007
Biblioteca de la Academia de la Historia:
        MS.   13
Biblioteca del Escorial:
        MS.   a.II.9.
        MS.   a. I.13.
        MS.   r.II.18.

Primary Sources
"Acta S. Honesto." Acta Sanctorum, February, t.
    II, p. 359.
"Acta S. Marthae Virg. et Mart." Acta Sanctorum,
    February, t. III, p. 361.
"Acta S. Turibio." Acta Sanctorum. April, t. II,
    p. 11.
"Acta S. Vincenti." Acta Sanctorum. January, t.
    II, p. 393.
"Acta S. Vincentii Martyris." Analecta Bollandiana
    I (1882), pp. 259-62.
"Acta S. Vincenti Presb." Acta Sanctorum. September,
    t. I, p. 206.
Antolín, Guillermo. "Vida de Santa Helia," Boletin
    de la Academia de la Historia, 55, 1909, pp.
    121-28.
Augustine. City of God, ed. David Knowles, Penguin,
    1972, Baltimore, Md.
    _____. "De Haeresibus," PL 42, c. 44.

_____. "In Natali martyris Vincenti," and
     "Sermo CCLXVII in festo martyris Vincenti,"
     PL 38, c. 1252-68.

_____. "Contra Mendacium ad Consentium,"
     PL 40, c. 517-48.

Avitus of Braga. "Abiti Bracarensis Presbyter
     Epistola," edited by H. Flórez, España Sagrada
     XV, Madrid, 1787.

Bachiarius. "Professio Fidei," "Bachiarii ad
     Januarium Liber de Reparatione Lapsi," PL XX,
     c. 1015-63.

Barlow, C.W., trans. The Fathers of the Church--
     Iberian Fathers, 1969, Catholic University
     Press, Washington, D.C.

_____., ed. Martini Episcopi Barcarensis
     Opera Omnia, 1950, Yale University Press,
     New Haven, Ct.

Biclarensis, Abbas Joannes. "Chronicon, Continuans
     ubi Victor Desinit," PL 72, 863-70.

Braulio of Saragossa. St. Braulio, Bishop of
     Saragossa: His Life and Writings, edited
     by Charles A. Lynch, Catholic University Press,
     1938, Washington, D.C.

Bruyne, D. De. "Fragments Retrouvés d'Apocryphes
     Priscillianistes," Revue Benedictine 24 (1907),
     318-35.

"Chronicon Conimbricense." Portugaliae Monumenta
     Historica, vol. I, 1856, Iussu Academiae
     Scientiarum.

"Concilia Hispaniae." PL 84, 301.

Corpus Inscriptionum Latinarium II: Inscriptiones
     Hispaniae, edited by E. Hubner, 1869, Berlin.

Cyprian, trans. by Sister Rose Bernard Donna C.S.J.
Saint Cyprian Letters, 1964, Catholic University
Press, Washington, D.C.

Cyprian. "Epistola LXVII," Corpus Scriptorum
Ecclesiasticorum Latinorum, vol. III, Part II,
pp. 735-43.

Deusdedit Papae. "Epistola ad Gordianum Hispalensem
Episcopum," PL 80, c. 361-62.

"Epistolae Wisigoticae" MGH, Epistolae Merowingici
et Karolini Aevi, Tomus III, pp. 658-90.

Etheria. The Pilgrimage of Etheria, trans. by
M.L. McClure and C.L. Feltoe, 1919, New York,
The Macmillan Co.

Ferontîn, D. Marius. Le Liber Mozarbicus Sacramentorum
et les manuscrits Mozarabes, 1912, Paris,
Librarie de Firmin-Didot.

_____. Le Liber Ordinum en Usage dans l'Eglise
Wisigothique et mozarabe d'Espagne du cinquième
au onzième siècle, 1904 Paris, Firmin-Didot.

Fortunatus, Venantius. "Carminum Libri," MGH,
Auctores antiquinui, IV, 101-06.

"Forum Judicorum," MGH, Legum I, 1890, Berlin.

Fructuosi Bracarensis Episcopi. "Regula Monachorum"
and "Regula Monastica Communis," PL 87, c.
1099-1130.

Gaiffier, Baudouin de, editor. "Vie et miracles
de S. Turibius," Analecta Bollandiana 59
(1941), pp. 34-64.

Garvin, J.N., trans. Vitas Sanctorum Patrium
Emeretensium, 1946, Catholic University Press,
Washington, D.C.

Grau, R. Dr. Angel Fábrega, editor. Pasionario
Hispanico, Siglos VIIXI, Madrid, 1953, Instituto
Enrique Florez.

Gregoire, Reginald. Les Homeliaires du Moyen
   age, Inventaire et analyse des manuscrits
   (Rerum eccl. documenta . . . Pontif. Ath.
   S. Anselmi, Series major Fontes VI), Rome,
   1966, pp. 161-85.
Gregorii Magni. "Homiliarum in Evangelia Lib. I -
   Homilia XI," PL 76, 1110-14.
Gregory of Tours. "De virtutibus S. Martini,"
   MGH scriptores rerum Merovingicarum I, 594-96.
Gregorii Turonensis opera ed. W. Arndt et Br. Krusch,
   MGH, SS. Rer. Merov. tomus I, 1885, Hanover.
Gregorius II. "Epistola no. 26," MGH Epistolarum
   c. III, Epistolae Merovingici et Karolini
   Revi t. I, pp. 275-77.
Idatii Episcopi. "Chronicon," PL LI c. 875.
Innocent I. "Epistola III: De dissensione corruptaque
   disciplina Ecclesiarum Hispaniae," PL 20,
   485-94.
Isidori. "De ecclesiasticis officiis," PL 83.
_____. "De Viris Illustribus liber," PL 83,
   p. 1084.
Isidori. History of the Goths, Vandals and Suevi.,
   trans. by Guido Donini and Gordon B. Ford, Jr.,
   Leiden: E.J. Brill, 1970.
Jerome. "Ep. XXII, XIX, Ad Eustachium," PL 22, 405-6.
_____. "Epistola LXXV," PL 22, pp. 685-88.
_____. "Epistola CXXIV: ad Avitum," PL 22,
   pp. 1059-72.
_____. "Epistola CXXVI ad Marcellinum et
   anapsychiam," PL 22, c. 1085-6.
Leander. "Homilia in Laudem ecclesiae ad conversionem
   gentis, post concilium et confirmationem
   canonum edita," PL 72, pp. 893-98.

_____. "Regula sive Liber de Institutione
     virginum et contemptu mundi," PL 72, pp. 873-94.
Leo the Great. "Epistola XV ad Turribum Asturicensem
     Episcopum," PL 54, pp. 677-92.
Morin, G. "Deux lettres mystiques d'une ascète
     espagnole," Revue Benedictine 40 (1928),
     pp. 289-318.
Nock, Sister Frances Clare., ed. and trans., Vita
     Sancti Fructuosi, 1946, Catholic University
     Press, Washington, D.C.
Orosius. "Epistola ad Augustinum de Haeresibus,"
     PL Supp. ii, c. 328-40.
_____. "Memoria Apostolorum," Corpus Scriptorum
     Ecclesiasticorum Latinorum, vol. 18, pp. 12-14.
_____. The Seven Books of History against
     the Pagans: Fathers of the Church (1964),
     Roy J. Deferrari, ed., Catholic University
     Press, Washington, D.C.
Pacianus. "Epistola Tres ad Sympronianum Novatianum,"
     PL 13, pp. 1051-81.
_____. "Paraenesis sive Exhortatorius Libellus
     ad Poenitentiam," PL 13, pp. 1081-89.
Priscillian. "Tractatus," PL, Supp. ii, c. 1391-1507.
Prudentius. The Poems of Prudentius, trans. by
     Sister M. Clement Eagan, 1962, Catholic University
     Press, Washington, D.C.
"Regula Consensoria Monachorun," PL 66, c. 993-96.
Ruiz Bueno, Daniel, ed. Actas de Los Martires,
     Biblioteca de Autores Cristianos, Madrid, 1962.
Scott, S.P., trans. The Visigothic Code (Forum
     Judicum), The Boston Book Co., 1910, Boston,
     Mass.

Strabo. The Geography of Strabo, trans. by Horace
     Leonard Jones, vol. 2, 1917, New York, Putnam's
     Sons.

Sulpicius Severus. "Sacred History," in A Select
     Library of Nicene and Post-Nicene Fathers
     of the Christian Church, 2d series, vol. XI
     1894, New York, the Christian Literature Co.

Tacitus. "Germania," Donald A. White, ed., Medieval
     History: A Source Book, 1965, The Dorsey
     Press, Homewood.

Turribi Asturicensis. "Epistola," PL 54, c. 693-95.

Valerius. "S. Valerii Abbatis opuscula," PL 87,
     pp. 431-37.

_____. Valerio of Bierzo-An Ascetic of the
     Late Visigothic Period, The Catholic University
     of America Studies in Medieval History, New
     Series, vol. XI, ed. by Sister Consuelo Maria
     Aherne, 1949, Washington, D.C.

Vigilius Papae. "Epistola Vigilis Papae ad Profuturum
     Episcopum," PL 84, 829-32.

Ward, Benedicta, trans. The Sayings of the Desert
     Fathers, 1975, Mowbrays, London.

Secondary Sources

Aherne, Sister Consuelo Maria. "Late Visigothic
     Bishops, Their Schools and the Transmission
     of Culture," Traditio 22 (1966) 435-44.

Akeley, T.C. Christian Initiation in Spain, c.
     300-1100, 1967, London, Darton, Longman and
     Todd.

Anderson, Robert T. Traditional Europe: A Study
     in Anthropology and History, 1971, Belmont,
     Wadsworth Publishing Co.

Antolín, P. Guillermo. Catálogo de los Códices Latinos
      de la Real Biblioteca del Escorial, vols. I-V,
      1910, Madrid, Imprenta Helénica.
_____. "El códice Emilianense de la Biblioteca
      del Escorial," Ciudad de Dios 72 (1907).
_____. "El códice ovetense de la Biblioteca
      de El Escorial," Ciudad de Dios (1917), 108.
_____. "Códices visigótica del Escorial," Boletín
      de la Real Academia de la Historia 86 (1925),
      605-38.
Antolín, P. Guillermo. "Historia y Descripcion de Un
      'Codex Regularum del Siglo IX' Escorial: a.I. 13"
      Ciudad de Dios LXXV (1908).
Arce Martinez, Javier. "Conflictes entre paganismo y
      christianismo en Hispania durante el s. IV,
      "Principe de Viana 32 (1971), 245-55.
Ariès, Philippe. Western Attitudes toward Death:
      From the Middle Ages to the Present, Johns
      Hopkins University Press, 1974, Baltimore, Md.
Arribas, Antonio. The Iberians, 1973, New York:
      Frederick A. Praeger.
Babut, E.C. Priscillien et le priscillianism, 1909,
      Paris.
Backman, E. Louis. Trans. by E. Classen, Religious
      Dances in the Christian Church and in Popular
      Medicine, London, Allen and Unwin, 1952.
Bakhtin, Mikhail. Rabelais and His World, trans. by
      Helen Iswolsky, 1965, MIT Press, Cambridge, Mass.
Barb, A.A. "The Survival of Magic Arts," in Paganism
      and Christianity in the Fourth Century, ed. A.
      Momigliano, 1963, Clarendon Press, Oxford.
Bateson, Mary. "Origin and Early History of Double
      Monasteries," Transaction of RHS, New Series,
      XIII, 1899.

Bell, Rudolph M. Fate and Honor, Family and Village,
        U. of Chicago Press, 1979, Chicago, Ill.

Benson, Robert L., The Bishop Elect, Princeton U. Press,
        1968, Princeton, N.J.

Bibliotheca Hagiographica Latina, ed. socii Bollandiani,
        Bruxelles, 1898-9.

Bishko, C.J. "The Date and Nature of the Consensoria
        Monachorum," American Journal of Philology 59
        (1948), pp. 377-95.

_____. "Salvus of Albelda and Frontier Monasticism
        in Tenth-Century Navarre," Speculum 23 (1948),
        pp. 559-90.

_____. "Spanish Abbots and the Visigothic
        Councils of Toledo," Humanistic Studies in
        honor of John Calvin Metcalf, University of
        Virginia Studies in Philology, 1941, pp. 139-50.

Bloch, Marc. "The Advent and Triumph of the Watermill,"
        Land and Work in Medieval Europe, trans. by
        J.E. Anderson, 1969, New York, Harper and Row.

Bosch, Gimpera, P. El Poblamiento Antigua la Formacion
        de los Pueblos de Espana, 1944, Mexico, Imprenta
        Universitaire.

_____. Two Celtic Waves in Spain, 1939, University
        Press, Oxford.

Braudel, Fernand. The Mediterranean and the Mediter-
        ranean World in the Age of Philip II, 1975,
        New York, Harper and Row.

Brehaut, Ernest. An Encyclopedist of the Dark Ages -
        Isidore of Seville, 1912, New York, Columbia
        University Press.

Brey, F. Bouza. "El Estado suevo en Galicia y su
        organizacion interna," Grial 27 (1970), pp. 29-39.

Brown, Peter. "The Rise and Function of the Holy Man
        in Late Antiquity," Journal of Roman Studies
        (1971), p. 80.

Bruyne, D. Donatien de. "Le Regula Consensoria une
    regle des moines Priscillianistes," in Revue
    Benedictine 25 (1908), p. 84.
Bugge, John. Virginitas: An Essay in the History of
    a Medieval Ideal, 1975, Martinus Nijhoff, The
    Hague.
Bullough, Vern L. Sex, Society and History, 1976,
    New York, Science History Publications.
_____. The Subordinate Sex: A History of Attitudes
    Toward Women, 1976, University of Illinois
    Press, Chicago.
Cantarino, Vincente. Entre monjes y musulmanes: El
    conflicto que fue Espana, 1978, Madrid, Alhambra.
Caro Baroja, Julio. Los Pueblos del Norte de la
    Peninsula Ibérica, (Analisis Historico-cultural),
    1973, San Sebastian, Editorial Txertoa.
Caspari, C.T. Martin von Bracara's Schrift de Correctione
    Rusticorum, 1883, Christiana.
Chadwick, Henry. Priscillian of Avila: The Occult
    and the Charismatic in the Early Church, 1976,
    Oxford, Clarendon Press.
Collins, Roger. Early Medieval Spain: Unity in
    Diversity, 400-1000, 1983, New York, St. Martins
    Press.
Colombas, Garcia M., O.S.B. El Monacato Primitivo,
    1974, Madrid, Biblioteca de Autores Cristiano.
D'Arnis, W.H. Maigne. Lexicon Mediae Latinitatis,
    ed. J.P. Migne, 1866, Paris.
Davies, Wendy. "Celtic Women in the Early Middle
    Ages," Images of Women in Antiquity, ed. A.
    Cameron and A. Kuhst, 1983, Detroit, Wayne
    State University Press.
David, Pierre. Etudes historiques sur la Galice
    et le Portugal du VI au XII Siecle, 1947,
    (Lisbon and Paris).

Delaurelle, E. "La Vie Religieuse populaire en Septi-
    manie pendant l'epoque Wisigothique," Anales
    Toledanos III (1971).
Delooz, Pierre. Sociologie et canonisations, 1969,
    Faculte de Droit Liege.
Diaz y Diaz, Dr. M.C. "El Códice monástico de Leo-
    gundia (a.I.13)," Cuidad de Dios 181 (1968),
    p. 567.
_____. "A Propósito de la Vita Fructuosi,"
    Cuadernos de Estudios Gallegos 25, 1952, pp.
    155-178.
_____. "San Agustin en la Alta Edad Media
    española a través de sus manuscritos," Augustinus
    50 (1968), p. 141.
_____. "Sobre le Compliación Hagiográfica de
    Valerio del Bierzo," Hispania Sacra vol. 4
    (1951), pp. 3-25. Also in same volume, "Un
    Nuevo Códice de Valerio," pp. 133-46.
_____. En torno a los orígenes del Cristianismo
    hispanico, Instituto Español de Antropología
    Aplicada, Madrid, 1968.
Dillard, Heath. "Rape, Seduction and Elopement in
    Reconquest Castile," Paper delivered at the
    Fourth Berkshire Conference on the History
    of Women, Mount Holyoke College, Mass., August
    25, 1978.
Domingúez Bordona, J. BRAH 140 (1957), "Diccionario
    de iluminadores Espanoles."
Durkheim, Emile. Elementary forms of the Religious
    Life, trans. by J.W. Swain, 1965, New York,
    The Free Press.
Elert, Werner. Eucharist and Church Fellowship in
    the First Four Centuries, trans. by N.E. Nage,
    1966, St. Louis, Mo., Concordia Publishing House.

Fernandez Alonso, Justo. "La disciplina penitencial
    en la Espana Romanovisigoda desde el punto
    de vista pastoral," 1951, Hispania Sacra, pp.
    243-311.

Fernandez Caton, Jose M. Manifestacion ascéticas
    en la iglesia hispano-romano del sigle IV,
    Leon, Archivo Historico Diocesano, 1962.

Flórez, Henrique. España Sagrada, 1759, Madrid,
    Antonia Marin.

Frend, W.H.C. The Donatist Church, 1952 Oxford,
    Clarendon Press.

Gaiffier, Baldinus de. "Hagiographic Hispanique,"
    Analecta Bollandiana 66 (1948), pp. 299-318.

_____. "Sermons latins en honneur de St. Vincent,"
    Analecta Bollandiana 67 (1949), p. 267.

García Gallo, A. "El Testamento de San Martin de
    Dumio," Anuario del Historia de la Derecha
    Española (1956), pp. 369-85.

García Alvarez, M. Ruben. Galicia y los gallegos
    en la Alta Edad Media, 1975, Santiago de
    Compostela, Editoriel Prio Sacro.

García Rodriguez, Carmen. El Culto de los Santos
    en la España Romana y Visigoda, CSIC, Madrid,
    1966.

García Villada, Zacarías. Historia Ecclesiastica
    de España, Razón y Fe, 1932, Madrid.

_____. "La vida de St. Helia Un tratado pris-
    cilianista contra el matrimonio?" Estudios
    Eclesiasticos, 2 (1923), 270-79.

Garrido Bonano, Manuel, O.S.B. Curso de Liturgia
    Romana, Biblioteca de Autores Cristianos
    Madrid, 1961.

Geertz, Clifford. The Interpretation of Cultures,
    1973, New York, Basic Books.

George, Katherine and Charles. "Roman Catholic Sainthood
    and Social Status--A Statistical and Analytical
    Study," The Journal of Religion (April 1955)
    Vol. XXXV, No. 21, pp. 85-98.

Gifford, A.E. "Mancipium. A propos de travaux récents,"
    Revue de Philologie, 1937, pp. 396-400.

Ginzburg, Carlo. "Cheese and Worms," Religion and
    the People, 800-1700, James Obelkevich, ed.,
    1979, Chapel Hill, University of North Carolina
    Press, pp. 87-167.

Glick, Thomas F. Islamic and Christian Spain in the
    Early Middle Ages, 1979, Princeton, Princeton
    University Press.

Gomes dos Santos, Domingos Mauricio, S.J. "Problems
    e hipóteses, na vida de S. Fructuoso," 1968,
    Bracara Augusta, Vol. XXII, pp. 63-66.

Gomez-Tabanera, José Manuel. Ethnogenesis of the
    Spanish People, 1966, Madrid, Instituto Espanol
    de Antropologia Aplicada.

_____. Las poblaciones prehistóricas de la
    Peninsula Ibérica, 1968, Madrid, Instituto
    de Antropologia Aplicada.

_____. Los pueblos antiguos de la Peninsula
    Ibérica, 1968, Madrid, Instituto Espanol de
    Antropologia Aplicada.

_____. Las religiones prehistoricas y antiguas,
    1968, Madrid, Instituto Espanol de Antropologia
    Aplicada.

Gonzales, F. and J. Fernandez, eds. San Fructuoso
    y su Tiempo, 1966, Leon, Imprenta Provincial.

Gougaud, L. "La danse dans les eglises," Rev. d'hist.
    eccles. XV (1914), pp. 229-45.

Hauschild, Theodor. "La Iglesia Martirial de Marialba
    (Leon)" Tierres de Leon, 1968, pp. 21-26.

Hillgarth, J.N. "Popular Religion in Visigothic Spain," Visigothic Spain: New Approaches, ed. E. James, 1980, Oxford, Oxford University Press.

James, E.O. Christian Myth and Ritual, 1933, London, John Murray.

Jenner, Henry, "Mozarabic Liturgy," Catholic Encyclopedia, X, p. 622.

Jernigan, Stephanie, R. "Origins of the Early Christian Architecture of the Iberian Peninsula," 1974 Ph.D. dissertation, University of MIssouri-Columbia.

Jiminez Duque, Baldomero. La Espiritualidad Romano-Visigoda y Muzarabe, 1977, Madrid, Fundacion Universitaria Espanola.

Jones, Hans. The Gnostic Religion, 1958. Boston, Beacon Press.

King, C.C. Preromanesque churches in Spain, 1924, Bryn Mawr College, PA.

Klauser, Theodor. A Short History of the Western Liturgy, 1969, London, Oxford University Press.

Kroeber, A.L. Anthropology, New York, Harcourt Brace, 1948.

Kurfess, A. "Textkritisches zu Martini espiscopi Bracarensi opera," Anthenaeum 32 (1954), pp. 404-09.

_____. "Zu Martini episcopi Bracarensis libellus de Ira." Athenaeum 32 (1954), pp. 250-58.

Lacarra, José Maria. Estudios de Alta Edad Media Española, 1971, Valencia, Anubar, Dario de Valcaral. "Panorama de la Historia Urbana en la Peninsula Iberica" desde el Siglo, Vol. X. "La Iglesia visigoda en el siglo VII y sus relaciones

con Roma," "La Peninsula Iberica del siglo
VII al X: Centrol y vias de irradiacion de
la civilizacion."

Ladurie, Emmanuel Le Roy. Montaillou, 1978, New
York, Braziller.

Lear, F.S. "The Public Law of The Visigothic Code,"
Speculum, 26 (1951), pp. 1-23.

Lerner, Robert. The Heresy of the Free Spirit in
the Later Middle Ages, 1972, Los Angeles,
University of California Press.

Linage Conde, Antonio. El Monacato en Espana e
Hispanoamerica, 1977, Salamanca, KADMOS.

_____.   Los Origenes del monacato Benedictino
en la Peninsula Iberica, Vols. I, II and III,
1973, Leon, Centro des estudios e investigacion
San Isidoro.

Lisón Tolosana, Carmelo. Antropología Cultural de
Galicia, 1971, Madrid, Siglo XXI de Espana
Editores, S.A.

Loomis, C. Grant. White Magic. An Introduction
to the Folklore of Christian Legend, 1948,
Cambridge, Mass., Medieval Academy of America.

Loos, Milan. Dualist Heresy in the Middle Ages,
1974, Prague, Martinus Nijhoff.

Lopez, Caneda, Ramon. Prisciliano; su pensamiento
y su problema historica, 1966, Santiago,
Cuadernos de estudios Gallegos.

Luengo, Luis Alonso. Santa Toribio, Obispo de Astorga,
1939, Madrid, Bibliotica Nueva.

Lutrell, C.A. "The Medieval Tradition of the Pearl
Virginity," Medium Aevum 31 (1962), pp. 194-200.

MacCulloch, J.A. The Celtic and Scandinavian Religions,
London, Fisher, Knight and Co.

Mac Kendrick, Paul. The Iberian Stones Speak, Archaeology
in Spain and Portugal, 1969, New York, Funk
and Wagnalls.

Madden, Marie R. Political Theory and Law in Medieval
Spain, 1930, New York, Fordham University Press.

Madoz, J. "Libellus Fidei de Baquiario," in Revista
Espanola de Teologia, 1941, Madrid, pp. 457-88.

Maldonado, Luis. Religiosidad Popular, Nostalgia
de lo Magico, 1975, Madrid, Ediciones Cristiandad,
Artes Graficas Benzal.

Malinowski, Bronislaw. A Scientific Theory of Culture
and Other Essays, Chapel Hill, 1944, The University
of North Carolina Press.

Manrique, Andres. "La Regla de S. Augustín en Espana
durante los primeros siglos de su existencia,"
Cuidad de Dios 182 (1969), pp. 485-513.

Manselli, Raoul. La Religion Populaire au Moyen
Age--Prolemes de method et d'histoire, 1975,
Paris, Librarie J. Vrin.

Marique, Joseph M.F., S.J. Leaders of Iberian
Christianity 50-650 A.D., 1962, Mass., St.
Paul Editions

Markale, Jean. Women of the Celts, 1975, London,
Gordon Cremonesi.

Martinez Diez, G. "Los Concilios de Toledo," Anales
Toledanos III (1971), pp. 119-38.

Martins, Mario, S.J. Correntes da Filosofia Religiosa
em Braga dos sec. IV and VII, 1950, Porto,
Libraria Tavares Martins.

_____. "A vida cultural de S. Fructuoso e seus
monges," Broteria 45 (1974), pp. 58-69.

_____. "A vida economica dos monjes de S.
Fructuoso," Broteria 44 (1947), pp. 391-400.

McBain, Alexander. Celtic Mythology and Religion,
    1917, Stirling, Eneas Mackay.
McKenna, Rev. Stephen. "The Monastic Rules of
    Visigothic Spain," unpublished dissertation
    at Catholic University of America, 1935,
    Washington, D.C.
    _____. Paganism and Pagan Survivals in Spain
    up to the Fall of the Visigothic Kingdom. The
    Catholic University of America Studies in
    Medieval History, New Series, Vol. 1, 1938,
    Washington, D.C.
McNeill, John T. The Celtic Churches, A History
    A.D. 200-1200, 1974, Chicago, University of
    Chicago Press.
Menendez Pelayo, Marcelino. Historia de los Heterodoxes
    Espanoles, 1963, Madrid, Consejo Superior de
    Investigaciones Cientificas.
Messenger, Ruth E. "Mozarabic Hymns in Relation to
    Contemporary Culture in Spain," Traditio 4 (1946),
    pp. 149-77.
Miller, B.D.H. "She Who Hath Drunk any Potion,"
    Medium Aevum 31 (1962), pp. 188-93.
Montalembert, Count de. the Monks of the West from
    St. Benedict to St. Bernard, 1860, New York,
    Kennedy and Sons.
Morales, Ambrosie de. Viage de Ambrosio de Morales
    por orden del Rey D. Philipe II a los Reynos
    de Leon y Galicia y Principado de Asturias,
    ed. Henrique Florez, 1765, Madrid, Antonio Marin.
Morin, D.G. "Un passage énigmatique de S. Jérôme
    contre la Peleaine Espagnole Eucheria?" Revue
    Benedictine 30, (1913), pp. 174-86.
    _____. "Pro Instantio--contre l'attribution
    a Priscillien des opuscules du manuscrit de
    Wurzburg," Revue Benedictine 30 (1913), pp. 153-73.

Morris, Joan.   The Lady Was A Bishop, 1973, New York,
    Macmillan.

Mundo, A.M.   "Estudis sobre el 'de Fide' de Baquiari,"
    Studia Monastica 1965, pp. 247-303.

Muñoz y Rivero, Jesus.   Paleografia visigoda. Metode
    téorico-practico para aprender a leer los códicas
    y documentos españoles de los siglos Val XII,
    1919, Madrid, Daniel Jorro.

Murguia, Manuel, Historia de Galicia, 1865, Lugo,
    Imprenta de Soto Freire.

Murphy, Francis X.   "Julian of Toledo and the Fall
    of the Visigothic Kingdom in Spain," Speculum
    27 (1952), pp. 1-27.

Nostrand, J. Van.   An Economic Survey of Ancient
    Rome: Vol. III, Roman Spain, 1937, Baltimore,
    Johns Hopkins Press.

Oakley, Thomas P.   "The Penitentials as Sources for
    Mediaeval History," Speculum 15 (1940), pp. 210-23.

Obermaire, H.   "Leichennagelung im Spanischen
    Mittelalter," Forschungen und Fortschritti,
    IX, (1933), pp. 169-71.

Obolensky, Dmitri.   The Bogomils, 1948, Cambridge,
    University Press.

Orella, José Luis, S.I.   "La Penitencia en Prisciliano,"
    Espana Sacra XXI (1968), pp. 21-36.

Orlandis, José.   "Las Congregaciones Monasticas en la
    Tradicion Suevo-Gotica," Anuario de estudios
    Medievales, (1964).

Orlandis, José.   La Iglesia en la España Visigótica
    y Medieval, 1976, Pamplona, E. Gomez.

_____.   "Traditio corporis et Animae, La
    'Familiaritas' en las Iglesias y Monasterios
    espanoles de la alta Edad Media," Anuario de
    Historia del Derecho Espanol 24, (1954), pp. 95-279.

Palmer, Harold F.   Martin of Bracara, De Correctione
    Rusticorum, Master's dissertation, Catholic
    University, Washington, D.C., 1932.

Park, Willard, Z.   Shamanism in Western North America,
    1975, New York, Cooper Square Publishers.

Pascual Pérez, Arturo.   La imagen de la Iglesia en
    la Liturgia Espanola, 1971, Instituto Superior
    de Pastoral Madrid.

Pérez de Urbel, Fray Justo, O.S.B.   Año Cristiano,
    1959, 5th ed., Ediciones Tax, Madrid.

_____.   "El Monaquismo. . .Posterior a San
    Fructuoso," 1968, Ciudad de Dios, pp. 882-910.

_____.   Los monjes espanoles in le edad media,
    2 vols., Madrid, 1933-34.

Piggot, Stuart.   Ancient Europe, 1965, Chicago, Aldine
    Publishing.

Pomeroy, Sarah B.   Goddesses, Whores, Wives and Slaves:
    Women in Classical Antiquity, 1975, New York,
    Schocken Books.

Porter, W.S.   "Early Spanish Monasticism," Laudate
    X (1932).

Potter, J.M. et al.   Peasant Society, 1967, Canada,
    Little, Brown and Co.

Redfield, Robert.   The Primitive World and Its Trans-
    formations, 1953, New York, Cornell University
    Press.

Reinhart, W.   "Los Suevos en tiempo de su invasion
    en Espana," Archivo Espanol de Arqueologia 19
    (1946), pp. 131-44.

Risco, Vincente.   Manual de Historia de Galicia,
    1952, Madrid, Editorial Galazia.

Russell, Jeffrey Burton.   A History of Medieval
    Christianity--Prophecy and Order, 1971, New
    York, Thomas Y. Crowell.

Salisbury, Joyce E. "Fruitful in Singleness," Journal
    Of Medieval History 8 (1982), pp. 97-106.

Sanchez Albornoz, Claudio. Del Ayer de Espana, "La
    Mujer Musulmana y la Mujer Christiana hace mil
    anos,"1973, Madrid.

Sandoval, Prudencio de. Antiguidad de la cuidad
    y Iglesia Cathedal de Tuy, 1974, Barcelona,
    Ediciones El Albin.

Schulenburg, J.T. "Sexism in the Celestial Gynaeceum
    from 500-1200," Journal of Medieval History,
    June 1978.

Serra Rafols, Jose de C. La Vida en España en la
    Epoca Romana, 1944, Barcelona, Alberto Martin.

Stark, Werner. The Sociology of Religion, 1966,
    New York, Fordham University Press.

Stephens, John Frank. Church Reform, Reconquest,
    and Christian Society in Castile-Leon, at the
    time of the Gregorian Reform (1050-1135),
    Doctoral dissertation at State University of
    New York at Binghamton, 1977.

Stoianovich, Traian. A Study in Balkan Civilization,
    1967, New York: Alfred A. Knopf.

Tamayo de Salazar, Juan. Anamnesis sive sommemorationes
    sanctoruno Hispanorum, pontificum, martyrum,
    confessorum, virginum (Martyrologuim Hispaniae)
    6 vols. 1659.

Thomas, Keith. "The Double Standard," Journal of
    the History of Ideas, 20, (1957), pp. 195-216.
    _____. Religion and the Decline of Magic, 1971,
    New York, Charles Scribner's Sons.

Thompson, E.A. The Goths in Spain, 1969, Oxford,
    Clarendon Press.

Thompson, E.A. "The Passio of Sabae and Early Visigothic
    Society," Historia, 4, 1955.

_____. "Peasant Revolts in Late Roman Gaul
and Spain," Past and Present 2, (1952), pp. 12-23.

Torres Lopez, Manuel. "La doctrina de las 'Iglesias
Proprias' en los autores Españoles," Anuario
del Historia del Derecho Español 2 (1925),
pp. 402-61.

_____. "El origen del sistema de 'Iglesias
Proprias,'" Anuario del Historia del Derecho
Espanol, (1929), pp. 83-217.

Torres Rodriguez, Casimiro. "Peragrinaciones de
Galicio a Tierra Santa en el s. V," Compostellanum
(April-June 1956), pp. 401-48.

_____. "Reckiario, Rey de los Suevos. Primer
ensayo de unidad peninsular," Boletin de la
Universidad de Santiago de Composteta 65 (1957),
pp. 129-77.

_____. "Situación juridica de los Suevos en
Galicia antes de la caida del impirio Romano
de Occidente (476)," Cuadernos de Estudios
Gallegos XXXIV (1956), pp. 181-203.

Tovar, Antonio. "Consideraciones Sobre Geografia
e Historia de la España Antigua, "Estudios Sobre
La España Antigua, 1971, Madrid.

Tranoy, A. La Galice Romaine, 1981, Paris.

Verheigen, Melchior. "La Regula Sancti Augustine,"
Vigilae Christianae (1953), pp. 27-56.

Vigil, Marcelo. "Romanizacion y permanencia de
estrutures sociales indigenes en la Espana
septentional," Boletín, Real Academia de Historia
152 (1963), pp. 225-33.

Vives, J. "Boletín de Hagiografia Hispanica,"
Hispania Sacra (1948), pp. 229-243.

_____. "Calendarios Hispanicos Anteriores el
Siglo XIII," Hispania Sacra (1949).

Vives, J. An Economic History of Spain, 1969, Princeton,
     Princeton University Press.

_____, ed. Historia Social y Economica de Espana
     y America, vol. I, 1972, Barcelona, Libres
     Viceus-bolsillo.

_____. Inscripciones cristianas de la Espana
     romana y visigoda, 1962, Barcelona, Balmeciana.

_____. "Santoral visigodo en calendarios e
     inscripciones," Analecta sacra Tarraconensis
     14 (1941), pp. 31-58.

Vizmanos, P. Francisco de B. Las virgenes cristianas
     de la iglesia primitiva, 1949, Madrid, Biblioteca
     de autores cristianos.

Warner, Marina. Alone of All Her Sex, 1976, New
     York, Knopf.

Weber, Max. Sociology of Religion, 1964, Boston,
     Beacon Press, trans. by Ephraim Fischoff.

Wedel, Theodore Otto. The Medieval Attitude Toward
     Astrology, 1920, New Haven, Yale University
     Press.

Ziegler, A.K. Church and State in Visigothic Spain,
     1930, Catholic University, Washington, D.C.

INDEX